Contention and Corporate Social Responsibility

This book examines anticorporate activism in the United States and includes analysis of anticorporate challenges associated with social movements as diverse as the Civil Rights Movement and the Dolphin-Safe Tuna Movement. Using a unique dataset of protest events in the United States, the book shows that anticorporate activism is primarily about corporate policies, products, and negligence. Although activists have always been distrustful of corporations and have sought to change them, until the 1970s and 1980s, this was primarily accomplished by seeking government regulation of corporations or through organized labor. Sarah A. Soule traces the shift brought about by deregulation and the decline in organized labor, which prompted activists to target corporations directly, often in combination with targeting the state.

Using the literatures on contentious and private politics, which are both essential for understanding anticorporate activism, the book provides a nuanced understanding of the changing focal points of activism directed at corporations.

Sarah A. Soule is the Morgridge Professor of Organizational Behavior at the Stanford Graduate School of Business. She received her BA from the University of Vermont in 1989, her MA from Cornell University in 1991, and her PhD from Cornell University in 1995. Before joining the faculty at Stanford, she was a faculty member at the University of Arizona and Cornell University. Her most recent articles have appeared in the *American Journal of Sociology*, *Administrative Science Quarterly*, *American Sociological Review*, *Annual Review of Sociology*, *Social Forces*, and *Mobilization*. She has recently completed another book (with David Snow) entitled *A Primer on Social Movements* and was a coeditor of *The Blackwell Companion to Social Movements*.

Cambridge Studies in Contentious Politics

Editors

Mark Beissinger, *Princeton University*
Jack A. Goldstone, *George Mason University*
Michael Hanagan, *Vassar College*
Doug McAdam, *Stanford University and Center for Advanced Study in the Behavioral Sciences*
Suzanne Staggenborg, *University of Pittsburgh*
Sidney Tarrow, *Cornell University*
Elisabeth J. Wood, *Yale University*
Deborah Yashar, *Princeton University*

Ronald Aminzade et al., *Silence and Voice in the Study of Contentious Politics*
Javier Auyero, *Routine Politics and Violence in Argentina: The Gray Zone of State Power*
Clifford Bob, *The Marketing of Rebellion: Insurgents, Media, and International Activism*
Charles Brockett, *Political Movements and Violence in Central America*
Gerald F. Davis, Doug McAdam, W. Richard Scott, and Mayer N. Zald, *Social Movements and Organization Theory*
Jack A. Goldstone, editor, *States, Parties, and Social Movements*
Doug McAdam, Sidney Tarrow, and Charles Tilly, *Dynamics of Contention*
Sharon Nepstad, *War Resistance and the Plowshares Movement*
Kevin J. O'Brien and Lianjiang Li, *Rightful Resistance in Rural China*
Silvia Pedraza, *Political Disaffection in Cuba's Revolution and Exodus*
Sidney Tarrow, *The New Transnational Activism*
Ralph Thaxton, Jr., *Catastrophe and Contention in Rural China: Mao's Great Leap Forward Famine and the Origins of Righteous Resistance in Da Fo Village*
Charles Tilly, *Contention and Democracy in Europe, 1650–2000*
Charles Tilly, *Contentious Performances*
Charles Tilly, *The Politics of Collective Violence*
Stuart A. Wright, *Patriots, Politics, and the Oklahoma City Bombing*
Deborah Yashar, *Contesting Citizenship in Latin America: The Rise of Indigenous Movements and the Postliberal Challenge*

Contention and Corporate Social Responsibility

SARAH A. SOULE

Stanford University

CAMBRIDGE
UNIVERSITY PRESS

CAMBRIDGE UNIVERSITY PRESS
Cambridge, New York, Melbourne, Madrid, Cape Town, Singapore, São Paulo, Delhi

Cambridge University Press
32 Avenue of the Americas, New York, NY 10013-2473, USA

www.cambridge.org
Information on this title: www.cambridge.org/9780521727068

First published 2009

Printed in the United States of America

A catalog record for this publication is available from the British Library.

Library of Congress Cataloging in Publication data
Soule, Sarah Anne, 1967–
Contention and corporate social responsibility / Sarah A. Soule.
p.   cm. – (Cambridge studies in contentious politics)
Includes bibliographical references and index.
ISBN 978-0-521-89840-9 (hardback) – ISBN 978-0-521-72706-8 (pbk.)
1. Corporations – United States.   2. Social responsibility of business –
United States.   3. Anti-globalization movement – United States.
I. Title.   II. Series.
HD2785.S59   2009
338.6–dc22   2009022131

ISBN 978-0-521-89840-9 hardback
ISBN 978-0-521-72706-8 paperback

For Alice, Ben, and Bill

Contents

Figures

Tables

Preface

This project on anticorporate activism began in the early 1990s when I became interested in understanding the diffusion of innovative protest tactics and the effects these can have on organizational decisions. This became the subject of my dissertation project, which was on the student divestment movement and its effects on university divestment from South Africa. But, like so many other projects, this was only the beginning. As an assistant professor at the University of Arizona, I watched the United Students Against Sweatshops take over the administration building in an effort to force the university to stop buying university apparel from companies using sweatshop labor. And I was in Tucson when the Earth Liberation Front took responsibility for torching a McDonald's restaurant in protest of that company's poor environmental and animal rights record. These and other events outside of Tucson in this period demonstrated to me that anticorporate activism was alive and well in the 1990s and was not something that collapsed with the fall of apartheid and the end of the student divestment movement. But, as someone drawn to the history of the labor, peace, and civil rights movements, I also recognized that anticorporate activism was not something that the student divestment movement had invented.

While at Arizona, I began collaborating with Doug McAdam, John McCarthy, and Susan Olzak on the daunting task of collecting protest event data on all public protests that occurred in the United States between 1960 and 1990 and was reported in the *New York Times*. In our deliberations about what to include on our coding mechanism, we decided to include a code for whether or not the protest event in question targeted a business or corporation. We did this in large part because of what we saw going on in Tucson and the rest of the nation at the time, but I don't think we imagined that so many of the protest events we would ultimately collect would, in fact, target businesses. This fact made me realize that the anticorporate protest I was watching in the 1990s and knew to exist in the civil rights, labor, student divestment, and peace movements, was more widespread than I imagined.

Thus, I decided to write this book to illustrate the continuity in anticorporate activism in the United States, from early events such as the Boston Tea Party, to current activism against corporate homebuilders. While the bulk of my data, as readers will see, come from the 1960 to 1990 period, I hope that this book illustrates commonalities in themes, claims, and tactics over a much longer period. And I hope that the book will provide some theoretical ideas for others interested in anticorporate activism, whether they are trained in sociology, political science, or organizational studies.

Along the road to completion of this book, I have had a great deal of support and assistance from colleagues, friends, and loved ones. The person who deserves the most thanks for his assistance, advice, and sound criticism is Sid Tarrow. Sid was present when I began my dissertation research in the early 1990s and shaped that work in important ways. But he was also present when I began this book many years later, offering advice on how to craft it, offering ideas on literatures, and offering much-needed moral support. I also owe a great deal of thanks to Christian Davenport, who encouraged me to think about writing this book to begin with and who, with his ability to see the big picture on such projects, offered invaluable advice on how to pull the many threads of it together. My collaborator and friend, Brayden King, deserves thanks for encouraging me to think about outcomes of protest that transcend state policy change and to look in more detail at the work of organizations scholars in business schools for different frameworks for understanding this phenomenon.

I am also deeply appreciative of my former colleagues at the University of Arizona. While historically and presently a terrific group of scholars, for the topic of this book I could not have asked for a better set of colleagues and friends with whom to talk about the core ideas herein. In particular, Lis Clemens, Joe Galaskiewicz, Kieran Healy, Doug McAdam, Miller McPherson, Woody Powell, Marc Schneiberg, Lynn Smith-Lovin, and David Snow all contributed to the formation of many of the ideas in this book, as did many of the other faculty members and graduate students at Arizona.

Along the way, others have served as sounding boards for my ideas and have provided comments or support and/or played a major role in the collection of the data used in this book. I owe these people thanks, too. They include: Jenn Earl, Jeff Larson, John McCarthy, David Meyer, Deb Minkoff, Mike Mulcahy, Susan Olzak, Huggy Rao, Alan Schussman, Verta Taylor, Nella Van Dyke, Liz Warburton, and Mayer Zald.

I also thank the Cornell Institute for Social Sciences and especially the members of the Contentious Knowledge Project, where I was a Fellow when I began this book, and I thank the National Science Foundation for providing funding for the collection of much of the data used in this book. I also thank Libby Wood and Lew Bateman of Cambridge University Press for their comments, insight, and support through this process. It has been a wonderful experience to work with the Cambridge team.

Finally, and perhaps most centrally, I wish to thank my family for their role in the completion of this book. David and Ivan Geraghty were the source of sanity throughout this process, forcing me to realize that there is, in fact, a world beyond the computer and the boxes and boxes of coded protest events. Their patience and love made this possible, despite a move from Cornell to Stanford when I was completing this book. And my sister, Elizabeth Soule, helped me immensely by picking up the slack with family matters in ways too innumerable to mention. I wish many thanks to you all for your guidance and support. While the book is dedicated to my parents and stepfather, I could not have completed it without the help of these family members who are present to read it and share my joy in its completion.

Palo Alto, California

1

Introduction

On December 16, 1773, three coordinated groups of New Englanders sneaked on board three of the East India Company's ships in Boston Harbor, located several hundred chests of tea (worth over a million U.S. dollars in today's currency), and flung the tea overboard. This action followed a boycott of the East India Company's tea and a pamphleteering campaign designed to raise awareness and consciousness of New Englanders about the Tea Act of 1773, which (among other things) raised taxes paid by colonists on tea. While most remember these as some of the key events kicking off the American Revolution and, as such, directed at the British crown, it is important to recognize that these events were also some of the first anticorporate events in American history.

What were the New Englanders so incensed about? At the heart of this early protest campaign was anger at a multinational company, which had all but achieved a monopoly, and the British government, which supported the East India Company. Because the East India Company had amassed a large surplus of tea in England and was competing with American tea smugglers in the colonies, the Company was at risk of losing a great deal of money. The King and many Members of Parliament held shares of the Company and thus passed the Tea Act of 1773, which increased taxes paid by colonists on tea, while simultaneously lowering taxes levied on the Company so it could offer its tea at a far lower price than smaller companies, thereby driving smaller companies out of business. The monopoly by the Company coupled with increased taxation (without representation) led the colonists to criticize both the Company and the government that had passed the Tea Act. Thus, they were incensed at the actions of a company that was able to influence the government to pass legislation that was arguably not in the best interest of the people.[1]

This set of events is remarkably similar to anticorporate events in more recent times. At the most basic level, the tea-dumping activists in 1773 were frustrated with the East India Company's ability to exert influence over the government and they were angry, more generally, at the unchecked growth of corporate power – power that was coupled with political influence. While the growth of corporate power and corporate influence in politics are not the only grievances that modern anticorporate protesters articulate, they are without doubt central ones. Much like many modern day anticorporate protesters, such as José Bové who led others in the destruction of a McDonald's restaurant in Millau, France and led farmers in Brazil to uproot genetically modified crops belonging to Monsanto, these protesters used tactics of direct action designed to halt the operations of the East India Company. More generally, the Boston tea activists' actions, while directed against a specific company, reflected a deep dissatisfaction with multiple targets, existing at different levels. The event (like many modern day anticorporate events) was about corporate malfeasance to be sure, but it was also about the government's inability or unwillingness to intervene and regulate a corporation that was, in their view, running amuck.

The Boston Tea Party was certainly a dramatic and early example of anticorporate sentiment and action. And if it were an isolated event, we might be tempted to dismiss it as unlike the recent wave of anticorporate activity in the United States. However, a broader historical view shows that there has always been distrust and fear of corporations in the United States – factors that have often led to collective action around the activities of corporations.[2] From the temperance movement, which targeted alcohol

---

[1] For lengthier discussions of the Boston Tea Party as an anticorporate protest event, see Hartmann (2002: 45–63) and Danaher and Mark (2003: 23–26).
[2] Lipset and Schneider (1987) discuss the general trend in declining confidence in corporations (as well as the other major societal institutions) over the course of the twentieth century, as does Vogel (1996) who connects the distrust in business and government to the growth of the public interest movement in the United States. More recent data from the General Social Survey in the United States show there has been a sharp decline in respondents' confidence and trust in corporations since the 1970s; about 31% of respondents reported that they had a great deal of confidence in corporations in 1973, but only 17–18% did so from 2002–2006. And, more recently, a November 2007 Harris poll found that less than 15% of respondents reported trusting corporations.

manufacturers, to the bloody labor strikes of the late 1800s and early 1900s; from the Bank of the United States controversy to the Populist Rebellion (that was explicitly anticorporate); from the "trust-busting" of the Progressive Era to the growth of the Labor Movement in the 1930s and 1940s, corporations have repeatedly come under activist-generated fire. And, when we think of the post-1960 period of activism in the United States, we soon recognize that corporations have been the targets of activism associated with the Civil Rights Movement (Vogel 1978; Chafe 1981; Luders 2006), the New Left Movement (Sale 1973),[3] antinuclear protests (Walsh 1986; Epstein 1991), the anti-Vietnam war movement (Vogel 1978), the nuclear freeze movement (Meyer 1992), the antitobacco movement (Wolfson 2001; Danaher and Mark 2003), the antiapartheid movement (Soule 1997; Massie 1997; Seidman 2007), the labor movement (Manheim 2001; Kay 2005; Martin 2008), and presumably many other social movements.

The subject of this book, as illustrated by the example of the Boston Tea Party, is activism directed at nongovernmental, for-profit corporations. Corporations, such as the East India Company, Ford Motors, Honeywell, McDonald's, Dow Chemical, and Nike, are frequently the targets of social movement actors and, if some observers are correct, the frequency with which corporations are targeted has increased in recent years. While in this book I focus on anticorporate activism, I will again and again note that much of this activism is not simply directed at corporations. As we will see throughout this book, there are often multiple targets of what we classify as anticorporate activism, just as was the case in the Boston Tea Party, which targeted both a corporation and a state. This multiplicity of targets, existing at different levels in several institutional domains, is a central theme of this book. And, in fact, this is the theme that leads me to situate the topic of this book as being of equal interest to sociologists, political scientists, and organizations scholars, all of whom have begun to pay more attention to anticorporate activism. The ultimate goal, then, is to draw on these disparate literatures and traditions in an attempt to offer a framework for understanding anticorporate activism. But, first, it is important to describe this form of activism in more detail and explore some of the reasons for its genesis.

---

[3] The 1962 Port Huron Statement explicitly called for "challenging the unchallenged politics of American corporations" (Danaher and Mark 2003: 58).

The Growth of Corporate Power and Social Movement Activity

A central claim made by scholars of anticorporate activism is that its frequency has increased markedly in recent years (e.g., see contributions in Doh and Teegan 2003) as a result of the fact that over the course of the twentieth century, corporations became larger and more powerful and that their reach over individuals increased dramatically (e.g., Vogel 1996; Nace 2003; Anderson and Cavanagh 2005; Jones, Comfort, and Hillier 2006). But what factors have led to the growth of corporate power? First and foremost is aggregation and economic concentration, which has led to the incredible growth of corporations. Simply put, through mergers and acquisitions, corporations have become much larger; that is, the largest corporations now control a higher share of the overall assets than they once did. For example, in the three years between 1998 and 2000, there were over $4 trillion in mergers; a dollar figure that is greater than that of the previous thirty years combined (Henry 2002). And it is clear that companies in the Fortune 500 dominate the U.S. economy: in the mid-1990s, over 25% of the assets of *all* corporations were controlled by these 500 companies (Grossman and Morehouse 1996).

This concentration of assets means that relatively few large corporations control many aspects of individuals' lives. Most of our food is produced and/or processed by a few large corporations (e.g., Kraft, Nestlé, Archer Daniels Midland) and most of the gas for our cars and oil for our heating comes from a few petroleum companies. Thus, the concentration of economic power among a few corporations means that a few corporations influence the products that are available to citizens, from what we eat, to what we wear, to what we drive.

But on top of this concentration in economic power, which is irksome enough to some anticorporate activists, most scholars of anticorporate social movements in the United States point to the way in which corporations increasingly influence the political process in America (Domhoff 1976; Kerbo and Della Fave 1979; Vogel 1996). Corporations achieve this through political campaign contributions, to be sure. But the government has reciprocated by appointing probusiness people to key regulatory and other governmental positions and by instituting policies that anticorporate activists charge amount to "corporate welfare," which might be defined as any state program or policy that benefits corporate interests over the interests of taxpaying citizens (Danaher and Mark 2003; Johnston 2007).

How bad is this? A few examples should suffice to make this point. Between 1989 and 2001, Enron contributed nearly $6 million to Republican candidates and the Republican Party (Danaher and Mark 2003). In return, Kenneth Lay and other Enron executives were able to meet with members of the government charged with writing energy policy – policies which, as we know, called for the break up of control over electricity transmission networks, a goal of Enron for many years (Danaher and Mark 2003).

On top of Enron, we also know that the big automobile manufacturers in the United States have given great sums of money in campaign contributions over the years. Some argue that such contributions, and the elected officials' fear of losing them, has led to the failure of the United States to ratify the Kyoto Protocol on Global Warming (despite the fact that public opinion polls indicate that citizens believe that the government should do more to halt global warming). More generally, critics charge that this has led to the government's historical reluctance to require better fuel efficiency standards in cars made in the United States. In other words, critics charge that the automobile industry has been able to influence U.S. policy via campaign contributions.

Another piece of this story is what some call the "revolving door" between corporate executives and public, regulatory positions (Danaher and Mark 2003). Essentially, many individuals in governmental positions also have ties to corporations and vice versa. For example, during the Clinton administration, Citibank and Travelers Group Insurance merged, despite the fact that it was then against the law for banks and insurance companies to merge (Danaher and Mark 2003). Citigroup, the resulting company of this merger, used its power to change this law and, within days, Treasury Secretary Robert Rubin resigned his government position and joined Citigroup.

During George W. Bush's presidency there were numerous other examples of appointments of business leaders and probusiness individuals to key governmental positions. For example, Bush appointee John Snow (Secretary of Treasury, 2003–2006) was the CEO of CSX Corporation, a transportation company that allegedly paid no federal income taxes during 1998, 2000, and 2001.[4] Or, James Baker (member of the Iraq Study Group, which was convened by Congress to make policy recommendations on the Iraq War) was a lawyer for the Carlyle Group, a global investment firm doing extensive business in the Middle East (Klein 2004). And, of course,

---

[4] http://oldamericancentury.org/bushco/cronyism.htm, Web site accessed June 11, 2008.

it is well known that between 1995 and 2000, Vice President Dick Cheney (while not an appointee) led the energy company, Halliburton, whose subsidiary was chosen to be the main government contract working to restore Iraq's oil industry. And, critics note that the $700 billion Wall Street bailout fund of 2008 was being managed by former Goldman Sachs employees (e.g., Treasury Secretary Henry Paulson, Steve Shafran, Kendrick Wilson III, Edward Frost, and Neel Kashkari) and that their decisions "directly impact[ed] the firm's own fortunes" (Cresswell and White 2008:1).

Also aiding in the growth of corporate power has been deregulation, which began in the 1970s and early 1980s in the United States. Deregulation is the governmental removal of rules and restrictions on businesses and is intended to encourage efficiency in the market via less encumbered competition. The idea behind deregulation can be traced to the University of Chicago's Department of Economics, and in particular Milton Friedman, who argued for a more laissez-faire brand of economics. Deregulation began in the United States under President Nixon who initiated the deregulation of transportation. This was continued in the administrations of President Ford and President Carter, the latter of whom eventually deregulated the airline industry. Deregulation continued throughout the Reagan administration, which deregulated the savings and loan industry, and continued through the first Bush administration. Importantly, at the same time, deregulation of the savings and loan and key bank and finance sectors was occurring, key posts in existing regulatory agencies were increasingly filled by probusiness individuals. The second Bush administration continued the trend of deregulation, most recently by issuing an executive order in 2007 dictating that governmental agencies (e.g., the Environmental Protection Agency and Occupational Safety and Health Administration) have a political appointee to oversee the guidance documents of regulated industries and that these documents must prove that there has been market failure before the government will intervene (Pear 2007). By forcing agencies to prove market failure, this executive order instituted an additional hurdle that must be cleared before the agency can issue protections for health and safety.

The increases in corporate power in both the political and economic realms are well documented, to be sure. And there is evidence to suggest that Americans are not unaware of these trends. For example, an October 2007 report issued by the Democracy Corps notes that the most often cited reason for Americans' discontent with the trajectory of their country was that "big business gets whatever it wants in Washington" (Greenberg,

Quinlan, and Carville 2007). But it is also important to note that at the same time corporate power was increasing, we also saw a decrease in the power of organized labor, one of the traditional opponents of corporations' unchecked growth. While union membership had been declining since the 1950s in the United States, the Reagan administration was known to be unfriendly to labor unions, as exemplified when Reagan fired striking air traffic controllers in 1981. In the wake of this event, Reagan also stacked the National Labor Relations Board (NLRB) with probusiness individuals, which led to further blows to labor organizing.

These changes – deregulation and decline in the power of organized labor – occurred at roughly the same time that the increase in mergers among corporations occurred. In effect, this was the perfect storm in the eyes of critics of corporations. The coincidence of the growth of corporations and corporate power and influence in matters of the government, with the decline in labor and increase in deregulation trends, underlies many of the grievances of modern-day anticorporate activists. In the past, activists attempted to indirectly influence corporations through targeting the government and/or regulatory agencies. Or, activists attempted to impact corporations through labor unions. However, since the 1960s, it would appear that activists often target corporations *directly* rather than through government regulation and unions (Vogel 1978). Thus, I argue that it is not that Americans are suddenly incensed with corporations and have begun to target them – they always have done so, at least since the Boston Tea Party. Rather, it is that Americans are targeting them *directly*, sometimes instead of targeting the government or via organized labor, and sometimes in addition to targeting the government and working through organized labor.

Direct versus Indirect Targeting of Corporations

What has led to this tendency to target corporations directly? There are a number of reasons worth highlighting. First, this can be a conscious strategy on the part of leaders of a given social movement who argue that it is more efficient and effective to target corporations directly (Lenox and Eesley 2006). For example, Paul Gilding, former head of Greenpeace noted in 2001 that, "Smart activists are now saying, 'O.K., you want to play markets – let's play.'" He further notes that targeting the government takes a long time and that mobilization by more powerful and resource-rich countermovements can undermine efforts of grassroots movements to target the government (discussed in Baron 2003: 34). Raeburn (2004) alludes to a similar process, noting that the gay and lesbian movement began targeting corporations *because* the government was viewed as less responsive to the claims of the movement.

Another reason that modern social movements target corporations directly is that certain technological changes have facilitated this (Davis and Zald 2005). While Internet and cellular phone technologies have made it much easier for most movements (including those that target the state and organized labor activity) to disseminate information, certain Internet-based tactics seem especially well suited for targeting corporations. An example is the "smart mob," which is a swarm of activists organizing on the Internet in an attempt to damage the reputation of a corporation (Hart and Sharma 2004). While certainly such tactics can be (and are) used to discredit governments, policies, elected officials, and political candidates, they are especially effective when trying to damage the image of corporations. Similarly, boycotts directed at corporations benefit from the wide and cheap dissemination of information on alleged corporate malfeasance via the Internet (Bennett 2003; Schurman 2004). Because of the sophisticated use of visual media (e.g., videos and photos), the Internet is especially useful for instigating "moral shock," which might induce otherwise agnostic people to participate in a boycott of a company (Jasper and Poulson 1995). All of this has led many to conclude that anticorporate activism on the Internet is a clear and present danger to corporations.[5]

A third reason has to do with the increase of globalization, which has led the power and importance of national governments to be eclipsed by the power of transnational entities, such as the WTO, World Bank, and International Monetary Fund (IMF) (Strange 1996; van Tuijl 1999; Schurman 2004; Hart and Sharma 2004). As well, as regulation of corporations moves from the purview of governments to that of various transnational bodies (e.g., the WTO, World Bank, and IMF), targeting the state has begun to make much less sense (van Tuijl 1999; Bennett 2003). While activists *do* target transnational bodies and agreements (e.g., Tarrow 2005; Kay 2005), it is substantially easier to target corporations. The result has been what Beck (2000) calls "sub politics," or politics directed at the

---

[5] On anticorporate activism and the Internet, see Kahn and Kellner (2003, 2004), Whysall (2000), and Jones et al. (2006). Also see my discussion in Chapter 5 of the Free Burma Coalition's use of the Internet.

political sphere *below* the traditional legislative, electoral, and regulatory spheres; that is, in this case, corporations.[6]

Finally, it is also important to note that one simple reason for targeting corporations rather than the government or state targets is that (at least in the modern era) doing so is associated with a lower likelihood of state repression. In Chapter 3, I will present evidence on this point – that is, protest events that explicitly target the government are more likely to be repressed than those targeting corporations. But for now, it is simply important to point out that while corporations can and do sometimes employ private security forces, the likelihood of violent police response is lower for protesters targeting corporations than those targeting the state.

The Tactics of Anticorporate Activists

If, in fact, there has been an increase in recent decades of anticorporate activism, it makes sense to ask what tactical forms this activism takes. In general, we might usefully conceptualize the various ways in which activists target corporations as either "insider" or "outsider" strategies, although this certainly is not a completely clean categorization. In the United States, corporate governance is characterized by a shareholder approach and dispersed ownership (Buhner, Rasheed, Rosenstein, and Yoshikawa 1998; Roe 2000; Guillen 2000), which necessarily means that a corporation answers first to its shareholders as it attempts to maximize returns for those individuals (Friedman 1970). Shareholders, then, may be thought of as insiders to the corporation, even if they opt not to participate in proxy votes and annual meetings. This means that other stakeholders (e.g., employees, communities, or social movement organizations) traditionally have a much weaker influence on corporations as they are outsiders (Mitchell, Agle, and Wood 1997; Frooman 1999). By this, then, it is possible to define corporate "insiders" as those who are shareholders and corporate "outsiders" as those who are not (King and Soule 2007).[7]

---

[6] This idea of sub politics is similar to that of "private politics" (Baron 2003), a subject that I take up in Chapter 2.

[7] A slightly different conceptualization is offered by Eesley and Lenox (2006) who use the terms "internal stakeholders" (employees, customers, stockholders) and "secondary stakeholders" (activists, advocacy groups, religious groups, NGOs).

Insider Tactics

At times, corporate insiders (e.g., shareholders) are able to use their position to attempt to change the corporation. One such strategy is *shareholder activism*, which is when a shareholder or group of shareholders in some corporation uses an equity stake to exert pressure on the corporation. There are several forms that this can take, ranging from publicity and letter-writing campaigns to petitioning. One particularly interesting form of shareholder activism is the *shareholder resolution*. Shareholders, as partial owners of the corporation, are entitled to bring nonbinding resolutions to others for a vote and, as such, the annual shareholder meeting can become a site of political contestation (Vogel 1978). The first usage of this tactic was in 1947, when two brothers, John and Lewis Gilbert, who owned stock in Transamerica, asked managers of this corporation to add a resolution to the proxy statement requiring the company to use outside auditors (Rao 2009). When Transamerica declined to do this, the Securities and Exchange Commission (SEC) intervened and eventually ruled that managers of corporations could not exclude such proxy resolutions from stockholders. This case provided a legal basis for subsequent resolutions to be introduced by shareholders.

Other early and notorious usages of this tactic include the 1966 campaign against Kodak for discriminatory hiring practices (which I will discuss in more detail in Chapter 3) or the campaign by James Peck against Greyhound, which was initiated in 1948 when he bought stock in that bus company so that he could raise the issue of segregation at the annual meeting of the company (Murray 2007). Evelyn Yvonne Davis is another person made famous by her colorful resolutions introduced at shareholder meetings, such as the one that she introduced at General Motors (GM), wearing a bathing suit and waving an American Flag (Murray 2007: 94).[8] These instances were applauded by Ralph Nader and Saul Alinksy, both of whom argued for the effectiveness of insiders to the corporation. Since the 1980s, the use of this tactic has grown so much, that by 2003, there were 299 proposed resolutions dealing with social and environmental issues, a number that would rise to 348 in 2005 (Social Investment Forum 2006).

---

[8] Ms. Davis did not always submit resolutions associated directly with social movement causes. For example, she submitted a resolution to General Electric to get that company to cease contributing money to charity until it could be proven that the charity actually achieved results (Waldron 1972).

One way that traditional social movement organizations have been able to use this tactic is to purchase (or otherwise procure, for example by bequest) stock in offending companies. The SEC has developed a number of procedural requirements for shareholder resolutions, which are summarized in "Rule 14a-8." This document specifies eligibility requirements for shareholders to sponsor a resolution, including ownership amounts ($2,000 or 1% of the company's stock), length of time of ownership (minimum of one year), and regulations requiring proof of ownership if the stock is held through a broker. As well, this document specifies procedures for submitting resolutions, including the requirement that the resolution be submitted more than 120 days prior to the release of the company's proxy statement and the requirement that a single shareholder can only submit one resolution in a given year.

One well-publicized case of a traditional social movement organization sponsoring a shareholder resolution occurred in 2004, when People for the Ethical Treatment of Animals (PETA) submitted a proposal to Proctor and Gamble, the makers of Iams pet products. The proposal called on Iams to cease testing on animals in their laboratories. PETA was able to use this tactic because a former Proctor and Gamble employee willed the organization $110,000 in stock in the company. The proposal noted that animal testing was not necessary, was cruel, and that implementing humane treatment of animals would actually increase profits for the company.[9]

A related strategy may be broadly thought of as *socially responsible investment* (SRI), which is essentially an investment process that holistically considers the social and environmental ramifications of an investment, while still being mindful of the financial picture of the investment (Social Investment Forum 2006). Socially responsible investment comes in a variety of forms. One form of SRI, *community investing*, attempts to provide financial services (e.g., credit, equity, basic banking services, and so on) to traditionally underserved populations. By choosing to bank with local credit unions and institutions dedicated to community investing, individuals and organizations make a commitment to help supply capital to underserved groups' small businesses, community services, and other public goods. Or by participating in the growing practice of *micro-lending*,

---

[9] As will be discussed in more detail in Chapter 2, anticorporate activists often frame their claims in terms of what will benefit a company's profits, a strategy that has proven effective in many cases.

individuals can directly invest in populations underserved by established lending institutions.[10]

Another form of SRI is *screening*, which is the process of locating and investing in companies that attempt to behave ethically and morally and try to give something back to society. This can involve both "positive screening," which entails seeking out stocks from firms that behave in such a way, or "negative screening," which entails divesting of companies with questionable records. For example, investors (e.g., individuals or organizations) may choose to invest only in socially responsible mutual funds, such as The Blue Fund, Domini Social Investment, and Calvert Funds, which invest in companies that behave in socially responsible and moral ways. Or, they can choose to invest in religiously based funds (e.g., The Timothy Plan Fund or Azzad), which also screen along moral and ethical lines.[11]

The idea of investing responsibly has its roots in Colonial America, when certain religious groups (e.g., Quakers and Methodists) refused to invest in enterprises that benefited the slave trade (Social Investment Forum 2006). This idea was seized on in 1928 by Pioneer Fund, which was the first mutual fund to screen stocks for social issues such as alcohol, cigarettes, and gambling. Since the 1970s, socially responsible investing has grown markedly: In 1995 there were 55 socially screened mutual funds – a number that had grown to 201 by 2005. Most socially responsible investing, as it exists today, grew out of the movements of the 1960s and, as such, involves paying attention to women's, environmental, gay and lesbian, ethnic minority, and antiwar concerns (Social Investment Forum 2006). But there has also been a growth in explicitly religious mutual funds since the early 1990s.

Outsider Tactics

Turning now to outsider (or nonshareholder) strategies, we might think of the *boycott*, which is perhaps the quintessential tactic used by those outsiders

[10] For example, individuals can make small loans to others via such websites as kiva.org, which provide a lending platform that connects entrepreneurs to potential lenders. Kiva also allows lenders to volunteer time to the website by helping with translation and general website support.

[11] In recent years, there has also been a lot of media attention to the opposite trend, that is screening *out* responsible companies and instead selecting companies that profit on vices, such as alcohol, tobacco, and so on (e.g., The Vice Fund).

12

who are displeased by the actions of a given corporation (Manheim 2001; Chasin 2001). Essentially, a boycott is the refusal to purchase a company's goods or services in an attempt to express dissatisfaction with the company and to ultimately influence the corporation by threatening to constrain revenues or impose costs (Chasin 2001; King 2008b). Boycotts also appeal to broader constituencies by broadcasting the reason for the boycott and by imposing various kinds of direct and indirect costs on firms, including damage to the public image of a company (Fischoff, Nadaï, and Fischoff 2001; Baron 2003). This may be especially true, as I noted earlier, when boycotts make use of the Internet.[12]

Corporate campaigns are "coordinated, often long-term, and wide-ranging programs of economic, political, legal, and psychological warfare usually, but not exclusively, initiated by a union or by organized labor in general" (Manheim 2001: xiii). The tactic is a lot like the boycott, but unlike the boycott does not require that consumers actually get involved (at least at first). Instead, activists typically target well-known companies and attempt to do real damage to its image in an attempt to force change. As we know, businesses are susceptible to attacks on image (Pfeffer and Salancik 1978; Hart and Sharma 2004) and there are certainly benefits to having a positive reputation or image (Fombrun 1996; Fombrun and Shanley 1990).[13] On top of this, those that have a reputation for being socially responsible are especially vulnerable to being targeted because activists wish to force companies to abide by past principles (Vogel 2005).

As well, the corporate campaign uses a strategy of directly targeting the chosen corporation and its key players. For example, the tactical repertoire of the corporate campaign includes such things as flying banners with anticorporate information over sporting events, attacking CEOs directly by leafleting their neighbors and alleging sexual misconduct of the CEO, attacking the safety and environmental record of the company, setting up websites with negative information, and encouraging ministers to deliver anticompany sermons (Manheim 2005). In sum, the goal of the corporate campaign is the attack the company's image in multiple ways, with the hope of getting the company to agree to a set of demands. While sometimes consumers join and take part in boycotting the company, the

---

[12] See Chasin (2001) for a description of numerous boycotts organized by the gay and lesbian movement in the United States.

[13] As well, there are some benefits to having some degree of name recognition; however, being a recognized name is a double-edged sword, as those with a higher profile may be more likely to be targeted by activists (Klein 1999).

threat of damage to a company's reputation is often enough to encourage the corporation to acquiesce to the demands of the campaigners.

The corporate campaign tactic was pioneered by the labor movement in the 1970s, but is now routinely used by environmental, health, student, and human rights groups (Bennett 2003). Manheim (2001) describes 162 of these between 1974 and 1999 that were sponsored by unions and thirty-two nonunion campaigns in the 1989 through 1999 period. An example of a union-led corporate campaign was the worldwide campaign against oil companies operating in South Africa in the mid-1980s, which began by boycotting Shell Oil because of its history of safety and health violations. This was a cross-border campaign, involving the United Mine Workers of America, National Union of Mineworkers, and several South African unions, who worked together with social movement organizations to boycott oil companies working in South Africa.

Examples of nonunion campaigns are those run by the Rainforest Action Network (RAN), which organized campaigns against eight different corporations in the 1989 to 1999 period. One of these was against Mitsubishi Industries for its lumbering practices (Manheim 2001). In 1989, RAN bought a full-page advertisement in the *New York Times*, which explained that Mitsubishi was importing rainforest wood from Indonesia and Malaysia and therefore was contributing to the destruction of the rainforest. This advertisement spurred environmental activists to write letters and threaten a boycott. By 1993, RAN began a campaign of protest and advertisement (including a second full-page ad in the *New York Times*) against Mitsubishi and its products and then began a national boycott of the company. The campaign continued through the mid-1990s and involved a coalition with Greenpeace and continued to use a mixture of tactics (e.g., banner hanging, boycotts, protest, video presentation, picketing, and civil disobedience). The attack on Mitsubishi was multifaceted, drawing on humor (for example, the use of a forty-foot Godzilla balloon at an auto show in California where Mitsubishi cars were on display), and the power of the purse via boycotts. As well, the campaign did a lot to damage the image of the company, the hallmark of the corporate campaign. Finally, the campaign was careful to target different levels of authority, from individual auto and electronics dealers, to company headquarters, to the Bank of Tokyo (which financed Mitsubishi projects). In response to this campaign, in the mid-1990s the company began taking steps to improve its record on lumber and even agreed to help improve the rainforest in exchange for RAN calling off the boycott.

Advocacy Science is another tactic used by outsiders and entails citizens instituting or commissioning a policy or scientific study to bring attention to a given issue (Baron 2003). An example of this is the case of the movement against the bovine growth hormone. In the early 1990s the FDA approved the use of bovine growth hormone (rBGH) to stimulate milk production in dairy cows in the United States. Following its approval, the Consumer's Union released a study by its Consumer Policy Institute, which reviewed the extant research on rBGH and called for more research on the hormone alleging that it was unsafe and that the federal government did not conduct enough research on it. The public outcry following the release of this report was enough to damage the reputation of both the hormone and Monsanto, the company that had purchased the technology from Genentech (Soule 2003).

In recent years, advocacy science (sometimes called "citizen science") has been combined with pubic art installations by social movement organizations concerned with genetically modified foods. In 2003 and 2004, the group "Critical Art Ensemble" conducted a project called Free Range Grains where they conducted "amateur research" in public labs near food markets to test for the presence of genetically modified organisms (GMOs) in products purchased at the markets (www.beatrizdacosta.net/freerange.php, website accessed January 28, 2008). The goal was to show consumers that the products they purchased were not safe (or at least not free of GMOs). Or, in 2007, they used methods of synthetic biology to alter the color of bacteria and yeast cells when exposed to pollutants. The group placed displays of these cells nearby potential polluting companies in urban neighborhoods to raise the awareness of air pollution (www.beatrizdacosta.net/yeast.php, website accessed January 28, 2008).[14]

Another form of outsider activism might be referred to as *tempered activism*, which is essentially activism directed at a corporation surrounding corporate issues, policies, and practices by members or employees of the organization (Meyerson and Scully 1995; Meyerson 2001; Raeburn 2004).[15] Tempered activists (or radicals, in Meyerson and Scully's terms) are

---

[14] Beatriz da Costa is currently an Associate Professor of Arts, Computation, and Engineering at the University of California, Irvine and does "interventionist art." She has run several projects that blend art, advocacy science, and activism. Some of these projects target corporations, while others target the state (da Costa and Philip 2008).

[15] This is where the categorization of "insider" and "outsider" strategies based on shareholder status is not so clean. Obviously, there are times when employees of a given corporation are *also* shareholders of that corporation. See Eesley and Lenox (2006).

organizational members who are committed to the overall organizational goals, but because of their connections to external groups and identities that conflict with those of the organization, they become agents of change (Meyerson and Scully 1995; Meyerson 2001). For example, female executives who identify with the broad goals of the feminist movement and/ or have connections to the feminist movement can be agents of change within their corporations, while still carrying out their duties and responsibilities. This is a strategy that was identified over twenty-five years ago by Zald and Berger (1978), who noted that social movements often take place within organizations and are initiated by organizational members. Hodson (1996) notes that this form of contention is often overlooked in studies of the workplace and, as noted by Raeburn (2004), few social movement scholars have adequately addressed this kind of contention (but see Meyerson and Scully 1995, Swan 1997, Scully and Creed 1998, Meyerson 2001, and Raeburn 2004).

An example of this kind of activism occurred in 1970 in Massachusetts, when an employee of Polaroid discovered the company was selling its instant camera technology to companies in South Africa who were using the technology to produce pass books, which identified citizens' race to governmental officials and were used to identify black and nonwhite South Africans as targets of discriminatory practices.[16] In an attempt to force Polaroid to sever its dealings with these South African companies, a small group of Polaroid employees founded the Polaroid Revolutionary Workers Movement (Morgan 2006). The Movement operated, at least initially, from within the corporation but eventually also organized rallies and protest events that drew students and others from the greater Boston community (Morgan 2006).[17] Polaroid was an interesting target of this movement, as the company had a record of being more liberal minded than other global companies (Massie 1997). For example, Polaroid was headed by Edwin Land, who believed in comprehensive benefits packages for workers, including educational support, and who generally instituted

[16] Pass books and pass laws were one of the chief policies of apartheid and will be discussed in more detail in Chapter 4.

[17] "Employee networks" are groups of employees, generally defined by race or gender, that get together for a variety of reasons, but which can sometimes act as advocacy or social movement groups (Friedman and Craig 2004). While these are not always activist groups, these networks can be mobilized when issues arise, thus may be important for movements just as preexisting networks in broader social movement are (see review in Schussman and Soule 2005).

progressive business policies (Morgan 2006).[18] The company reacted swiftly to this movement by taking out advertisements in newspapers acknowledging their wrongdoing and by sending a team of experts to South Africa to study the situation therein (Massie 1997). As well, they instituted an experiment in South Africa that entailed actively trying to improve the working and living conditions in South Africa by increasing wages and benefits and donating funds to education and community groups.

Collective legal maneuvers are often used by outsiders to the corporation, too. For example, in the mid-1980s, W. L. Gore and Associates was sued (unsuccessfully) by former workers who claimed that the chemical toluene diisocynate, used in making Gore-Tex fabric, harmed their health (*New York Times* 1989). In the 1980s, several women sued the A. H. Robbins Company, the maker of the Dalkon Shield contraceptive device, for pelvic infections, which sometimes led to infertility (*New York Times* 1984a). Or, in the 1970s, Ford and GM were both sued by former workers who claimed that these companies discriminated against pregnant women (*New York Times* 1979).[19] And, in a large study of lawsuits and legal maneuvers, Lenox and Eesley (2006) code 144 civil suits targeting companies because of environmental infringements in the 1971 to 2003 period. They report that such suits are the most effective means used to influence corporate behavior (when compared to protest, boycotts, letter-writing campaigns, and proxy votes).

Finally, *protest demonstrations* are perhaps the quintessential tactic used by social movements who are outsiders to the corporation. Protest, like the boycott, is available for use by people outside of the corporation who may be unable to use shareholder resolutions or who do not have the capital to invest in socially responsible funds (King and Soule 2007). Protest is also explicitly a public action as protesters choose to broadcast grievances to broad audiences, rather than going to authorities with expressions of desired changes and keeping this information and debate

---

[18] However, as was mentioned earlier and will be discussed in more detail in Chapter 5 with respect to Nike, often it is precisely such corporations that are targeted by anticorporate activists. That is, those with a reputation for behaving responsibly are often quite likely to be targeted by anticorporate activists.

[19] Critical readers may wonder if lawsuits brought by workers are *insider* or *outsider* tactics. Recall the way I have categorized these types of actions: Insider actions are conducted by those who own stock in a company. Thus, while it is possible that the workers at W. L. Gore, GM, and Ford held stock in these companies, in these lawsuits they were not drawing upon their insider (e.g., shareholder) status.

Table 1.1. *Tactics of Anticorporate Activists in the United States*

Insider Status	Outsider Status
Shareholder Activism	Boycott
Shareholder Resolutions	Corporate Campaigns
Socially Responsible Investment	Advocacy Science/Citizen Science
Community Investment	Tempered Activism
Microfinance	Collective Legal Maneuvers
Positive and Negative Screening	Protest

in a more enclosed environment. Protest thus calls for the involvement of various audiences in the change process, appealing as much to the masses as to internal decision makers. As such, protest may go hand-in-hand with corporate campaigns, in that both are able to change the image of the company – one mainly through the use of the Internet (Bennett 2003), the other through the use of mobilizing people to gather collectively to express grievances (King and Soule 2007). As well, protest is often used jointly with shareholder activism, as was the case of the movement directed at the Cracker Barrel chain restaurant because of their dismissal of all gay and lesbian employees following a memo from the CEO stating that the restaurant would not "continue to employ individuals ... whose sexual preferences fail to demonstrate normal heterosexual values" (Niebuhr 1991: C1). The National Gay and Lesbian Task Force (NGLTF) and other gay and lesbian groups began staging protests and pickets outside of restaurants, framing the dismissals as egregious and socially irresponsible. At the same time, shareholder resolutions were introduced in an effort to make the company cease its policy of discrimination against gay and lesbian employees. During the period, Cracker Barrel stock fell 26% below the expected rate of return, suggesting that such actions can impact a company's bottom line.

To summarize, anticorporate activism takes many forms and sometimes draws on the status of activists as insiders and sometimes as outsiders to the corporation. Drawing on these two statuses, there are multiple ways that activists target the corporation. These are summarized in Table 1.1.

The chief subject of this book is the outsider form of public protest, but it is important to note that, as was the case in the Cracker Barrel example, in many instances, activists take a multipronged approach. This multipronged approach combines tactics falling into *both* the insider and outsider categories summarized in Table 1.1 and described previously. Thus, while I focus primarily on protest in this book, I do also discuss the combinatorial reality of the set of tactics used when targeting corporations.

Thus far, I have described some of the reasons for increases in activism directed at corporations and noted that this is increasingly done via targeting corporations directly, rather than through some intermediary institution (e.g., the government or labor). And I have also described the chief tactical forms used by insiders and outsiders to the corporation. I turn now to a general discussion of what it is that anticorporate activists are trying to change with these actions.

What Are They Incensed About? The Growth of Claims about Corporate Social Responsibility

The New Englanders who took part in the raids on the East India Company's tea stores, the Polaroid workers who protested the company's business ties to South Africa, the PETA activists who submitted the shareholder resolution at Proctor and Gamble, the RAN's campaign against Mitsubishi, and the NGLTF activists who picketed Cracker Barrel were angry about the unchecked growth of corporations and corporate power, corporations' mistreatment of workers (and animals), corporations' environmental records, and sometimes corporate ties to the government. In general, they were angry that corporations were not behaving in a way that benefits the greater society. We might say that all of these activists were upset that a given company was not acting in a socially responsible way.[20] This issue, while obviously not framed as such in 1773 during the Boston Tea Party or even in 1970 when the Polaroid workers were mobilizing, is the root of anticorporate activism today. Thus, any book on the subject anticorporate activism would not be complete without some discussion of *corporate social responsibility.*

While notions of the moral imperative of private business have been around for a very long time, it has not been until rather recently that the

---

[20] In Chapter 3, I will examine *specific* claims articulated at anticorporate protest events in the United States. As we will see, these fall into three primary categories: anticorporate policy, antiproduct, and antinegligence. I argue that all three of these categories are part and parcel to the broader issue of corporate social responsibility.

idea of social responsibility of businesses has been palatable to businesses themselves and shareholders alike. To illustrate this change, in 1977 less than half of Fortune 500 firms mentioned corporate social responsibility in their annual reports, but by the end of the 1990s, nearly 90% of them did (Lee 2008). More recently, the *Economist* Intelligence Unit found that nearly half of the firms it surveyed felt that corporate social responsibility is a necessary cost of doing business and that it might actually give them a distinctive position in the market (*Economist* January 17, 2008). What is corporate social responsibility and why are so many corporations interested in it?

The term "corporate social responsibility" (CSR) implies "... the commitment by business to behave ethically and contribute to economic development while improving the quality of life of the workforce and their families as well as of the local community and society at large" (World Business Council for Sustainable Development 2002).[21] While this idea had been around previously, the term itself was first used in 1953 by Howard Bowen, in his book *Social Responsibilities of the Businessman*. As Bowen (1953) notes, the idea that businesses should be socially responsible was promoted before him by religious (especially Puritan and Protestant) writers; however, his work was perhaps the first attempt to systematize the set of beliefs and rationale for CSR. In the book, Bowen argues unequivocally that the scope and consequences of business decisions obligate them to consider the social effects such decisions have.

Just after the time Bowen was writing, the consumer rights movement in the United States grew in prominence, often dramatizing cases of corporate malfeasance. For example, the 1965 publication of Ralph Nader's *Unsafe at Any Speed: the Designed-In Dangers of the American Automobile*, blamed American automobile companies' lax safety standards on the number of injuries and deaths on the nation's highways. This best-selling book and the broader consumer rights movement played a critical role in governmental regulation of the auto industry (especially via the National Traffic and Vehicle Safety Act of 1968).

As illustrated by this example, during these early stages, the consumer rights movement attempted to exert influence on corporate behavior via

---

[21] Recently the term "corporate sustainability" has come to be used nearly synonymously with corporate social responsibility. Corporate sustainability was used initially to refer to attempts of companies to behave in an environmentally responsible way, but recently it has grown to encompass much more (*The Economist* Intelligence Unit 2008).

targeting the government, primarily by fighting for greater regulation of firms (Vogel 1978). That began to change in the 1960s, when movements began to target businesses directly, as I noted earlier. For example, the sit-ins at Woolworth's and Kress stores directly targeted these establishments for their practices of segregation and reportedly had a dramatic effect on the revenues of these chains (Luders 2006). And, as I will discuss in Chapter 3, during the Vietnam War, Dow Chemical was targeted directly by activists for its production of napalm, while Honeywell was targeted for its production of weaponry used during that war.

Events such as these in the 1960s highlighted Americans' growing distrust of corporations, although they probably never really fully trusted them to begin with (Vogel 1978). Nonetheless, in the late 1960s and 1970s, corporate leaders could not ignore the pressures of citizens for more accountability. In this early era, corporate response was often little more than symbolic, and many classical economists objected vehemently to the idea that corporations could and should act in ways that would benefit anyone other than shareholders. Milton Friedman, for example, called corporate social responsibility a "fundamentally subversive doctrine," the acceptance of which "... involves the acceptance of the socialist view that political mechanisms, not market mechanisms, are the appropriate way to determine the allocation of scarce resources to alternative uses" (Friedman 1970: SM17).

In 1970, a study was commissioned by the Committee for Economic Development, which was entitled *A New Rationale for Corporate Social Policy*. This publication urged economists, business leaders, and the public to consider ways in which corporate social responsibility could be seen as less at odds with profits of shareholders. In particular, one of the articles in the study suggested that because most shareholders by 1970 owned stock in many companies (as opposed to just one), they could be less concerned with profit motives of a single company and more interested in spreading social expenditures evenly over a number of firms in a way that does not, overall in a diverse portfolio, compromise the benefits (Wallich and McGowan 1970).

The publication of this study led to something of a sea change in the literature on corporate social responsibility. Rather than debating whether or not companies should engage in socially responsible behaviors, the literature began to explore how corporations could implement socially responsible actions in ways that would not compromise the best interests of stockholders (Lee 2008).

In the wake of this study, scholars began to better articulate ways in which corporations could simultaneously make money and be attentive to legal, ethical, and social issues involved in their policies and practices. This coincided with an increase in attention to the *stakeholder approach* in management studies, which will be discussed in more detail in Chapter 2. Essentially, the stakeholder approach views the economic goals of the corporation to be less important than organizational survival. As such, shareholders are no longer seen as the only – or even the main – stakeholder in the corporation. Instead, it has become commonplace to recognize that unions, employees, customers, social movements, and governments have direct effects on corporate survival, and as such, should no longer be ignored by companies.

In fact, strategic management scholars have increasingly promoted the benefits to corporations for behaving in a responsible fashion. For example Hart (1997), focusing on the environment, notes that if corporations can couple the concept of sustainability to their development, they can achieve a competitive advantage over other corporations. Others (e.g., Kotler and Lee 2005) suggest that corporations broaden their charitable activities and suggest ways to frame such actions to increase their competitive advantages. In essence, this line of scholarship has tapped into public perceptions about the appropriate role of the corporation as socially responsible and argues that corporations will lose legitimacy by damaging their image or reputation if they do not behave in socially responsible ways.

A recent op-ed in the *New York Times* (Barbaro 2008) discusses this very issue with respect to Wal-Mart. Wal-Mart, according to the piece, has moved from its former pariah status as a corporation (e.g., low wages and lack of health insurance for employees, discrimination against women, and so on), to a much more favorably perceived company. Barbaro argues that this transformation was set in place by Wal-Mart's conscious efforts at damage control in the face of mounting negative publicity. In addition to attempting to clean up their act as an employer, Wal-Mart also adopted a proactive CSR stance when it responded to Hurricane Katrina by delivering water and food to victims of the tragedy (in advance even of the federal government). Wal-Mart has also remade its image by becoming something of a leader on environmental sustainability issues (Denend and Plambeck 2007). In short, Wal-Mart, according to Barbaro, has learned that CSR can be good for its bottom line.

This is fundamentally a different way of thinking about corporate social responsibility than was the case in the 1960s. Rather than framing corporate behavior as morally right or wrong, in the more recent era, companies are urged to consider the damage to their reputation or image if they do *not* behave responsibly. For example, as I just noted, in the 1960s activists targeted Dow Chemical in an attempt to get the company to cease production of napalm. Their argument was framed in terms of the immorality of war, broadly, and the use of napalm, specifically, and there was little or no mention of how napalm production would impact Dow's earnings. However, Dow has recently been targeted by activists in an attempt to encourage the company to reduce emissions. In this more recent campaign, activists frame their arguments in terms of how behaving in an environmentally responsible fashion will increase Dow's earnings (Vogel 2005). In sum, coupling social responsibility with a corporation's bottom line differs markedly from how activists framed claims in earlier periods, and in so doing may have a far greater impact on what corporations actually do.[22]

Lee (2008) argues that it is precisely this different framing of what corporate social responsibility *is* (and, more importantly, how it can benefit the corporation's financial performance) that has led to the growth of discussion of the concept in academic and strategy circles, as well as by the broader public. This growth can be seen in Figure 1.1, which shows the count of different articles mentioning corporate social responsibility in several different venues in the 1970 to 2007 period: scholarly journals, trade publications, and newspapers and magazines.[23] Figure 1.1 shows a dramatic increase in attention to corporate social responsibility in the 1990s in all of these venues.[24]

---

[22] In Chapter 2, I discuss Raeburn's (2004) ideas on "frame blending," or the use of two or more frames, at least one of which appeals to the target and at least one of which appeals to potential activists. In her case, activists successfully framed the issue of domestic partnership benefits in terms of ethics for potential activists *and* in terms of the bottom line for the companies targeted.

[23] Note that between 1950 and 1970, there were only two mentions of corporate social responsibility in these venues, one in 1960 and the other in 1969, both in scholarly journals.

[24] The growth in attention to corporate social responsibility is also evidenced by the way in which most Americans now believe that companies should operate in a morally responsible manner by doing things such as ensuring that workers in other countries have safe working conditions, are paid a living wage, and are allowed to unionize (Gereffi, Garcia-Jones, and Sasser 2001).

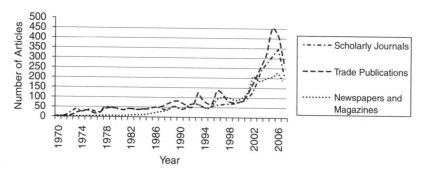

Figure 1.1 Media Attention to Corporate Social Responsibility, 1970–2007.
Source: ABI/INFORM Global Database of Periodicals.

Another example of the popularity of CSR is the UN Global Compact, which is a set of principles for companies that are committed to the ideas of CSR, especially with regard to the Compact's "Ten Universally Accepted Principles" related to human rights, labor, the environment, and anticorruption. The Global Compact is the world's largest "corporate citizenship" initiative and, by October 2007, over 3,500 companies had signed onto the Compact. The rhetoric produced by the Global Compact promotes the idea that CSR can enhance profits via enhancing trust, social capital, and contributing to sustainable markets. Firms that decide to participate in the Global Compact provide the Compact with annual reports and "stories" about actions that the company is taking to act more responsibly. In return, the company can use the Global Compact logo, which serves as a legitimating device and signals that the company believes in the principles of the Compact and perhaps CSR more broadly.

As one might imagine, this growth and acceptance of the CSR concept has been highly contested. In the academic and popular literatures on corporate social responsibility, questions about whether or not corporations should engage in socially responsible activities and abide by socially responsible principles are often hotly debated. In the popular press, the debate was played out very clearly in a 2005 *Reason* magazine forum in which Milton Friedman (whose historical opposition to CSR is highlighted above) and T. J. Rodgers, the founder and CEO of Cypress Semiconductor and fellow opponent of CSR, were invited to comment on an article written by John Mackey, the cofounder and CEO of Whole Foods Markets. Rodgers, like Friedman, articulated his view that shareholders do not necessarily invest in companies so that managers can use proceeds to better the world. In fact, Rodgers (echoing Friedman's 1970 sentiments) went as far as to equate CSR ideas with those of Karl Marx and Ralph Nader. On the other side of the debate, Mackey articulated his view that companies should pay attention to various constituencies, such as customers, employees, vendors, and local communities, and not merely to investors. One of the issues debated in this forum was the difference between the ethics of CSR and the potential profit that can be made by businesses operating in accordance with CSR principles.

The debates in the academic literature mirror these two dimensions of the debate surrounding CSR, with business ethics scholars (e.g., Solomon 1983; Donaldson and Preston 1995; Fort 2001) and management scholars (e.g., Hinings and Greenwood 2002; Margolis and Walsh 2003) arguing for CSR on moral grounds, and others (e.g., Orlitzky, Schmidt, and Rynes 2003) arguing for CSR on business grounds. Thus, as activists using both insider and outsider tactics target companies around issues of CSR, it has become abundantly clear that companies must do something about CSR or risk losing legitimacy, which can damage their reputations.

Summary and Conclusion

This chapter argued that throughout the history of corporations in the United States, there has been anticorporate sentiment and distrust, which has periodically led activists to revolt against corporations. Often, this has been accomplished through directing complaints toward the government to encourage the passage of policy designed to regulate corporations. Or, sometimes such sentiments have been channeled through organized labor, which can challenge corporations directly on behalf of workers. In fact, throughout much of U.S. history, most challenges to corporations were launched in these indirect ways; that is, through channeling these other, more powerful institutions.

I argue in this chapter, however, that this has changed in recent times. With the erosion of governmental regulation of businesses and the decline in the power of labor, often the most effective strategy – and sometimes the *only* strategy – is to target corporations directly. This chapter reviewed the tactics that anticorporate activists use and how the term "corporate social responsibility" has come to crystallize the various grievances and complaints of these corporate stakeholders.

In the next chapter, I will step back from specific cases of anticorporate activism and review some of the theoretical approaches to understanding how social movements matter to the institutions that they target. I will draw heavily on the broader literature on movement outcomes or consequences and describe how these approaches are making their way into analyses of anticorporate activism. The goal is to synthesize ideas on this topic from political science, sociology, and organizational studies to suggest both a theoretical framework and some analytical tools appropriate to the study of anticorporate activism.

In Chapter 3, I examine thirty-one years of data on anticorporate protest events in the United States (1960–1990). I describe how these events were often connected to other social movements, such as the civil rights or the peace movement, how many of these events also target various governmental institutions and authorities, and how often times protest is coupled with other strategies and tactics, both insider and outsider forms. Finally, I discuss findings of an analysis of how these events have impacted the financial picture of targeted firms; findings that point to the effectiveness of anticorporate protest.

In Chapter 4, I turn to an examination of how activism impacted college and university divestment decisions during the 1980s. Faced with criticism for investments in firms doing business in South Africa, colleges and universities began to adopt policies of divesting of these firms. In this chapter, I will present findings that indicate that student activism impacted university decisions in very specific ways, suggesting again that protest can matter to issues related to corporate social responsibility. I also discuss the broader literature on divestment and how divestment may impact corporations and their activities, with an eye toward understanding the ultimate effects of the student divestment movement (that is, ending apartheid).

In Chapter 5, I turn to the post-1990 era and profile several different instances of activism directed at corporations. This chapter highlights the point made in this chapter that much of this activism, while directed at corporations, is also directed at governmental policies. In particular, Earth Island Institute's campaign for dolphin-safe tuna, the Free Burma Coalition's campaign to get multinational enterprises to divest from Burma, and the Laborers' International Union's campaign against corporate homebuilders were all directed simultaneously at corporations and the government.[25] Alongside these three cases, I also discuss the United

[25] Note that in 1989, the Burmese military changed the name of the country to Myanmar. The name change is considered controversial because it is seen as less inclusive of

Students Against Sweatshop's campaign against Nike, the Amnesty International and Students for Bhopal campaign against Dow Chemical, and the Greenpeace campaign against the Gerber corporation as examples of protest directed primarily at corporations.

The final chapter of this book, Chapter 6, will offer some conclusions for sociologists, political scientists, and organizations scholars and will propose some questions for future research.

The message of this book should be a positive one. That is, a major theme in this book is that citizens can and do matter to corporations – with respect to their financial picture (e.g., corporate financial performance) and with respect to the policies and practices that they adopt (e.g., corporate social performance). As such, the major message of this book speaks to some of the work by John Kenneth Galbraith who, in the 1950s, argued that there are four ways to counter the ill effects of rampant corporate power and to force them to behave in ways that reflect the best interests of society.[26] The first is to maintain free competition between corporations, which acts as a natural check on the tendency for corporations to cease serving the public good. The second is to encourage and enforce governmental regulation of corporations.[27] And the third is to strengthen organized labor. As we have seen in this chapter, these first three legs of Galbraith's "countervailing corporate power" are presently quite shaky. However, Galbraith also suggested that citizen activism and organization can be used effectively to help keep corporate power in check. This is the point of this book as well and, as such, is a positive message for those interested in the power of citizen action.

As well, my message about corporations and corporate response is one of optimism. Any longer, corporations are finding that they must attend to issues of CSR. While cynics may charge that corporate action is mere lip service and that substantive changes are not possible, I prefer a more optimistic interpretation. In many cases, corporations *are* behaving in a

---

minorities and was also never formally approved by any legislative body in Burma. Moreover, the U.S. Government (along with Great Britain and Ireland) has not adopted the name change. Thus, I follow the convention of the U.S. Government and of other academics (e.g., Schock 1999) and use "Burma" rather than Myanmar.

[26] See Galbraith's (1952) *American Capitalism: The Concept of Countervailing Power* for a more in-depth discussion of these points.

[27] These first two points made by Galbraith are echoed nicely in Yaziji and Doh (2009), who link the emergence of nongovernmental organizations targeting corporations to failures in the market and in traditional (i.e., state) regulatory bodies.

far more ethical and responsible fashion than they once did. And, they are doing so for both financial reasons and for reasons perhaps not directly connected to their bottom line (Mackey, Mackey, and Barney 2007). The duel trends, then, of citizen action and corporate social responsibility are, I believe, good reasons for optimism.

2

Understanding Social Movements, Contentious and Private Politics, and Their Consequences

In a recent synthetic discussion of two of the most active areas of sociological inquiry – organizational studies and social movement studies – McAdam and Scott (2005) show that there is a great deal to be learned by crosspollination between these two distinct areas. One key area of inquiry at this nexus is the *consequences* that social movements have on corporations. While Zald and Berger (1978) made this observation over three decades ago, it has become an even more critical area of inquiry given the enormous growth in corporate economic and political power alongside the decline in power of regulatory agencies of the government and organized labor (as I discussed in Chapter 1). As I noted in the previous chapter, citizen anticorporate activism may be the last remaining way to influence corporate behavior and by all indicators, this type of activism shows no evidence of waning (Galbraith 1952; Yaziji and Doh 2009).

If scholarship on this topic is accurate, in the past few decades there has been an increase in activism directly targeting firms (e.g., Vogel 1978; Doh and Teegan 2003). For example, as I discuss in Chapter 5, a number of firms – including Pepsi and Unocal – have been targeted because of their investments in Burma (Spar and La Mure 2003). Nike has been targeted by a number of different social movement organizations because of its alleged mistreatment of workers in foreign factories, a campaign that I also discuss in Chapter 5. Such campaigns directed at firms for alleged malfeasance, harmful policies and products, exploitation, and scandalous behavior have been referred to as the left-leaning "Biz-War" (Manheim 2004); however, it is important to note that right-leaning social movements have also targeted firms. For example, the prolife movement in the United States has sponsored a boycott of pharmacy chains that dispense birth-control pills and emergency contraceptives. And, the boycotts of the Walt Disney Corporation by Christian groups for their products (e.g., the film *Priest*, which was released by Miramax in 1995) and for extending domestic partnership benefits to gay and lesbian workers are other examples of right-leaning movements targeting corporations.

The increase in interest in social movements that target corporations is reflected in the concept of *private politics* (Baron 2001; Baron 2003; Baron and Diermeier 2007). Private politics are collective interactions between parties attempting to advance their interests that do *not* rely on the law, public order, or the state (Baron 2003). As such, they are similar to what Beck (2000) refers to as subpolitics, which as mentioned in Chapter 1, are those that exist below the level of the state. The concept of private politics has been applied most fruitfully to corporate-directed social movement activity when the state does *not* become involved and is not targeted in any obvious way. This concept may be contrasted with *contentious politics*, which, as will be discussed in more detail shortly, are collective interactions between parties seeking to advance their interests, but in which one of the parties *is* the state or some element thereof (McAdam, Tarrow, and Tilly 2001: 5). Typically, as we will see, the state is the target of collective action in contentious politics.

The purpose of this chapter is to discuss what we know about how social movements, and by this I mean *both* contentious and private politics, matter to corporations. To do this, we must recognize that much of what we have learned about movement consequences or outcomes has come from scholarship on the effects of movements on *state* targets. Nonetheless, this scholarship is useful as we begin to understand the effects of movements on corporations. I begin this chapter by offering a working definition of what I mean by social movements, contentious politics, and private politics. I argue that all three of these terms are essential to understanding anticorporate activism and its effects on corporations.

Following this definitional matter, I describe the types of outcomes or consequences that social movement scholars have focused on, with an eye toward reviewing scholarship on corporate and organizational outcomes.

Finally, I review the major theoretical approaches to the study of social movement outcomes and sketch out how these theories can be adapted and imported into the study of organizational and corporate outcomes. In this final section, I focus on how both characteristics of the movement and characteristics of the context or environment impact movement outcomes. A major theme in this final section is that corporations and the movements that challenge them exist in a multilayered, nested set of environmental factors that impact whether a movement ultimately challenges the corporation solely (i.e., private politics), or whether it also targets some government or agency thereof (i.e., contentious politics).

Defining Social Movements, Contentious Politics, and Private Politics

When thinking about the Boston Tea Party as I described in Chapter 1 and other more recent events of anticorporate activism that I will describe in subsequent chapters of this book, it is helpful to conceptualize what social scientists mean by a "social movement" and offer a working definition of one. Of course, definitions of social movements abound in the literature, especially in edited volumes based on conferences, texts on the subject, and in scholarly papers and books.[1] For example, some simply state that social movements are "collective attempts to promote or resist change in a society or group" (Benford, Gongaware, and Valadez 2000: 2712). While others specify a number of different "systems of authority" (Snow 2004; Snow and Soule 2009), such as the broader culture, organizations, educational and religious institutions, and so on, all of which may be targeted by social movements.

It is useful to have an expansive definition of social movements, such as those offered by Snow (2004) and Snow and Soule (2009), because it allows us to consider the phenomenon of interest in this book using concepts, terms, and theories germane to the study of social movements. That said, there are times when a more limited definition (that is, either contentious or private politics) is useful, such as when we wish to isolate the mechanisms and processes driving anticorporate activity. In such cases, it is helpful, if not necessary, to limit our phenomena of inquiry in some fashion. Thus, following a discussion of some of the points of agreement in the extant definitions of social movements, I will say more about the two specific *types* of social movement activity briefly defined above: contentious politics and private politics, both of which are essential to the subject of this book.

The first point of agreement in most definitions is that social movements are collective enterprises with a common goal that operate, at least part of the time, outside of institutional channels. The qualification

---

[1] This discussion is based on the Introduction to the *Blackwell Companion to Social Movements* (2004), which I wrote with my coeditors of that volume. Please see this work for an elaboration of the points made herein (Snow, Soule, and Kriesi 2004).

that social movements must sometimes operate outside of institutional channels helps us to specify what we are interested in more clearly. If we consider goal-directed, collective action, *without* specifying that some of the action must take place outside of institutional channels, then we would include lobbying, interest group activity, and some activities of political parties.[2] Similarly, if we remove the condition that social movements must have some common goal but keep the noninstitutional dimension, then we might include various kinds of collective behavior that we normally do *not* think of as part and parcel to social movements, such as fads or stampedes at sporting events.

A second point of agreement in the various definitions of social movements is that social movements promote or resist change, but there is some debate in the literature about what the locus or level of this change is. In fact, as I will describe, this debate reflects the major difference between contentious politics and private politics. But for now, it is sufficient to point out that social movements attempt to change a situation or resist a change to a system thought to be desirable by the movement.

A third point of agreement in these definitions is that social movements have some degree of organization and coordination. While there has been a great deal of debate on the degree and form of the organization needed for social movement activity, most scholars agree that at least some kind of organization is necessary for social movements. On one side of this debate are scholars who follow the claims of Piven and Cloward (1977), who argue that too much organization is the death knell of effective mobilization, particularly among the poor. According to Piven and Cloward (1977), the power of social movements lies in their ability to disrupt. Because more formally organized groups are less likely to be disruptive, a high degree of organization necessarily means that the group will be less effective. On the other side of this debate are those who follow McCarthy and Zald (1977) who argue that social movement organizations (SMOs) are fundamental not only for assembling and deploying resources necessary for effectively mounting movement campaigns, but they are also key to the realization of a movement's objectives.

More recently, some scholars have argued that SMOs are not the most important unit of analysis for studying social movements; instead, it is important to focus on the networks of individuals that may or may not

---

[2] Note that Burstein (1999) argues that all of these types of activity, including social movement activity, are best thought of as "interest organization" activity.

constitute formal organizations (Della Porta and Diani 1999). That is, organization is best viewed as a continuum; on one end, there are loose, informal networks of people, while on the other end there are highly structured networks of individuals that are characteristic of formal organizations. The issue of organization of social movements is probably best clarified by Tarrow (1998), who distinguishes between social movements as formal organizations, the organization of collective action, and social movements as connective structures or networks. The basic point is that, regardless of how we think about organizations, the existence of social movement activity implies some degree of organization, whether that is formal or informal, structured or unstructured.

A fourth and final point of agreement in most definitions of social movements is that they operate with some degree of temporal continuity; in other words they last for some length of time. Usually the kinds of changes movements pursue require some measure of sustained, organized activity. Some movements are fairly short-lived, when people mobilize for a very specific reason and demobilize when the issue has been resolved. Other movements last a great deal longer, sometimes for generations (e.g., the Women's Movement). Others cluster temporally within broader "cycles of protest" that wax and wane historically (Tarrow 1998).

Based on these four points of agreement, it is now possible to offer a working definition of a social movement. Social movements are collectivities acting with some degree of organization and continuity outside of institutional channels for the purpose of seeking or resisting change in some extant system of authority. By this definition, contentious politics is an important and common form of social movement – one in which actors challenge or defend the state or some unit thereof. And, by this definition, private politics is another important and common form of social movement – one in which actors challenge another private actor, without the help or intervention of the state or public order. In its most common empirical usage, private politics has been used to understand corporate-directed social movement activity, the subject of this book.[3]

Scholars of contentious politics have been criticized for too narrowly defining their subject by including only cases of social movement activity

---

[3] In Baron's (2003: 7) terms, private politics are when an activist group "seeks to change the production practices of a firm for the purpose of redistribution to those whose interests it supports."

in which the government is either an object or a target of the activity (Snow 2004; Van Dyke, Soule, and Taylor 2004). This is not surprising, of course, as the term was developed by political sociologists. But, we might also criticize scholars of private politics for too narrowly defining their concept so as to mean that there is no state action involved. This is not especially surprising either, given that the term was developed by a scholar in a business school (Baron 2001; 2003a; 2003b).[4]

The problem is that anticorporate activism sometimes *is* pure private politics, wherein there is no discernible state action or target. For example, in Chapter 5, I will describe the United Students Against Sweatshops campaign against Nike for its use of sweatshop labor in foreign factories. In this case, there was no apparent attempt to seek governmental intervention into Nike's doings.

But, sometimes there *is* some attempt to target the state either through corporations, alongside corporations, or as a means to impact corporations via regulation. This was illustrated in the case of the Boston Tea Party, as discussed in Chapter 1, when the proximate target was a monopolistic company, but the ultimate target was Britain. Similarly, in the case of the Free Burma Coalition (which will be discussed in Chapter 5), activists targeted corporations directly, but hoped to ultimately influence the ruling government of Burma. As well, as the movement progressed, it began to expand its targeting beyond corporations to also include state and local governments in the United States in an attempt to influence decisions on selective purchasing agreements.

Thus, it is my hope that this book can offer something to both sets of scholars – private politics scholars should note that some of their subject is missed with a narrow focus on nongovernmental interactions, and contentious politics scholars should note that some interesting and important activity is missed when focusing solely on interactions in which one party is the state. Straddling the line between two literatures and intellectual fields is not always easy; however, I believe that the subject of this book is one in which it is absolutely necessary to do so and that the ultimate payoff will be a much deeper understanding of anticorporate activism and how corporations (and the state) respond to it.

---

[4] To be fair, Baron (2001: 7) compares private politics to public politics, which (like contentious politics) is when "groups attempt to influence officeholders to the benefit of the groups themselves or those whom they support." But, the empirical work coming out of this tradition has focused on private politics and, more specifically, activism directed at firms.

34

Now that I have laid the basic conceptual groundwork for thinking about this class of movement activity, it is important to outline what we know about how movements matter. To this end, I briefly review the literature on social movement consequences or outcomes, especially with respect to the outcomes of anticorporate activism.

Conceptualizing Outcomes or Consequences of Movements

Most scholars of social movements, private politics, and contentious politics assume that social movements have *some* impact, whether that impact be direct or indirect (Cress and Snow 2000), intramovement or extramovement (Earl 2000), intended or unintended (Deng 1997), or comes in the form of "new advantages" or "acceptance" (Gamson 1990). However, until recently, there was little research that actually looked empirically at the outcomes, consequences, impacts, or effects of movements; instead, researchers were content with working out explanations for the emergence of, and fluctuations in, movement activity.[5] And, in the late-1990s, several other scholars picked up on this point and issued a call for research into this very question (Giugni 1998; Soule et al. 1999; Giugni, McAdam, and Tilly 1999; Earl 2000).

In answer to the call for research about outcomes, research on the subject has proliferated in recent years. Much of the empirical research in the social movement literature on movement outcomes falls into four broad categories: *state response, cultural outcomes, personal or biographical consequences*, and, most recently, *corporate-level outcomes*.[6]

The bulk of research on outcomes examines how movements impact the state. The most commonly studied type of state response is a *policy change*; for example, McCammon, Campbell, Granberg, and Mowery (2001) examine how women's suffrage activism, organization, and framing impacted state-level women's suffrage laws (see also King, Cornwall, and Dahlin 2005) and Soule and her colleagues (Soule and Olzak 2004;

---

[5] I use the terms "outcomes," "impacts," and "consequences" interchangeably throughout this book. These terms refer to the effects that social movements have on something else and they avoid the more narrow terms "success" and "failure" because, of course, not all of the effects of movements are about the realization (or nonrealization) of stated goals.

[6] These are clearly the most prevalent types of outcomes studied. However, some studies do not fall neatly into these categories. For example, a growing area of research looks at the effects movements have on other movements (Meyer and Whittier 1995; Soule 1997; Strang and Soule 1997).

Soule and King 2006) study how activism impacted states' decisions to ratify the Equal Rights Amendment in the United States. Another form of state response is *congressional hearings* and *roll call votes* on a subject. For example, Soule, McAdam, McCarthy, and Su (1999) examine the effect of feminist movement organizations and activism on congressional hearings on women's issues. McAdam and Su (2002) examine the effect of peace movement activism on congressional hearings and roll call votes related to war, and Olzak and Soule (2009) examine the effects of environmental activism on congressional hearings on the environment. A third type of state response is *repression* or *policing of protest*. Repression takes many forms, from policing of protesters by the state or by private policing agencies, to blacklisting of protesters, to investigation and surveillance of protesters. For example, Earl, Soule, and McCarthy (2003), Earl and Soule (2006), and Soule and Davenport (2009) study how the various characteristics of both protest events and police agencies impact levels of police response to protest. Finally, others have looked at *levels of state spending* on various social welfare programs as a result of movement activity and other factors (Amenta, Carruthers, and Zylan 1992; Amenta, Dunleavy, and Bernstein 1994; Andrews 2001).

There is much less research on the effects of social movements on culture, in large part because *cultural outcomes* are notoriously difficult to study because there is little agreement on what is meant by 'culture' and even less agreement on how one might measure cultural change (Earl 2004). Those who have examined cultural outcomes have conceptualized cultural change in three main ways. First, several researchers study changes in *values, opinions, and beliefs* as a function of movements (Gamson and Modigliani 1989; d'Anjou 1996; Rochon 1998). Second, others study changes in *cultural practices* (e.g., literature, music, media, fashion, discourse, and so on) as a function of social movements (Gamson and Modigliani 1989; Eyerman and Jamison 1995; Pescosolida et al. 1997; Gamson 1998; Rochon 1998). Finally, some scholars have studied changes in *communities and collective identities* as a function of social movements (Taylor and Whittier 1992; Polletta and Jasper 2001).

Personal and biographical consequences are the effects on the lifecourse of individuals who have participated in movement activities or contentious politics, effects that are at least in part due to involvement in those activities (McAdam 1999; Goldstone and McAdam 2001; Giugni 2004). For example, Wilhelm (1998) studies the effect of political activism on nonmarital cohabitation and Nagel (1995) studies its effects on levels of American Indian ethnic identity. And, Sherkat and Blocker (1997) investigate the political and personal consequences of participation in antiwar and student protests of the late 1960s.

Finally, and of course most central to this book, a growing body of research examines how movements matter to *organizations*, such as universities, corporations, and businesses. Note that most of this work has implicitly or explicitly conceptualized anticorporate activism as private politics, though at times it may have been more accurately conceptualized as contentious politics.

Some of this research has focused on how movements matter to *policy decisions* by organizations, including policy decisions of both corporations and non-profit organizations. For example, Scully and Segal (2002) examine employee activism associated with a number of issue areas (e.g., diversity, women's and minority issues, and so on) in a high-tech firm and how this affected the firm's policy decisions. They identify over twenty-three different accomplishments cited by activist groups in the firm they studied. In a similar vein, Raeburn (2004) examines the effect of lesbian and gay mobilization for workplace rights on decisions regarding domestic partner benefits of Fortune 1000 companies and Loundsbury (2001) studies the effect of student movements on recycling practices of universities and colleges. More recently, King (2008b) finds that the announcement of a boycott in the 1990 to 2005 period is associated with firm concessions when the boycott received more media attention. And, with respect to the environmental movement and environmental issues, Eesley and Lenox (2006) examine the relative impacts of protest, boycotts, proxy decisions, and lawsuits on the policy responses of companies and Maxwell, Lyon, and Hackett (2000) argue the environmental movement has successfully encouraged firms to adopt voluntary emissions controls. Finally, Fineman and Clarke (1996) find that social movement environmental campaigns can matter to various industries, so long as they are perceived of as legitimate.

In addition to studying how movements targeting organizations affect policy response, some scholars have turned to the question of how such movements impact the *financial performance* of firms. For example, Epstein and Schnietz (2002) find that Fortune 500 firms suffered declines in equity following the 1999 Seattle WTO protests and that the losses were greatest among those firms suspected of mistreating labor and damaging the environment. Related, King and Soule (2007) study the effect of protest on stock price returns over a thirty-year period (1960–1990), surrounding multiple issues, and conclude that protest events are associated with negative stock price returns.[7] And Luders (2006) reports that the 1960s sit-ins at department store lunch counters led to substantial financial losses for those stores targeted. Finally, Vogel (1995) argues that shareholder activism, including introducing resolutions, is associated with a drop in stock value and can result in some percentage of shareholders selling off their stock.

Several studies have also shown that the announcement of an organized boycott by a social movement organization appears to negatively affect the financial performance of targeted firms. While Friedman (1985) concluded that only about a quarter of ninety separate consumer boycotts were successful, additional quantitative studies using his data have shown boycotts to be more effective. For example, Pruitt and Friedman (1986) studied twenty-one consumer boycotts that took place between 1970 and 1980 in the United States and found that these boycotts resulted in both a decrease in stock price and in the overall market value of firms targeted. And, Pruitt, Wei, and White (1988) examined union-sponsored boycotts and found they led to financial losses in the targeted firm.[8]

A growing body of literature looks at how socially responsible investment (an insider form of activism described in Chapter 1) impacts financial performance. While somewhat mixed, the bulk of the evidence seems to suggest that financial performance is not harmed, and may actually be improved, by socially responsible investment choices (Margolis and Walsh 2003).

It is important to note that beyond impacting the financial performance and policy decisions of organizations, social movements can also have effects on activists and movement groups themselves, such as the dismissal of workers involved in workplace activism (Scully and Segal 2002: 150).[9] For example, one of the cofounders of the Revolutionary

[7] This research, and the data used by King and Soule (2007), will be described in far greater depth in Chapter 3.
[8] But note that Koku, Akshigbe, and Springer (1997) found that the value of fifty-four targeted firms actually *increased* following the announcement of a boycott. However, they attributed this finding to the damage control that firms engage in to counter the potential negative effects of boycotts. As well, Friedman's (1999) study of twenty-four boycotts by environmental and animal rights organizations concluded that only 40% of these were successful at getting company concessions and that there was little evidence that boycotts hurt the sales of the targeted company.
[9] We might consider this a form of repression and, of course, to be a negative consequence of activism. Note that sometimes repression can ultimately have positive effects, such as

Workers Movement described in Chapter 1 was dismissed by Polaroid for her activism (Massie 1997). Her letter of suspension from the company cited her "public advocacy of a boycott of Polaroid corporation" as grounds for the company's actions (cited in Massie 1997: 237).

Another effect of activism on activists themselves is the development of collective identity (Creed and Scully 2000; Raeburn 2004). For example, Raeburn (2004) analyzes how "coming-out" stories and personal narratives of gay and lesbian activists within corporations can work to build collective identity within employee networks in Fortune 1000 firms. While the ultimate goal of gay and lesbian activists in these firms was domestic partnership benefits, building solidarity and collective identity were equally important goals.

Explaining the Consequences of Contentious and Private Politics and Social Movements

As I noted earlier in this chapter, much of the extant research and theorizing about social movement outcomes has come from scholarly work on state-oriented outcomes. But, one of the chief arguments of this book is that the insights from this rich literature can be applied (sometimes directly and sometimes with modification) to the study of organizational and corporate outcomes. In fact, as I will argue in this section of this chapter, several notable pieces of scholarship on organizational outcomes has done just this and, as such, has brought us closer to reconciling how we might situate anticorporate activism and outcomes in the broader social movements and contentious politics literature. The chief goal, then, of this section is to describe what we know about movement outcomes from the literature on state outcomes and to illustrate how these insights can be usefully applied to the study of outcomes of anticorporate activism.

The factors identified by the literature to help explain *how* corporate outcomes are achieved exist both internally and externally to a given movement. On the *external side*, scholars emphasize the role of the *political opportunity structure* (POS) or overall political context on the state-level outcomes sought by social movements.[10] Of course, when considering

the diffusion of a policy or procedure deemed favorable to employees beyond the targeted organization to other organizations (Briscoe and Safford 2008).

[10] It is important to note that there have been a number of interesting modifications of the "political opportunity structure" concept. For example, some argue for the importance of the "cultural opportunity structure" (Johnston and Klandermans 1995; Taylor

corporate-level outcomes, some adjustments must be made to the POS concept, as we will see shortly. On the *internal side*, scholars emphasize the role of social movement organizational resources, tactics, and frames used by activists. Recent research argues for the careful assessment of the *relative impact* of internal and external factors and for the examination of the *joint and mediated effects* of both sets of factors on movement outcomes. Before discussing how factors internal and external to the social movement may interact and combine to produce desired outcomes, I will discuss internal and external factors separately, with an eye toward drawing analogies to research on organizational outcomes.

Internal Factors

In thinking about what leads to movement success, many scholars point to the importance of the characteristics of the movement itself, such as the structure of the organizations within the movement, the tactics and strategies employed by the movement, the use of collective action frames, and the level of resources that the movement is able to obtain.

One of the most frequently studied internal characteristics is the organizational structure of the movement and, related to this, how the organizational structure impacts the tactics used by the movement. Social movement theory and research emphasizes how the strength of supportive social movement *organizations* can impact policy decisions at the state, local, national and, presumably, at the organizational level. Beyond their capacity to mobilize protest, social movement organizations are able to influence policy makers by their use of institutional channels such as litigation and lobbying. In other words, organizations both mobilize adherents to take part in collective action (McCarthy and Zald 1977) *and* influence policy makers directly through institutional means. This suggests that movements with a greater organizational capacity will be more effective than those lacking a strong organizational infrastructure.

1996), others for the "legal opportunity structure" (Pedriana 2006). But, to my knowledge, the only one of these modifications that has been used to help us understand *outcomes* of social movements (as opposed to the mobilization of social movements) is the "gendered opportunity structure" (McCammon et al. 2001). The gendered opportunity structure includes the characteristics of the political system that might make political actors more or less favorable to claims by women. For example, favorable public opinion about women's roles and women legislators has been used to operationalize this concept (McCammon et al. 2001; Soule and Olzak 2004; Soule and King 2006).

This basic model is known as the "access influence" model (Gamson 1990; Andrews 2001).

At the organizational or corporate level, groups such as employee networks (Friedman and Craig 2004; Raeburn 2004) and other kinds of employee associations (Scully and Segal 2002) may be important for effecting change. Not only are these groups or associations able to provide free spaces for dialog and discussion, which are essential for building collective identity and solidarity, but they also provide a network of individuals that can be mobilized should the opportunity arise. For example, Raeburn (2004) shows that the majority of the Fortune 1000 corporations that adopted domestic partnership benefits had gay and lesbian employee networks.

The "access-influence" model may be contrasted with the "action-reaction" model, which holds that movements matter to policy outcomes because they threaten political and corporate elites and disrupt normal operating procedures (Piven and Cloward 1977; Gamson 1990; Andrews 2001). The "action-reaction" model posits that it is not organizational capacity that influences targets, but protest and other activities of social movements that are disruptive and threatening to those in power. In particular, frequent and vociferous protest is hypothesized to matter more to elites at the state and organizational levels, as these tactics are more likely to disrupt (or threaten to disrupt) normal operations of the state or company.

Disruption of normal operating procedures might be especially important at the organizational or corporate level. Consider, for example, how direct action against companies, such as the tactics advocated and practiced by Earth Liberation Front (ELF), impact the normal operating procedures of companies. In 2001, ELF helped to burn down a McDonald's restaurant in Tucson, Arizona, and burned eight SUVs at a Ford dealership in Detroit, Michigan (Rosebraugh 2004). Such actions, which can lead to lost business due to closures but also can damage the image or reputation of a firm, may be very effective at getting companies to give in to protesters' demands.

In addition to organizational resources and tactics used by activists, social movements scholars also argue that the *collective action frames* used by social movements are an important part of the outcomes story (Cress and Snow 2000; McCammon et al. 2001; Halebsky 2007). As used within the social movement and contentious politics literatures, framing refers to the meaningful construction engaged in by activists and leaders in social movements, which is relevant to the interests of the movement and may be used to mobilize supporters, influence public opinion, and effect change. Frames are essentially signifying devices that help people understand complex issues and integrate these with their own prior experiences and knowledge. Activists use these to help buttress their claims and win supporters, thus frames are an essential part of recruiting participants and they are likely an important factor impacting the outcomes of activism.

In examining how frames impact outcomes, some scholars look at the level of *specificity* of a given frame and make claims about how this impacts outcomes. For example, Cress and Snow (2000) find that favorable outcomes of the homeless movement across seventeen U.S. cities were more likely when the movement articulated specific frames (e.g., shelter conditions) rather than more diffuse frames (e.g., homelessness). As well, the status and expertise of the person articulating the frame may matter to outcomes, such that more authoritative and higher status individuals are considered more credible (Benford and Snow 2000). At the organizational level, King (2008a) notes that the frames used by activists are also likely important, with more specific frames associated with a higher likelihood of success.

Alternatively, McCammon (2001) points to the importance of the *content* of a frame; those that resonate more with the existing culture are more likely to be met with success. In her case, the Suffrage Movement in the United States, it was important to frame the right to vote in terms of women's unique place in politics as feminine and thus able to help heal the country's problems, rather than in terms of women's equal rights. At the organizational level, Raeburn (2004) also argues that the content of the frame matters to outcomes, such that the "blended" frame of the ethical nature of domestic partnership benefits *and* the importance of these benefits for the profits of the company was more easily understood by corporate leaders, because they are fundamentally concerned with the bottom line of the company. That is, successful activists framed the issues around domestic partnerships in ways that would both encourage mobilization of workers *and* resonate with the chief concerns of corporate leaders.

These factors – frames, tactics, and resources – are all characteristics of social movements or social movement organizations and have all been shown to impact the attainment of goals. Because these are internal to the social movement itself, I refer to these as internal characteristics or factors, as summarized in Table 2.1.

At a most basic level, the insights offered by scholars interested in the internal characteristics of social movements resonate with those offered

Table 2.1. *Internal Factors Influencing the Consequences of Anticorporate Social Movements*

Characteristic of Social Movement	Examples from Literature
Resources	Raeburn (2004) on employee networks
Tactics	Rosebraugh (2004) on disruptive tactics
Collective Action Frames	King (2008a) on frame specificity, Raeburn (2004) on frame content

by the *stakeholder theory* in organizations. The stakeholder theory of the corporation redefined how scholars consider corporations, from an older view, which held that corporations take input from employees, suppliers, and investors and in turn, produce some output for consumers, to a much less simplistic view of what a corporation is and what its relationship to the broader environment is. The newer view offered by stakeholder theory notes that employees, suppliers, investors, and customers do not merely provide inputs, but they also receive outputs. But, more importantly for my purposes here, stakeholder theory explicitly recognizes that corporations are embedded in a web of entities – all of which need to be considered when thinking about inputs and outputs of a corporation. Stakeholder notions of the corporation, thus, seek to broaden the definition of who matters to corporations, such that employees, customers, labor unions, interest groups and the broader community can be seen as important constituents of the corporation (Donaldson and Preston 1995; Jones 1995; Frooman 1999). The name of the game, then, becomes figuring out which characteristics of these entities make corporations more interested in listening to their claims (King 2008a). Because the stakeholder theory of the corporation focuses on characteristics of groups that target the corporation, it resonates with those social movement scholars who examine internal characteristics of activist groups, such as resources, tactics, and frames, and how these impact organizational outcomes. King (2008a) makes this connection explicit by arguing that stakeholder theory can be deeply enriched by social movement theories on outcomes or consequences.

External Factors

In addition to such internal factors or characteristics of social movements, others point to the importance of the larger, external environment, which shapes *both* mobilization *and* chances of success of this mobilization. Most

43

central to these arguments when applied to state outcomes is the *political opportunity structure*. Tarrow (1994: 85) defines the political opportunity structure as the "consistent ... dimensions of the political environment that provide incentives for people to undertake collective action by affecting their expectations for success or failure." Political opportunity theory contends that social movement mobilization is a function of changes in the level of elite receptivity to protesters, changes in elite ability and willingness to repress movements, and the presence of elite allies (McAdam 1996; Tarrow 1998). While POS theory has been used to explain protest mobilization in a number of contexts, researchers argue that the concept should also be used to understand *policy outcomes* (Jenkins and Perrow 1977; Kitschelt 1986; Kriesi et al. 1995; Tarrow 1998; Soule and Olzak 2004; Soule and King 2006). Essentially, the same set of factors that stimulate protest should, in turn, affect the outcomes sought by the movement. For example, open political systems in which there are sympathetic elites should be more responsive to movement claims than are more closed systems in which elites are hostile to the movement.

Recent work on the concept of the political opportunity structure has noted that in addition to the domestic opportunity structure, there is also a transnational or international political opportunity structure, which affects how movements operate (Keck and Sikkink 1998; Stillerman 2003; Kay 2005; Della Porta and Tarrow 2005; Van der Heijden 2006). Whereas the political opportunity structure, as described previously, refers to characteristics of a given nation state, when we move to the global level, we need to consider nonstate characteristics that impact social movements and their outcomes. The international or transnational political opportunity structure, then, may be thought of as the set of international governmental associations (e.g., UN, EU, WTO, World Bank), which establish treaties, agreements, and norms (Van der Heijden 2006). The transnational or international political opportunity structure may be especially important for some corporations, namely multinational enterprises, which operate within these and are governed by international treaties and agreements. In fact, multinational enterprises exist within a domestic opportunity structure, the opportunity structure of the host country in which they operate, and the transnational opportunity structure, thus social movements against such corporations and their outcomes are governed by multiple levels of opportunity. This is an important point that I will raise throughout this book.

Arguments about the political opportunity structure have taught us a great deal about what external factors matter to state outcomes and some of these factors are also likely important to corporations. But there are additional external factors that are also essential to corporate outcomes. Importantly, corporations exist in a wider environment that (of course) includes the political opportunity structure, but it also includes what Raeburn (2004: 107) calls the "sociopolitical field." To Raeburn, this includes the broader legal and regulatory framework that governs what a corporation can and cannot do, industry-level norms, the level of competition within the industry, as well as the broader social movement for, in her case, gay and lesbian civil rights.

It is useful to think about external factors that facilitate both mobilization and the outcomes of that mobilization as a multilevel, nested phenomenon (Khagram et al. 2002; Meyer 2003; Raeburn 2004; Schneiberg and Soule 2005). At the most distant level is the transnational political opportunity structure, as defined previously. Beneath this level, there are state-level changes in laws, policies, and regulatory frameworks that affect corporations (Raeburn 2004; Pedriana 2006). For instance, Edelman and Suchman (1997) discuss the way in which organizations look to the law for guidance on contested issues that are often promulgated by social movements. This was the case, as discussed by Raeburn (2004), when the San Francisco Equal Benefits Ordinance requiring employers with city contracts to provide domestic partnership benefits was passed in 1997. Not only did other cities follow suit (by 2004, 153 localities had adopted such ordinances), but certain corporations immediately adopted domestic partnership benefits to comply with this legislation.

At a more proximate level, there are characteristics of the industry in which the corporation is embedded, such as the level of competition therein, which can make corporations more likely to imitate what others are doing with respect to some set of policies. This was the case in Raeburn's (2004) analysis of domestic partnership benefits among Fortune 1000 companies. For example, when United Airlines adopted domestic partnership benefits in 1999, US Airways and American Airlines quickly followed suit and did so within two weeks. And, within just two years, nearly all other U.S. airlines had done so, as well (Raeburn 2004).

Other facets of the industry also impact how corporations respond to social movements and contentious politics. As defined by Schurman (2004), the "industry opportunity structure" is the set of "economic, organizational, cultural, and commodity-related" factors that facilitate and constrain movements and their effects on corporate targets" (Schurman

2004: 251).[11] Other key dimensions to the industry opportunity structure include the relationships among actors in the industry's organizational field and the nature of the goods or services produced by the industry, which, to the extent that these can be harmful, may offer more opportunities for activism than do others (Schurman 2004).

Then, beneath the industry-level, there is the most proximate level, the corporate environment itself, which Raeburn (2004) calls the *corporate windows of opportunity*. A corporate window of opportunity is the set of organizational characteristics that constrain and facilitate activism from within the confines of the corporation. Specifically, Raeburn (2004) points to various realignments within the corporation, signals from the elite within the corporation, and to alliances between the elite and others outside the corporation in favor of a given movement's goals. For example, Raeburn (2004) discusses how official recognition by the corporation of gay employee networks is both an outcome of the movement *and* a signal that the corporate leaders are open to the claims of the network. Sometimes these networks were even given a budget, further signaling the openness of the corporate leaders to the group.

Related, in a recent article, King (2008a) argues that facets of the *corporate opportunity structure* both encourage mobilization against corporations and shape the effects of that mobilization. King, like Raeburn, directs us to look at such characteristics of the corporation as changes in corporate leadership, mergers and acquisitions, corporate restructuring, new officers, supportive allies in the governance of the corporation, and the effect of governmental intervention and regulation. King (2008a) also points to organizational performance as an important element of the corporate opportunity structure. Performance declines may lead to splits among organizational leaders, elite turnover, and elite sensitivity to outsider claims.

Another related argument is the "internal corporate polity" model proffered by Weber, Rao, and Thomas (2009). In their analysis of the anti-biotech movement in Germany, Weber and his collaborators find that the "internal corporate polity" of Germany's pharmaceutical firms was a chief predictor of the extent to which the anti-biotech movement impacted firm decisions regarding investment in new biotechnologies. They argue that movements, as outsiders to these firms, challenged the legitimacy of

---

[11] A related concept is the *economic opportunity structure* (Luders 2006), which focuses on both the disruption costs incurred on a target by a given protest event and the costs to the target of conceding to the social movement responsible for organizing the protest event(s).

these new technologies and led to divisions within the elites at these firms, therefore undermining the firms' commitment to biotechnology.

Finally, while the authors did not use the terminology "opportunity structure," Ashford and her colleagues (1998) find that female managers are more likely to speak out and "sell" the issue of gender equality to those above them when the organizational context is favorable and they perceive that they will be successful. Schurman (2004) echoes this in her discussion of the importance of corporate culture to mobilization and its outcomes. While this study was not explicitly about the opportunity structure, it nicely illustrates my point that the attention to the context in which "tempered activists" operate is analogous to arguments about the political opportunity structure, only at a lower level: the corporate opportunity structure.

This discussion highlights the hierarchical or nested (Khagram et al. 2002; Meyer 2003; Raeburn 2004; Schneiberg and Soule 2005) levels of factors exogenous to social movements and is depicted in Figure 2.1.

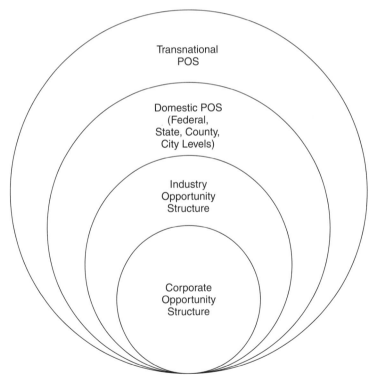

Figure 2.1 The Nested Nature of Factors External to Social Movements.

Figure 2.1 shows that private and contentious politics exist within the greater transnational political opportunity structure, the domestic political opportunity structure (which itself exists at multiple levels, including the state, county, and city levels), the industry opportunity structure, and the corporate opportunity structure. All of these are relevant to the outcomes of anticorporate activism. Thus, movements directed at the corporation operate in an extremely complex environment in which favorable opportunities at one level may not exist at another level. As well, as I will discuss in the next section, there are likely joint and interactive effects between these levels, just as there are between external factors and internal factors.

Joint and Mediated Effects

While some scholars of movement outcomes have focused on either internal or external factors and how these affect whether or not a movement will have the desired effect, other scholars have pointed to the importance of the contingent and interactive nature of internal and external factors. Building on the insights of the POS approach, the *political mediation model* argues that while the openings in the POS may stimulate protest, these openings also dramatically influence the possibility of success of challengers (Amenta et al. 1992; 1994). According to this view, movement mobilization and organizational strength provide the necessary, but not sufficient, conditions for social movement activists to achieve their desired outcomes. For example, the political mediation model suggests that successful mobilization by social movement actors depends on the presence of sympathetic elites whose presence is critical in determining policy outcomes of movement activity (Cress and Snow 2000). Strong versions of the political mediation model hold that movements will *only* matter to policy outcomes when the political opportunity structure is favorable (Amenta et al. 1994), while weaker versions argue that the effects of movements are intensified when the political opportunity structure is favorable (Soule and Olzak 2004; Soule and King 2006).

Building on these insights, King (2008b) offers the *corporate mediation model*, which is analogous to the *political mediation model* in that the chief insight is that when trying to explain how movements matter to corporations, we need to consider the interactive and contingent nature of movement activities and the corporate opportunity structure. Strong versions of this argument might be that movements *only* matter to corporations when the opportunity structure is open, while weaker versions of the argument would hold that the effect of movements on corporate outcomes is *amplified* when the opportunity structure is open.

But just as we can think of the interactive nature of internal and external factors, it is also important to recognize that interactions likely exist *between* the various, nested levels of external characteristics that are depicted in Figure 2.1. This is a complex set of relations that determine both the emergence of anticorporate mobilization and also condition the outcomes of this mobilization. The contentious politics literature, and especially the idea of *scale shift*, is particularly useful for understanding how this multilevel, nested system of opportunity both encourages anticorporate activism and conditions its impacts on corporations.

Anticorporate Targets and Shifting the Scale of Contention

The previous discussion highlights the core elements of social movement theories of policy change and how both internal and external factors impact whether or not a movement will impact its chosen target. However, when we return to my earlier distinction between private and contentious politics (two different kinds of social movements), we note that the chief difference between these two is that private politics are those interactions *without* the government or state, while contentious politics involve the state as an actor. In empirical practice, this most often means that contentious politics target the state and private politics target corporations. But, as I have noted previously, anticorporate activism sometimes (though obviously not always) targets *both*.

The contentious politics literature describes the concept of *scale shift*, which is useful to understanding the targets chosen by anticorporate activists. Scale shift is the "change in the number and level of coordinated contentious actions to a different focal point, involving a new range of actors, different objects, and broadened claims" (McAdam, Tarrow, and Tilly 2001: 331). While the examples of scale shift provided by McAdam, Tarrow, and Tilly tend to focus on "upward" scale shift (that is, they focus on examples of contentious politics that expand outward and upward from the local level to the transnational level), Tarrow (2005: 121) elaborates also on the idea of "downward" scale shift, or when "a generalized practice is adapted at a lower level."

Most of the literature on scale shift seems, thus far, to focus on the connection of scale shift to diffusion processes, such as when a movement campaign diffuses from the national to the transnational level (e.g., Tilly 2001; Tarrow 2005; Tarrow and McAdam 2005). And, much of the empirical illustrations and applications focus on how a movement that emerges at the local level spreads outward to other, supralocal levels (Tarrow and McAdam 2005) or, sometimes, downward (Tarrow 2005), via diffusion, attribution of similarity, and emulation. But, I wish to argue that another aspect of scale shift is important and hitherto underutilized in the extant literature – the targets or "focal points" of contentious politics.

Corporate targets (or focal points) exist at each of the levels depicted in Figure 2.1. That is, sometimes anticorporate activism targets the corporation directly for some injustice or instance of malfeasance, such as when activists target an employer around diversity issues (e.g., Scully and Segal 2002; Raeburn 2004). At other times, activism can target the broader industry, as exemplified by environmental movements targeting the automobile industry to encourage better fuel efficiency of automobiles.[12] Anticorporate activism is also sometimes directed at the domestic government, such as when activists attempt to get Congress to pass regulatory policy. Sometimes anticorporate activism indirectly targets the government or a foreign government via intermediary actors or institutions, such as in the cases of the South African and the Burmese divestment movements, which are discussed in later chapters. And, sometimes anticorporate activism targets transnational bodies and agreements, such as when activists targeted the WTO during the "Battle of Seattle" in 1999 (Gillham and Noakes 2007) or the G8 (Waddington and King 2007) or NAFTA (Kay 2005). Of course, many times there are simultaneous targets of anticorporate activism. For example, the antisuperstore/antibig box store movements target both local level city councils and zoning boards in an effort to block the placement of these large stores, but they also target large, multinational corporations directly.[13] Or, in Kay's (2005) case, a transnational system (NAFTA) was the ultimate target of activists, but the movement she describes in Mexico also targeted corporations directly. In her case, General Electric (GE) in Juarez was targeted to improve working conditions and wages (Kay 2005: 730).

---

[12] As another example, Sine and Lee (2009) show that the environmental movement also impacted entrepreneurship within the wind energy industry.

[13] On the anti-Wal-Mart movement in the United States, which has mobilized in at least 100 cities and towns, see Halebsky (2007). On the history of the movement more generally, see Rao (2009) and Ingram and Rao (2004). See also Neumark, Zhang, and Ciccarella (2007) for evidence on how Wal-Mart impacts local economies.

Targeting corporations, thus, is an interesting and illustrative case of the process of scale shift, as it exemplifies both upward and downward scale shift. On the one hand, when we consider many of the examples of this phenomenon that I describe in this book, we see that activists moved from targeting the state to targeting the corporation because the state was seen as less powerful than corporations or because the state was seen as more likely to repress dissidents. Thus, as I discussed in Chapter 1, we saw activists move downward from attempting to influence the state in order to ultimately affect corporations via regulation, to targeting corporations directly, where business practices could be impacted directly.

On the other hand, targeting business interests has also more recently become transnational, as corporations have globalized. Whereas once social movements targeting businesses relied on local networks and acted locally, now social movement organizations work across national borders, coordinate a lot of different people, and target multiple levels of both organizations and governments (Doh and Teegan 2003). For example, Widener (2007) examines the transnational campaign against multinational oil companies working in Ecuador. This campaign involved local, grassroots activists in oil-saturated regions in that country as well as transnational advocacy organizations interested in environmental conservation. The campaign targeted oil companies directly, but it also targeted the government of Ecuador.

The concept of scale shift, coupled with work on the political opportunity structure, is useful as we examine anticorporate activism because it allows us to more neatly consider how various levels of external factors impact mobilization and its outcomes, but also how these various levels represent the targets (or focal points) of this activism. Just as the external factors conditioning both anticorporate mobilization and outcomes of the mobilization exist at various, nested levels, the *targets* of anticorporate activism exist within the company itself, the broader industry, some level of state government, transnational bodies, or some combination of these nested, external factors. The concept of scale shift nicely taps the reality of what anticorporate activists do. Not only do they move up and down the scale for strategic reasons (including the avoidance of repression), but they also do so in response to changes in their targets. That is, many corporate targets are best described as "moving targets" in that they change with mergers and acquisitions (as we will see in Chapter 5, in the case of the movement against Dow Chemical for Union Carbide Company's (UCC) role in the Bhopal disaster, and in Chapter 3, in the case of the movement against Chevron for Texaco's past misdeeds) and with globalization.

Summary and Conclusion

This chapter presented a consensual definition of social movements and compared this to the somewhat narrower, but no less useful, concepts of contentious and private politics. I have argued that all of these terms are useful for understanding anticorporate activism and, in fact, that we cannot understand this phenomenon fully without drawing on ideas from both private and contentious politics and from the larger social movements literature. I have also described the different kinds of outcomes that are typically studied by scholars of movements and reviewed two broad classes of factors affecting the ability of movements to have an impact: factors internal to the movement and factors external to the movement.

With respect to external factors, I have built on the concept of the political opportunity structure to describe the nested or multilevel nature of the reality in which corporations are embedded, from the most proximate factors related to the structure of the corporation itself, to the most distant factors related to the international or transnational opportunity structures. I have noted that these different levels of external factors impact both mobilization of anticorporate activists and attainment of the outcomes that these activists seek. Finally, I have argued that the concept of scale shift can be usefully applied to the study of anticorporate activism in that this concept allows us to sort out the different kinds of targets as well as better understand how anticorporate sentiment has been channeled in different ways, to different focal points, throughout the history of corporations.

3

Anticorporate Protest in the
United States, 1960–1990

In Chapter 1 I argued that in the United States there has always been some level of distrust of big business and corporations and that throughout our history, this distrust has periodically manifested itself in protest against these entities. While historically anticorporate protest has often been directed at the government with the goal of increasing regulation, or channeled through organized labor, it has been a pretty consistent facet of U.S. history. When we consider *all* protest in the United States reported in the *New York Times* between 1960 and 1990, we see that nearly 18% of public protest events targeted one or more business interest, sometimes alongside other targets, such as the government, religious organizations, or educational institutions. Figure 3.1 shows how the proportion of anticorporate protest varied by year during this period.[1]

Figure 3.1 shows a dramatic peak in 1960–1961, when about 40% of all reported protest events targeted business interests. The bulk of these were associated with sit-ins at restaurants and department store lunch counters, as well as protest events staged in sympathy or as an expression of solidarity for the participants of the sit-ins.[2]

Throughout the 1960s, we see a decline from this early peak, but in the late 1960s and early 1970s, we see this trend reverse, as protesters began

---

[1] The data used to generate this figure come from a comprehensive dataset of all protest events in the United States, as reported in the *New York Times* (See Appendix A for a description of these data).

[2] It was commonplace for protesters to demonstrate outside of northern branches of the department store chains targeted by the sit-ins in the South as a show of solidarity for the civil rights activists who were risking arrest and physical harm at lunch counters in other locales.

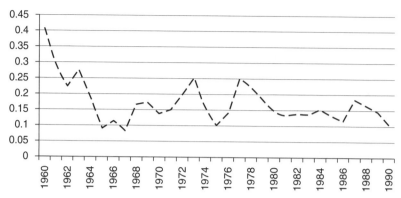

Figure 3.1 Proportion of Protest Targeting Businesses in the United States, 1960–1990.

to target companies making weapons used in the Vietnam War. As well, in the mid to late 1960s, protesters began to target companies doing business in South Africa, charging that such businesses helped to support that country's racist system of apartheid (as will be described in greater detail in Chapter 4). In the early 1980s, we see a continuation of protest directed at companies with ties to South Africa and we see another upsurge of protest again directed at weapons manufacturers, but this time associated with the Nuclear Freeze movement.

We might again ask the question I posed in Chapter 1: What were these protesters so incensed about? While an underlying theme of most anticorporate protest reported in the *New York Times* involved the growth of corporations and how this has adversely affected the way that corporations conduct business, it is useful to look at what kinds of *specific claims* were raised at individual protest events. When we consider the different kinds of claims articulated at these events, it turns out that nearly all of these events may be categorized as complaints surrounding a company's *product, policy,* or some instance of *corporate negligence.* This may not seem like an especially novel observation, but it is a useful way to categorize protest directed at corporations as these three types of anticorporate protest were prevalent across this entire time period and, as I will discuss in Chapter 5, in the post-1990 period as well. In the following three sections of this chapter, I treat each of these categories of complaints separately, drawing on specific examples from the data described in Appendix A.

Antiproduct Protest Events

The most commonly cited grievance at public protest events directed at corporations in the United States during this period is some company product; in fact, 44% of the anticorporate events made some claim about a company's product (including a service) that was perceived of as morally bad, physically harmful,[3] or discriminatory in some way. In essence, corporate protesters charge that corporations, because of unchecked growth and eroding regulatory principals, are free to produce items and provide services that are bad for the consumer, the broader citizenry, animals, the environment, or some other entity that may or may not even be aware of the protest.

An example of an antiproduct protest event was the 1983 protest directed at Burger King, which then offered a veal sandwich at some of its restaurants. Critics charged that the calves (the source of the veal used in the sandwiches) were not treated humanely, thus should not be consumed by humans (Shenon 1983). In this case, animal rights groups such as PETA and American Vegetarians worked together to encourage Burger King to drop the veal sandwich from its menu. The veal sandwich, in this case, was a specific product and the events surrounding this issue generally did not articulate any number of other issues around which Burger King could conceivably be targeted (e.g., labor issues, their use of beef tallow, their environmental record, or their recent refusal to pay a price for tomatoes that would allow farmworkers to be paid a decent wage).[4]

Another example of an antiproduct protest event was when, in 1971, Nabisco was protested because one of its subsidiaries (Aurora Products) produced toys that were dubbed "torture kits" by activists because they depicted hangings and other forms of violence (*New York Times* 1971a; 1971b). The company was protested not only by activists concerned about violent toys for children, but also by women who found many of the toys

[3] Harmful products and policies should be differentiated from negligence (which I treat in detail later) in that events in the "antiproduct" category articulate some complaint with something that a company *actively* and *knowingly* produces and attempts to sell to consumers. This includes a service in some cases, as we will see. However, "negligence" events focus more on some byproduct of the production process (or process of delivering a service) which harms individuals, sometimes with, and sometimes without, the company's direct knowledge of the harm.

[4] A paradigmatic case of antiproduct protest is the campaign against Nestlé for their marketing of infant formula in lesser developed nations. This case is discussed in some depth in Chapter 5.

in its "monster" line to be sexist (e.g., the Vampirella, which was based on a comic book character, and the "Pendulum," which depicted a seminude woman being tortured). Again, these protest events were very specific to the offending line of toys and did not typically articulate any other conceivable issues or problems related to other aspects of Nabisco or Aurora.

But why do antiproduct events represent the highest proportion of anticorporate events in my data? The chief reason that antiproduct claims are so prevalent during this period is that so many of these events targeted corporations (e.g., Dow Chemical, Honeywell, General Electric) for their role in producing weapons used in the Vietnam War and, a bit later, for producing nuclear weapons. Dow was one of the first corporations targeted for weaponry used in Vietnam, and in particular for its development and production of napalm, a substance that, when mixed with gasoline, becomes flammable. Howard Zinn (1997: 305) quotes a physician's description of napalm:

Napalm is a highly sticky inflammable jelly which clings to anything it touches and burns with such heat that all oxygen in the area is exhausted within moments. Death is either by roasting or by suffocation. Napalm wounds are often fatal (estimates are 90 percent). Those who survive face a living death. The victims are frequently children.

Activists, especially on campuses, were incensed about the cruelty and brutality of this particular weapon and the fact that it was apparently being used on civilians. And, they took to the streets in an effort to force Dow to discontinue manufacturing napalm. The first protests against Dow were in 1966 at Stanford University, but these rapidly spread across college campuses in 1966 and 1967, often as a result of Dow Chemical recruitment visits to these campuses. A notable such protest event occurred at the University of Wisconsin in Madison in October of 1967 when several hundred students blockaded themselves in a room where recruiting interviews were taking place, spawning similar protests shortly thereafter on other campuses across the country (*New York Times* 1967a). The police ended up beating these Madison students, injuring close to fifty of them and arresting more than seventy (Fraser 1967).[5] Executives at Dow confessed that the student movement against the company hurt its stock price and also tarnished the company's image as a potential

---

[5] This event is depicted in the photo on the cover of this book.

employer, making it more difficult to recruit talented employees (*New York Times* 1967b).[6]

Dow was not the only company targeted for producing weaponry for the war. In April 1972, fifty antiwar demonstrators dressed in black and carrying black balloons protested General Electric's development of new weapons to be used in Vietnam and other conflicts (Waldron 1972). And, two years earlier, protesters broke into GE's offices in Washington to protest the company's role in the war (Vienna 1970).[7] In the 1980s, Diamond Shamrock Corporation was protested in New Jersey for its collaboration in the making of "agent orange," the herbicide used in military operations (especially in Vietnam) to destroy the protective cover that plants provide for opposing soldiers (*New York Times* 1984b). Interestingly, the makers of agent orange were protested by peace activists and veterans alike, the latter group protesting the companies who made it because of the alleged health problems they experienced due to exposure to the chemical (*New York Times* 1984b).

One of the best-known (and longest-lasting) campaigns against a corporation for its production of weapons used in Vietnam was the Honeywell Project. Founded in the late 1960s by Marvin Davidov in Minneapolis, the Honeywell Project sought to explicitly target Minnesota's largest military contractor, Honeywell, which produced conventional weapons and guidance systems for nuclear weapons. Early on, the Project practiced various kinds of civil disobedience at Honeywell plants and was allegedly infiltrated by the FBI's Covert Intelligence Program (*New York Times* 1976) leading to a suit filed by the American Civil Liberties Union (ACLU) in the late 1970s (Jensen 1977).

In the 1980s, the Honeywell Project was rejuvenated by the nuclear freeze movement (Meyer 1990). In 1983, for example, the Project organized a blockade of the company's headquarters, leading to the arrest of 130 protesters, including the wife of the then Minneapolis police chief, who was actually arrested multiple times over the years for her activism at Honeywell (*New York Times* 1983). Over the 1981 to 1987 period,

---

[6] Readers will see that this was not the last time Dow's image was tarnished by protesters. In Chapter 5, I discuss the ongoing campaign against Dow because of its now ownership of Union Carbide, the company responsible for the deadly gas leak in 1984 in Bhopal, India. And, in Chapter 1, I mention the campaign against Dow designed to encourage the company to reduce emissions.

[7] This act of protest imitated earlier such actions at Dow Chemical, when the "DC-Nine" broke into Dow's offices and vandalized files therein (Vienna 1970).

there were over 1,800 arrests at similar antinuclear events at Honeywell (Dugger 1987).

The Honeywell Project was joined by other nuclear freeze groups in protests directed at weapons manufacturers across the country. In September 1980, for example, the members of the Plowshares Eight, a group organized by a former Catholic priest, Philip Berrigan and his brother, Daniel, broke into a General Electric plant in King of Prussia, Pennsylvania, and destroyed the nosecones of Minutemen missiles, spilled their own blood on tools and weapons blueprints, and damaged other materials used in the production of these missiles (Meyer 1990; Nepstad 2008). These tactics were borrowed by other groups who targeted additional nuclear weapons producers. For example, the maker of the Trident missile, General Dynamics in Groton, Connecticut, was the target of many attacks that used markedly similar tactics such as blood spilling and destruction of property (Meyer 1990; Meyer 2007; Nepstad 2008).

The Honeywell Project often combined direct action tactics with shareholder resolutions to target the companies responsible for weapons production, thus, blending what I referred to in Chapter 1 as "insider" and "outsider" tactics (*New York Times* 1969c). This will be a theme throughout this book; that is, activists targeting corporations typically take a multipronged approach involving both insider and outsider strategies. Another example of this two-prong approach is that of the campaign against Dow. In addition to the protests described previously, in the late 1960s, the Medical Committee for Human Rights requested that the SEC allow them to introduce a proxy calling for Dow to cease its production of napalm (Welsh 1988). Initially refused, the Medical Committee finally persuaded the U.S. Circuit Court of Appeals to rule in its favor in 1970. The ultimate goal of this two-pronged strategy of protest and resolutions is to disrupt normal operating procedures of the companies, while also damaging the image of the company.

These are but a few examples of antiproduct protest events that occurred from 1960 to 1990 and were directed at corporations. While prevalent, these represent just one type of protest against corporations. They tend to be fairly narrowly focused on a specific product and tend to articulate specific goals of ending the production of the product or the provision of a service. But, they are often linked to much larger causes (e.g., peace, environmentalism, vegetarianism), even if the activists do not spend an inordinate amount of time drawing out these linkages. The next category of events, antipolicy protest events, includes those events that are directed at a corporation for some policy or practice. As we will see, these tend to be more explicitly connected to broader issues and concerns.

Anticorporate Policy Protest Events

Beyond some product or service, the next most commonly cited grievance at the events in my data is some policy or practice of a corporation; 41% of these events fell into this category. Again, the underlying narrative of these events is one of how corporations, because of unchecked growth and declining regulation, behave immorally without any regard for workers, consumers, the broader society, or some class of people adversely affected by corporate policy. As well, these events are explicitly about the offending policy and do not typically articulate other issues that activists may have with a given corporation.

For example, in 1969, a Sears, Roebuck, and Company department store in New York City was protested by people charging that its practice of not issuing credit to welfare recipients was discriminatory (*New York Times* 1969a). The following year, welfare recipients staged a "shop-in" at Macy's for that company's refusal to extend credit to the poor (Blau 1970).[8] These events highlighted the practice of discrimination in the extension of credit to lower income people and were connected, often explicitly, to the broader Poor Peoples Movement (Pivan and Cloward 1977).

Other examples from my data include the protest of Pepsi in 1972 by Jewish people for the company's trade agreement with the former Soviet government, which allegedly refused to allow Soviet Jews to emigrate to Israel (*New York Times* 1972). This event was connected to the broader Zionist movement that was active at the time. Or, General Motors was protested in 1977 for its business interests in Chile (Stuart 1977), as was Kennecott Cooper in 1975 (*New York Times* 1975). These events were part of a movement that wished to punish the repressive, military regime of Augusto Pinochet via exerting leverage over corporations with ties to that country, thus, they are similar to the student divestment movement discussed in Chapter 4 and the Free Burma Coalition discussed in Chapter 5.

This short discussion highlights the fact that there are clearly many different kinds of policies that protesters might become incensed about

---

[8] The "shop-in" protest tactic was used at a variety of other department stores during this period and involved shoplifting items from a store in protest of these stores' policies of not issuing credit to poor people.

and deem protest worthy. However, the bulk of the antipolicy events in my data are those directed at a given company for discriminatory hiring and promotion practices. GM, for example, was protested in the 1960s by the National Association for the Advancement of Colored People (NAACP) for discriminating against African Americans (Jones 1964) and in that same decade, Pepsi was protested by African Americans led by Jesse Jackson for not hiring more black executives (*New York Times* 1969b). Similarly, in 1971, A&P was protested by the Southern Christian Leadership Conference (SCLC) for failing to hire African Americans (*New York Times* 1971c). In 1981, Operation PUSH (People United to Save Humanity), Jesse Jackson's organization (now the Rainbow PUSH Coalition), issued a list of soft drink companies (including Pepsi, Coca Cola, Royal Crown, and Seven-Up) to be boycotted because of their failure to hire and promote African Americans (*New York Times* 1981a).

One of the best known campaigns against a discriminatory corporate policy was the 1966–1967 campaign against Kodak sponsored by FIGHT (Freedom-Integration-God-Honor-Today). FIGHT was originally organized by Saul Alinsky and Minister Franklin Delano Roosevelt Florence in response to a race riot that occurred in Rochester, New York, in 1964. FIGHT was a coalition of religious and community groups dedicated to the cause of civil rights. In 1966, FIGHT asked Kodak (as Rochester's largest employer) to develop an employment and training program for poor people, who in Rochester at that time were mainly African American. As was the case with Polaroid, which was targeted by activists for providing film to South African companies making pass books (see Chapter 1), Kodak also had a decent record of being a progressive and community-minded company that offered very good benefits to its workers. Initially Kodak was willing to listen to a proposal by FIGHT to institute a job training program, however negotiations soon broke down and a near agreement was nullified by Kodak (Kifner 1967). FIGHT responded with a series of protests, including a large demonstration at the annual stockholders' meeting in Flemington, New Jersey, in April of 1967 (Kifner 1967). At this event, over 700 supporters of FIGHT showed up to protest Kodak's refusal to institute the job training program nearly agreed upon in December 1966. In the wake of the meeting, Kodak and FIGHT reached an agreement to set up a training program and eventually Kodak helped to set up Rochester Business Opportunities Corporation to help provide assistance to minority and disadvantaged businesses.

While the FIGHT campaign and many others like it were organized to correct the pervasive problem of employer discrimination against African Americans, not *all* of the collective action events about workplace discrimination in my data were initiated by (or on behalf of) African Americans. For example, there are many protest events focusing on discriminatory policies directed at women, such as when the National Organization for Women organized a "National Day of Protest" in 1983 against Allstate Insurance Company for its failure to pay women the same as they then paid men.

As well, there are protests focusing on discrimination of gays, lesbians, and transgendered individuals, such as the one in 1975 organized by the National Gay Rights Advocates that involved a suit against Pacific Bell because of their policy of discriminating against gays and lesbians. The suit named 250 people whose job applications were marked "code 48 – homosexual" (an indication that the Company believed the applicant to be gay) and then rejected for employment at the Company (*New York Times* 1986a).[9]

Finally, there were a fair number of events related to age discrimination. For example, in 1989, 1,000 older employees of General Motors filed a class action lawsuit against the Company, arguing that the merit-pay program implemented at GM penalized older workers (Ross 1989). As well, there were several events directed at universities for forced retirement policies of professors (*New York Times* 1986b; 1990).

Much like the antiproduct events described earlier, the antipolicy events in my data also often reflect a multipronged strategy used by protesters that involves combining insider and outsider tactics. For example, the FIGHT activists described previously successfully convinced shareholders of Kodak to sign over proxies to them in protest of Kodak's refusal to institute the program described previously (Welsh 1988). Again, the goal of this two-pronged strategy is to disrupt normal operating procedures of businesses as well as damage the image of the company.

Also, much like the antiproduct events described previously, antipolicy events tended to be narrowly focused on a specific policy but connected

[9] Although not in my data because it happened after 1990, another example is about discrimination against a transgendered person. In 2000 a long-time employee of Winn Dixie grocery store was fired because he admitted to sometimes wearing women's clothing at his home. This event, and the lawsuit that the employee subsequently filed, sparked the "Shame on Winn Dixie" protest campaign, which involved protest demonstrations outside of Winn Dixie stores in Georgia and Florida and a media campaign on the Internet.

to a larger issue (e.g., discrimination against minorities). And, like the antiproduct protest events, an undercurrent of these events is the sentiment that corporations, because of unchecked growth and increasing power, are able to institute policies and abide by practices that are not fair and may be downright immoral.

Antinegligence Protest Events

Finally, 11% of these events made explicit claims about corporate negligence. Once again, a common undercurrent in these events is one of corporate growth and lack of governmental regulation that has led corporations to willingly and knowingly cut corners, leading to accidents, loss of life, destruction of the environment, and, in general, the harming of health and welfare of citizens. For example, in 1985, 400 protesters demanded to know more from Union Carbide about a poisonous gas leak in West Virginia, charging that the company was not training workers properly, and that its negligence would lead to another Bhopal-like disaster (*New York Times* 1985a).[10] Or, in that same year, eight Greenpeace activists were arrested for attempting to plug underwater pipelines belonging to Chevron alleging that this company had illegally dumped hazardous chemicals (e.g., ammonia, cyanide, zinc, lead, and so on) into the ocean (*New York Times* 1985b). In 1969, General Motors was protested by Ralph Nader and others who charged that this company was in violation of federal standards on air pollution. Despite meeting emissions standards, the protesters argued that GM ignored the impact of lead, nitrogen, and rubber-tire pollutants (Millones 1969).

Perhaps one of the most infamous examples of protest directed at a corporation's negligence is the protest campaign in the wake of the Exxon Valdez oil spill. This spill was one of the largest to have occurred in the world and is considered to be the most environmentally destructive. The oil tanker, the Exxon Valdez, was captained by Joseph Hazelwood who was accused of being drunk when the ship ran aground in Prince William Sound on March 24, 1989 and spilled eleven million gallons of crude oil (Egan 1989). The damage to sea life was immeasurable and the initial cleanup was slow and ineffective; in September of 1989, Exxon disbanded its cleanup efforts leaving beaches still covered with oil (Egan 1989).

---

[10] In Chapter 5, I discuss the current campaign against Dow Chemical, which acquired Union Carbide, and is now being targeted for the latter's past wrong doings.

Almost immediately following the spill, Greenpeace and other groups began protesting the negligence of Hazelwood and Exxon for hiring him. Protests against Exxon for negligence associated both with the spill *and* its ineffective cleanup of the spill continued for years. For example, in 1993, Alaskan fishermen blockaded the Valdez narrows with their boats, preventing oil tankers from entering, in an effort to bring publicity to the declining population of pink salmon (*New York Times* 1993). And, in 2005, students in Oregon protested Exxon for failing to pay Alaska residents and fishermen for damages due to the accident (Sylwester 2005). However, these efforts were apparently not especially effective; in 2008, nearly twenty years after the accident, the Supreme Court cut the punitive damages against Exxon from what was once $5 billion to $500 million (Liptak 2008).

As was the case with the antiproduct and antipolicy events, protesters espousing antinegligence claims often couple outsider (or protest) tactics with insider tactics by introducing shareholder resolutions. For example, Chevron has recently been targeted by various organizations for Texaco's (which is now owned by Chevron) operations in the Ecuadorian Amazon. Between 1964 and 1992, Texaco operated a joint venture with Petroecuador to extract and transport oil through a pipeline.[11] Critics charge that over this period, about nineteen million gallons of oil (nearly twice as much oil as the Exxon Valdez spill described previously) were spilled around the pipeline. As well, critics charge that Texaco knowingly and improperly disposed of toxic and industrial waste in the area. While Texaco cleaned up some of this waste in 1998, critics charge that they left far more than they removed and that this waste has contaminated soil and groundwater and is making Ecuadorians ill. Protesters, sometimes organized by the Rainforest Action Network discussed in Chapter 1, have used direct actions of various sorts, both in Ecuador but also in the United States. These actions have been joined by Amnesty International and other organizations that have introduced several resolutions over the years directly related to the Ecuadorian controversy.

The data on protest directed at corporations over the 1960–1990 period, then, show that the activists were incensed about very specific issues related to policies, products, services, and corporate negligence. However, when we step back from the often colorful and exciting tactics

---

[11] For a discussion of the transnational social movement coordinating local struggles against oil companies in Ecuador, see Widener (2007).

used at protest events, we see that there is usually a common narrative of these events – a narrative that places the blame squarely on corporations, their unchecked growth, and the failure of the government to step in and ensure that corporations will not trod on basic human and civil rights of citizens, animals, and the environment. It seems reasonable to turn next to the question of identifying who anticorporate protesters in this period were.

Initiators of Anticorporate Protest

Just as I have been asking what protesters are incensed about, it is also interesting to consider who these protesters *are*. When examining this, it is critical to note that there are often many different kinds of people who come together to protest. For example, we see many events in the data that involved coalitions of African Americans and some religious organization or group, or women and some occupational group, or students and some resident group. However, if we examine the *dominant* characteristic of protesters identified by the writers of the news, we see that the group represented most frequently at anticorporate protest events in the 1960–1990 period in the United States are African Americans. In fact, when we examine the *full* dataset (in other words, not just the events directed at corporations as I describe in Appendix A), we see that African Americans initiated about 21% of the 21,000+ protest events. But, when we look only at the 3,632 anticorporate events, we see that African Americans initiated over 30% of these events. Remarkably, in many years, African Americans initiated over 50% of the anticorporate events in the United States. For example, in 1960, over 76% of the anticorporate protest events in the United States were initiated by African Americans and in 1963 this figure was close to 68%. While the proportion of events initiated by African Americans declines over this period (as it does within the full dataset), throughout the 1960s and early 1970s African Americans were incredibly active at targeting businesses in the United States.

What is going on here? As I noted previously, many of the anticorporate events in my data were associated with the civil rights movement and involved protesting against various businesses for discriminatory policies. But, later in this period, African Americans initiated events directed at Shell Oil for its operations in African countries, Korean grocery store owners in Brooklyn for allegedly discriminating with respect to service, a myriad of different companies for discriminatory hiring and promotion policies, and other companies for their involvement in South Africa. Thus, it would be a mistake to conclude that African Americans ceased targeting U.S. businesses after the civil rights movement.

Occupational or worker groups also initiated a great deal of anticorporate protest, as we might expect. In fact, while 15% of the events in the full dataset were initiated by an occupational or worker group, 17.5% of the anticorporate events involved some kind of group of people united by their occupation or profession (and, importantly, the events in these data do *not* include organized strikes and union organized events, as I note in Appendix A). Some of these events were actually sponsored by professional associations, such as when the New York State and American Psychological Associations protested NBC's television series "The Eleventh Hour" for its inaccurate portrayal of treating mental illness and its presentation of violations of confidentiality (*New York Times* 1962). Others were sponsored by loosely organized groups of people sharing the same occupation, such as when physicians picketed and protested GM automobile shows in 1964 and in 1965 because of their concerns with automobile safety (Stengren 1964; Ingraham 1965). Another such example is when writers organized a letter-writing campaign against Houghton-Mifflin Company and Western Pacific Industries because of fear that the latter's purchase of 6.7% of the former's shares would allow the conglomerate to influence the publishing decisions of Houghton-Mifflin (Mitgang 1978).

While students initiated about 17% of the protest events in the full dataset, only about 13% of the anticorporate events were initiated by students, who sometimes targeted their universities as an intermediary to a corporation and other times targeted companies directly. Students were active in environmental protest directed at companies, civil rights protest directed at businesses for their segregation policies, events directed at companies for investments in South Africa and Rhodesia, and, as noted before, the movement against companies producing weapons for war.

Importantly, students often initiated protest events directed at companies for reasons not directly related to their status as students. For example, in 1978, about 180 students at Princeton staged a protest of the textile giant, J. P. Stevens and Company, as part of a then ongoing national boycott of that company organized by the Amalgamated Clothing and Textile Workers Union. The Union was trying to organize workers in plants located in the South, but was also boycotting the company for discriminating against African Americans and women and for substandard working conditions in its factories. The protest at Princeton was directed at the University for using J. P. Stevens linens in its infirmary and dining halls (*New York Times* 1978). Or, in 1964, the Berkeley Students' Ad Hoc Committee Against Discrimination helped initiate campaigns against merchants who would not sign nondiscrimination agreements (Heirich 1968).[12]

While in the full dataset 8% of the events were initiated by some residential group, about 13% of the anticorporate events were. Typically these events targeted a company believed to be harming a given locale, such as when residents work together to block landfills and the trucking of garbage through a neighborhood. An example of this kind of event is found in 1965, when the residents of Monterey, California, organized a petition drive and pamphleteering campaign against Standard Oil, arguing that this company's proposed refinery would cause too much pollution and that it would cause scenic areas and agricultural valleys to become smog filled and hazardous due to potential spillage (Davies 1965: 55). Such events came to be known in later years as "NIMBY" (Not In My Back-Yard) protests, though as this example shows, their occurrence clearly predates the development of this acronym.[13]

Other fairly common anticorporate events that were sponsored by residents were those directed at rental companies for increasing rents or declining conditions of rental properties. For example, in 1966, residents of a luxury apartment building in New York City owned by the Alcoa Residence, Inc., hung laundry out their windows in protest of an increase in rent (*New York Times* 1966a). Also in 1966, New York City residents built a giant bonfire in the middle of the street to protest the lack of heat in their apartments (*New York Times* 1966b). The bonfire disrupted ordinary traffic flows, but also drew the press, which publicized the plight of the tenants and potentially damaged the reputation of owners of the building.

Finally, while about 6% of the events in the full data were initiated by women, about 8% of the anticorporate events were initiated by women. The bulk of the female-initiated events, as might be imagined, were related to employment discrimination, such as in 1975, when eleven New York

---

[12] See Meier and Rudwick (1973) for a general discussion of student activism in the 1960s, much of which was directed at corporations.

[13] After 1990, we also see the growth of the antibig box store movement, another kind of NIMBY protest movement (e.g., Whysall 2000; Jones and Comfort 2006). Examples include such protest campaigns as those directed at Wal-Mart and Home Depot (Ingram and Rao 2004; Halebsky 2006).

City restaurants were targeted because they did not hire women (Campbell 1975). One restaurant owner admitted at the time to not hiring women as a matter of business practice, while other owners made excuses for their behavior, ranging from lack of locker room facilities for women, to conflict with male waitstaff who would not like to work with women (Campbell 1975). Or, in 1981, thirty women protested outside of the shareholder meeting of Morgan Guaranty and Trust Company, charging that the company discriminated against women in hiring and promotion (*New York Times* 1981b).

However, many of the female-initiated events were directed at corporations for other, unrelated, feminist and nonfeminist concerns. For example, in 1977, women (feminists and more conservative women alike) joined together to target vendors and producers of pornography, especially pornography that also depicted violence (Ivins 1977). Or, in 1966, thousands of "housewives" in Denver, Colorado, boycotted and picketed five major supermarket chains (Safeway, King Soopers, Furr's, Red Owl, and Miller's) for their high prices (*New York Times* 1966c). Similar protests organized by women took place that same year in Oregon (*New York Times* 1966d). And in 1970, "mothers" organized a campaign against the toy maker, Remco Industries Incorporated, for producing a line of toy trucks that emitted real smoke from exhaust pipes (*New York Times* 1970). Or, in 1968, feminists organized to boycott the corporate sponsors of the Miss America Pageant (Pepsi-Cola, Toni, and Oldsmobile), as well as the pageant itself. The protesters displayed a giant puppet dressed as a bathing beauty, but in chains, to symbolize "the chains that tie [women] ... to these beauty standards against [their] ... will" (Curtis 1968: 81). The protesters also carried a "freedom trash can" into which they threw bras, girdles, high-heeled shoes, dish detergent, cosmetics, *Playboy* magazines, and hair curlers (Curtis 1968).

Thus, it is important to note that women organized a great many different kinds of events directed at corporations. While many of these drew directly on their status as women and/or women workers, many events drew on women's status as mothers or as feminists or as antifeminists. I make this point because it would be wrong to conclude that women only organize against corporations for issues related to discrimination in employment.

This section has described the most prevalent groups initiating anticorporate protest events in my data drawn from the *New York Times* in the 1960–1990 period: African Americans, students, occupational groups, women, and residents. To be sure, other groups initiated protest directed at corporations and should not be overlooked. The most obvious of these are religious groups, which were also very active during this period (as evidenced in my earlier discussion of protest directed at weapons manufacturers). Thus, it would be incorrect to draw the conclusion from my discussion that no other groups protested firms during this period. Rather, it is simply that the bulk of these events during this period were organized by African Americans, women, students, occupational groups, and residents.

Shifting the Scale of Contention and the Targets of Anticorporate Activism

Much of the previous description of specific protest events in my dataset brings us back to my earlier observation (from Chapter 2) about the fact that many of these anticorporate events, while proximally targeting a corporation, also target a governmental unit.[14] In fact, when we examine this duality of targets in my data, we see that nearly 18% of the 3,632 events that target a business *also* target some governmental unit. Most of these are domestic governmental units, but certainly some also make claims against foreign governmental units (as we'll see in Chapter 4, especially, but also in Chapter 5). Therefore, if we accept my earlier (Chapter 2) distinction between contentious and private politics, we might then note that 18% of the anticorporate events in my data may be accurately categorized as "contentious politics" because, in addition to targeting a corporation, they also target some governmental unit. There are many examples of this in my data.

First, as I described previously, in the early 1960s there were many protests associated with the civil rights movement that took part at restaurants and other businesses and articulated claims about desegregation. While the proximate target of these events may have been some corporate policy, practice, or product, the more distant target was the state and its policies. As we know from the history of the civil rights movement, in 1964 Congress passed the Civil Rights Act (Pub. L 88–352, 78 Stat. 241)

---

[14] Interestingly, nearly 23% of the events that targeted a business also targeted some other entity (e.g., government, educational institutions, or medical facilities). Thus, it is not uncommon at all for protest events to target multiple systems of authority (Van Dyke, Soule, and Taylor 2004).

outlawing segregation in schools and public places including restaurants, which until this time often had rules specifying where, in relation to white Americans, African Americans could sit to dine. Thus, we might consider the protest events at restaurants to have targeted both businesses and the state. Viewed as such, these events can be classified as contentious politics.

Or, another example from my data are the riots of the late 1960s that took place in over 128 cities in the United States (U.S. Riot Commission 1968). The 164 "civil disorders" studied by the Kerner Commission usually involved African Americans targeting symbols of white America, such as white property in black neighborhoods. One of the notable characteristics of this wave of riots is that in many of them, businesses were damaged and/or looted. While the initial reports of damages tended to be exaggerated, the Kerner Commission still estimates the costs of damage in some cities to be in the tens of millions of dollars, and that 80% of this was typically related to losses by businesses (U.S. Riot Commission 1968). The riots clearly targeted both the state and business interests, as the grievances noted by the Kerner Commission included the unfair commercial practices of primarily white-owned businesses, as well as crime, poverty, and poor sanitation of the neighborhoods in which the rioters lived (U.S. Riot Commission 1968). So, again, viewed in this way, the riots that targeted businesses may also be seen as contentious politics.

In the 1970s, protest events that targeted both businesses and the government tended to focus on weapons production and were proximally directed at companies (such as Dow Chemical and Honeywell) making weapons for use in the Vietnam War. But they also targeted the U.S. government for its involvement in the war, as I described previously. Interestingly, many of these events took place on college campuses, such as the one I described in Madison, adding yet another target to the mix: the university.

There were also a fair number of protest events in the 1970s that targeted stores that sold pornography and movie theaters showing pornographic films.[15] These events typically targeted the businesses directly, but also made claims directed at the state in an attempt to increase regulation of

[15] These events were certainly not the first antipornography events in the United States. In my data, one particularly active group was Operation Yorkville (later renamed Morality in the Media), which organized protest events in the 1960s and early 1970s in New York and sought to "keep suggestive magazines out of bookstores and newsstands in the area" (*New York Times* 1965: 80).

pornographic materials.[16] For example, in 1976, a Utah group organized against pornography in that state, staging rallies and demonstrations, as well as smaller scale picketing events outside of establishments selling pornographic materials (Lichtenstein 1976). The group claimed that the campaign was successful and that its coordinated actions shut down several movie theaters, encouraged Safeway and Albertson's to stop selling some pornographic magazines, and forced theater production companies to begin editing their plays to reduce potentially offensive material (Lichtenstein 1976).

While we may think that most of the antipornography events in the data are staged by more conservative or traditional groups and actors, it is interesting to note that one of the most active campaigns in the data was not. In 1979, gay men in New York City organized a series of events directed at Lorimar Productions/United Artists for the film *Cruising*, which was produced by Jerry Weintraub and directed by William Friedkin. The film, starring Al Pacino, depicts a police officer trying to solve a series of brutal sex crimes in which gay men were the victims. Protesters attempted to get the then mayor of New York City (Ed Koch) to withdraw support for the film, charging that the film portrayed gay men as "psychopathic murderers or pathetic victims who invite victimization" (Ledbetter 1979: B2).[17]

Thus, as these examples show, one interesting facet of many of the antipornography (sometimes referred to as "antismut") events is the way in which they simultaneously target businesses and local governmental authorities. Another such example is when, in 1977 in New York City, a number of groups mobilized under the banner of the Mayor's Midtown Citizens Committee with the explicit goal of "stamping out smut" in New York. Through a series of rallies and marches, the group hoped to simultaneously shut down peep shows, massage parlors, topless and bottomless bars, and pornographic book shops *and* convince the Board of Estimate to pass a zoning law on pornography (Klemesrud 1977: 31).

---

[16] Related to these events were those that targeted movie theaters for showing violent films and bookstores for selling racist and Nazi literature. Again, while the proximate targets of these events were the actual business establishments, in many cases we see that protesters also make claims against the government for greater regulation of the entertainment industry.

[17] And, of course, throughout this period antipornography events were also staged by feminists who protested pornography for reasons not related to the conservative or traditional groups that also staged such events.

These examples – sit-ins, riots, and antiweapons and antipornography events – all targeted multiple entities, including the state and at least one business interest. As such, they highlight the importance of recognizing the way in which activists move up and down the scale when determining who and what to target, as described in Chapter 2. In the antipornography case, we see protesters moving up the scale from the local businesses to the city level to encourage zoning laws against businesses selling pornography. In the case of students targeting universities for allowing recruiters from weapons manufacturers, we see protesters moving up the scale from the university to the corporate level, to eventually (of course) the ultimate target of the state's military policy. And, as will be discussed more in Chapter 4, protesters moved down the scale from targeting a foreign government (South Africa), to the U.S. government, to eventually corporations with investments in South Africa, to finally universities whose portfolios held investments in corporations with investments in South Africa.

As I discussed in Chapter 2, shifting the scale of contention has mostly been discussed as part and parcel to the diffusion process, but I also argue that it is also part and parcel to the process of strategically choosing targets and experimenting with which targets are more likely to grant concessions to groups. In some cases, it may be the corporation, in others the state, and in others the university is considered to be more likely to grant concessions. Strategically choosing which scale to target is an essential part of the dynamics of contention and one that is well demonstrated with my data. But one issue that is *not* reflected in my discussion is the issue of how state repression may drive scale shift, at least with respect to choice of targets. I address this in the next section, asking how state repression of protesters might force them to seek targets less likely to respond with force, violence, and arrests.

Repression and Scale Shift

In Chapter 1, I noted that with duel trends of both deregulation and the declining power of organized labor, activists have moved to targeting corporations directly rather than indirectly through the government or via organized labor. These are all compelling reasons for why activists might shift the scale of contention, at least with respect to focusing on targets other than, or in addition to, the government.

But, I also noted that another reason that has yet to be explored in the literature on this subject is that the state may be less likely to repress activists targeting businesses than they are those targeting the state. And, businesses may be less likely, or less able, to repress activists. While repression of labor unrest by private security forces of companies certainly exists, corporations do not control the same repressive capacity as does the state. The state has the ability to repress dissidents directly via the police, the national guard, and other, more covert entities, such as the FBI's Covert Intelligence Program (Cunningham 2004).

Most studies of repression of public protest in the United States context examine *overt* forms of repression, namely policing, as data on overt repression are easier to come by (Earl 2003; Earl et al. 2003).[18] But, to my knowledge, these studies have not connected the instance of repression or policing to scale shift. I argue here that repression can lead activists to seek other focal points – focal points that may be less likely to respond with force. Much like McAdam's (1983) discussion of tactical innovation, which links the deployment of new tactics to state repression of previously used tactics, I argue that activists may also innovate with respect to what targets they choose. In essence, repression can lead to strategic innovation, which in turn leads to a shift in scale, as activists opt to target different focal points – those that either cannot or will not, respond with repression. Before I present some evidence to support this claim, it is critical to step back and talk briefly about repression and the policing of protesters more generally.

The Policing of Protest in the United States

What leads to police repression of public protest? Research on this question typically focuses on the particular characteristics of protest events. The most prevalent work in this area employs a "threat approach," which argues and finds that policing responds to the manifestation of "threat" directed against the government and/or the citizenry (Earl et al. 2003; Soule and Davenport 2009). That is, the more threatening the protest is to state agents and citizens, the more aggressive the response of the political

---

[18] There is some notable scholarship on *covert* repression of protesters (Earl 2003). For example, it has historically been fairly common for police departments and the FBI to use surveillance as a way to harass and intimidate members of civil rights and black power movements (Davenport and Eads 2001). Or, Cunningham (2004) discusses the general use of surveillance to intimidate activists and Beckles (1996) describes how the FBI used surveillance outside of community institutions (such as movement-focused book stores) to intimidate activists and discourage protest.

authorities will be. Two primary types of threat have been identified in this literature: situational threat, or the behavioral threats posed to police at the protest event (e.g., protesters use of violence, projectiles, property damage, and the presence of counterdemonstrators) and diffuse threat, or the level of threat that the protesters pose to the legitimacy of the state (e.g., targeting the government and articulating radical goals). While scholarly work on repression also identifies other factors that affect levels of policing, such as the perceived weakness of protesters, diffusion of policing protocols, and the character and strength of the police force, I focus here on the threat approach, as this has been the one that has received the most empirical support (Earl et al. 2003; Davenport 2007; Soule and Davenport 2009).

Taking this literature into account, I examine a number of different measures of threat at a protest event and assess how these impact the likelihood that police will attend a protest event and the likelihood that they will use force or violence at the event. Then, in addition to these characteristics, I examine whether or not events targeting corporations are more or less likely than events targeting the state to be met with police presence and police force and/or violence.[19] If they are less likely to be repressed than are those that target the state, then this lends support to my argument that one of the reasons that activists target corporations is that they are less likely to be repressed when so doing.

In the models presented in Table 3.1, the first measure of the level of threat posed by a protest event to authorities is the size of the event, measured by the number of participants, logged (Tilly 1978; Earl et al. 2003).[20] The logic here is that larger events are more threatening to police because they are more difficult to control, they present more opportunities for violation of laws, they harbor a greater potential to harm police officers at the event, and because they signal to police that there is a larger number of aggrieved individuals. In the dataset used in the analysis herein, a specific

---

[19] The data used for the analysis presented in Table 3.1 come from my data on all protest events in the United States, as reported in the *New York Times* (See Appendix A for a description of these data). Note that earlier sections of this chapter primarily use data on a subset of these events; that is, those that target businesses. Here, I compare such events to the full set of all protest events in the dataset.

[20] In Table 3.1, I limit the analysis to those events that might plausibly draw police presence. In other words, I remove events such as lawsuits and other legal activities that, under normal circumstances, will not be at risk of drawing police presence and action. I did run the same analysis on all events and the results were consistent with those presented in Table 3.1.

Table 3.1. *Logistic Regression Models Predicting Police Presence and Police Use of Force and/or Violence at Protest Events in the United States, 1960–1990. (Robust Standard Errors in Parentheses)*

	Model 1 Police Presence	Model 2 Police Force and/or Violence
1960s	.534*** (.131)	1.092*** (.174)
1970s	.124 (.141)	1.05 (.162)
Number of Protesters (log)	.021 (.023)	.154*** (.036)
Protester Use of Violence	1.392*** (.098)	1.818*** (.143)
Property Damage by Protesters	.483*** (.125)	.166 (.125)
Counterdemonstrators Present	1.012*** (.084)	.460*** (.114)
Confrontational Tactics	1.176*** (.083)	.647*** (.082)
Extremely Confrontational Tactics	1.126*** (.158)	.804** (.165)
Multiple Tactics	.444*** (.057)	.311** (.076)
Business Target	−.335*** (.055)	−.439*** (.084)
Cases	15,087	15,091
Model Log Likelihood	−8401.484	−4577.704

$^{*} p < .05,$ $^{**} p < .01,$ $^{***} p < .001$ (two-tailed test)

number of protesters was reported in the news article for about 51% of the events. In the remaining 49% of the events, coders were asked to estimate the number of protesters based on verbal cues in the article (e.g., "small," "few," or "handful" of protesters were estimated to be in category 1, fewer than ten protesters).[21] For events in which there was *not* a specific number reported, I imputed a number by choosing the midpoint of each category. In the dataset, the average size of all protest events in the 1960–1990 period was 1,533 participants.[22]

I also include a dichotomous variable that is coded 1 when there were counterdemonstrators present at the event as a second measure of threat. I include this variable because research shows that the presence of counter-demonstrators increases the probability of conflict at an event and therefore increases the level of threat to police agents (Waddington 1994; Earl

[21] The specific categories are as follows: category 1 = fewer than 10, category 2 = 10–49, category 3 = 50–99, category 4 = 100–999, category 5 = 1,000–9,999, and category 6 = over 10,000 participants.

[22] As a robustness check, I ran the analyses on two different sets of events: those for which the number of participants was reported in the news article and those for which coders estimated the number of participants. The pattern of results was the same on both sets and is in line with the findings presented herein.

and Soule 2006). Over this period, 6% of events had counterdemonstrators present.

Next, I include several aspects of the behavioral challenge presented by protesters. The first of these is a dichotomous variable coded 1 when protesters used *extremely confrontational tactics* (such as attacks, riots, melees, and/or mob violence). Between 1960 and 1990, protesters used such tactics at 16% of events. The second of these is a dichotomous variable coded 1 when protesters employed *confrontational tactics* (such as civil disobedience, demonstrations, and rallies). Protesters used such tactics in 71% of events in this period. The third measure of the behavioral threat presented by protesters is a dummy variable coded 1 when protesters damaged property at an event. Over this period, protesters damaged property at about 10% of the events. The fourth is a dummy variable coded 1 when protesters used violence (e.g., threw bricks, fought, and so on) at the event. This occurred in about 15% of the events. Finally, the last measure of the behavioral threat of protesters is a measure of tactical variety, which ranges from 1 to 4 and is a count of the number of different protest tactics used by protesters at the event. When greater numbers of tactics are used, authorities are confronted with a more complex scenario and are forced to improvise and employ personnel with greater variation in training and preparation – dynamics which frequently lead to greater levels of police use of force and violence (Davenport 1995).

Finally, once controlling for the level of threat present at a given event I include a dummy variable, which I coded 1 whenever an event *explicitly* targeted a business firm. This variable is included to test the argument that events targeting businesses are *less* likely to be repressed and/or repressed heavily than are other events, such as those that target the government or an educational institution. If it is the case that anticorporate events are less likely to be policed and/or policed heavily, then this will lend support to my argument that repression can lead to a shift in scale, as activists strategically ferret out new targets that are less likely to respond with force and violence.

The results presented in Table 3.1 are largely as expected with respect to how threat affects the likelihood of police presence and police use of force or violence at a given protest event. That is, violent events, those in which protesters damage property, use extremely confrontational tactics, and that use many tactics are all more likely to be met with policing. This is true in both models in Table 3.1, showing that threat does, in fact, lead to police presence and deployment of force and violence.

But, even when I control for the level of threat at a protest event, business targets are much less likely to draw police presence and police force/violence than are those that target the government or other institutions (educational, religious, and so on).[23] This is an important finding in that it suggests that a central element of the opportunity structure (state repression) can impact the choice of targets and thus lead to scale shift, at least with regard to the focal point or target chosen by activists. That is, targeting corporations may be due in part to their immense growth and to the simultaneous decline in regulation and organized labor, as Galbraith (1952) and Yaziji and Doh (2009) have argued. But, it may also have something to do with the fact that authorities are less likely to repress these events than they are those that target the government or other institutions. This fact could lead activists to strategically innovate with respect to target choice (hence to the observed shift in the scale of the targets).[24]

More broadly, scholars of policing and repression of protesters will likely be intrigued by this finding. In this literature, repression has been shown to impact subsequent protest levels[25] and tactical innovation (McAdam 1983), but less research has examined how repression affects other social movement phenomena. While my findings cannot show that repression directly impacts the strategic choice of targets, they do hint that this process may be at work.

---

[23] Just how much less likely are they to draw police presence and force/violence? The coefficients presented in Table 3.1 indicate that events targeting businesses have a predicted probability of .31 of police presence, while those targeting other entities have a predicted probability of .39. Events targeting businesses have a predicted probability of .07 of police force/violence, while those targeting other entities have a higher predicted probability (.10).

[24] Of course, my findings can really only suggest this as a possibility. To adequately test the causal nature of this argument, one would need to have sequential data on given protest campaigns showing that activists switched targets once they were repressed for targeting the government. Nonetheless, this is an intriguing possibility and one that should be investigated more deeply by scholars working in this area.

[25] On the question of how repression affects subsequent protest rates, some scholars find support for negative monotonic effects, others find support for positive monotonic effects, while still others debate between opposing versions of nonmonotonic effects, such U-shaped and inverted U-shaped effects. Some scholars have even suggested countervailing effects that net to a null effect (see Koopmans 1997, Moore 1998 and Davenport 2007, for reviews of recent work and Zimmerman 1980 for a review of classic work).

Epilogue: Does Anticorporate Protest Matter?

It would be difficult with the kind of data used in this chapter to examine how anticorporate protest impacted all of the corporations targeted herein. Because these data are from news accounts of protest events, they do not always (or even most of the time) describe corporate reactions or concessions to activist claims. However, one way to gauge the effectiveness of anticorporate protest is to examine how it affects the stock price of a targeted corporation. This assumes, of course, that corporations care about their stock price and pay close attention to factors that affect it – whether positively or negatively. To this end, Brayden King and I have published a study that shows that protest is associated with a decline in stock price of targeted corporation (King and Soule 2007).

Specifically, in King and Soule (2007), we employ methodology used by finance scholars to measure the impact of a given event on the stock price change of a corporation. We examine 342 different protest events in the 1960–1990 period that explicitly targeted a named corporation for which we could also find accompanying stock price data.[26] Following finance scholars, who use data on *abnormal stock returns* to assess value created as the result of corporate actions, such as takeovers (e.g., Travlos 1987), stock repurchases (Zajac and Westphal 2004), and corporate restructuring (Markides 1992), we examine the effect of a protest event directed at a corporation on its abnormal stock returns. To do this, we used event study methodology, which uses the past performance of the firm's stock to calculate the extent to which the current performance of the stock deviates substantially from expected performance (see MacKinlay 1997 for a review).

Thus, the dependent variable in our study, abnormal stock price returns, measures investor reaction to an unanticipated corporate event, in our case a protest event directed at the company (McWilliams and Siegel 1997). Positive abnormal returns indicate that investors perceive an event favorably, while negative returns suggest the opposite. The underlying theory of event studies suggests that abnormal stock returns reflect new information about the firm's value (MacKinlay 1997). Thus, we argue that protest events can broadcast to the public new information – usually

---

[26] While this may seem like a small number, it is many more than those reported in comparable studies of the effect of protest and boycotts on stock price change (see review in King and Soule 2007).

negative information – about a firm. This information can affect investor perceptions, which in turn affect stock returns.

Findings from our analysis suggest that protest is, in fact, associated with negative stock price returns. That is, even controlling for other kinds of market fluctuations and confounding events, a protest event directed at a corporation negatively affects its stock price. Thus, by demonstrating that protest affects abnormal stock returns, we provide evidence that investors consider protest to be consequential to the firm, independent of previously available information.

This study provides important evidence that I hope will foreshadow my discussion in subsequent chapters about the efficacy of anticorporate protest. That is, activists targeting corporations can have profound effects on firms' financial performance. The hope, of course, is that these effects may drive the corporation to remedy the underlying problems identified by protesters; that is, the hope is that corporate financial performance may drive decisions regarding policies, products, and behaviors that are commensurate with principles of corporate social responsibility. Thus, the hope is that corporate financial performance (CFP) will lead to corporate social performance (CSP).[27]

Summary and Conclusion

In this chapter, I have used data on thirty-one years of anticorporate protest in the United States to explore a number of important themes. It seems reasonable to conclude this chapter with some reflections on what this analysis might tell us about current day anticorporate protest. First, one of the themes that emerged herein is that protesters often use both insider and outsider tactics in a multipronged approach when targeting corporations. They draw on their status as outsiders to corporations when they protest, but when they can, they also draw on their insider status, such as when they submit shareholder resolutions in conjunction with this protest. I suspect that this multipronged approach remains true today and, in fact, I will explore this in Chapter 5.

Second, I noted that anticorporate activists often have multiple focal points or targets. I brought up the importance of understanding the focal

---

[27] The connection between CFP and CSP has been explored by several scholars and, while the results are mixed, the consensus seems to be that there is a weak positive relationship between the two (see review Baron, Harjoto, and Jo 2008).

points of anticorporate activism and discerning whether or not specific protest events and campaigns are best understood as private politics or contentious politics. And, I demonstrated with my data that the literature on both private and contentious politics should be used when studying anticorporate activism. I return to this theme in Chapter 5.

Third, I suspect that the issues around which activists mobilize – antipolicy, antiproduct, and negligence – remain important today. Overall, as I noted in Chapter 2, we might think of these as part and parcel to corporate social responsibility concerns. And, in Chapter 5, I will return to the issues of anticorporate protest in the post-1990 period.

Finally, I argued that one of the reasons that activists may target corporations directly is that anticorporate events are far less likely than others to be policed heavily. The analysis presented in Table 3.1 hints that this process may be at work. This finding is important because it suggests that anticorporate activists strategically change their targets or focal points in response to changes in elements of the opportunity structure (here, repression or policing). As such, it would appear that scale shift can be driven by changes in the opportunity structure, an important empirical finding.

In the next chapter, I examine the student antiapartheid movement in depth focusing on its effects on university divestment policy. This movement provides a nice illustration of my points on scale shift, but it also illustrates my points about the various outcomes or consequences of social movement activity.

4

The Effect of Protest on University Divestment

During the late 1970s, in the wake of the Soweto Uprising of 1976, students in the United States began protesting, demonstrating, signing petitions, building blockades, staging sit-ins, building shantytowns, and participating in a movement designed to encourage pension funds, insurance companies, and other organizations to disinvest of their South African-related securities. This movement, known to most as the student *divestment* movement, had its roots in earlier student *antiapartheid* activism, which began after the Sharpeville Massacre of 1960, but fluctuated throughout the 1960s and 1970s.[1] But, by the mid-1960s, student activists (many of whom were from seminaries in and around New York City and also from colleges in western Massachusetts), had organized a boycott against the First National City Bank (later Citibank) and Chase Manhattan, both of which ran branches in South Africa. The boycott was followed by demonstrations in March 1965 led by Students for a Democratic Society (SDS), Congress on Racial Equality (CORE), the Student Nonviolent Coordinating Committee (SNCC), and several other student and civil rights organizations outside of Chase Manhattan's downtown headquarters (Jones 1965). These events were joined by protest marches in the

[1] On March 21, 1960, the Pan African Congress organized a peaceful protest against pass books and pass laws, which were used to limit the movement of nonwhites in South Africa and were one of the hallmarks of the system of apartheid. In response to the peaceful gathering of several thousand people, police forces opened fire on the crowd and killed sixty-nine people. A wave of protest both within and outside of South Africa followed the massacre and the South African government declared a state of emergency. The event marks a turning point in South Africa's relationship with the rest of the world, as the international community (including the United Nations) condemned the actions of the police and apartheid more generally. For a complete history of activism directed at South Africa, see Massie (1997).

Spring of 1968 at Princeton, the University of Wisconsin, and Cornell, all of which explicitly called for banks and corporations to disinvest from South Africa (Massie 1997).

Thus, by the early 1970s, student antiapartheid activists had begun to reframe their goals from the very broad goal of ending apartheid, to the narrower goal of ending corporate investment in South Africa, to (eventually) the very specific goal of divestment *by their own universities* of holdings in corporations with ties to South Africa.[2] This winnowing of the goals of the movement was aided by a group called "Catalyst," which in 1976 and 1977 sponsored speakers and informational forums about divestment at colleges and universities (Vellela 1988). These speakers drew the attention of students to the fact that college portfolios routinely held stock in companies entrenched in South Africa – a fact that galvanized support among students and led them to begin targeting their universities directly to divest of their South African-related stocks and bonds.

At the same time students were engaging in prodivestment activism of various sorts, administrators at colleges and universities were debating the role of the university in divestment activity. As will become clear later in this chapter, in many ways, this debate mirrored some of the arguments for and against corporate social responsibility, which I discussed in Chapter 1. But, the outcome of this debate was the fairly rapid rate of university divestment: Between 1977 and 1989, 167 educational institutions agreed to divest in South Africa-related companies through the sales of stocks and bonds in these companies. Hampshire College was the first to divest, followed closely by Howard University and Michigan State University and then by many others.

The coincidence of the rise of the student divestment movement and the wave of university divestment raises the question of whether or not student activism mattered to university decisions and, if so, in what ways it mattered. These issues are the subject of this chapter. As such, this chapter provides a clear example of a point raised in earlier chapters; that is, when we think about activism directed at corporations, we need to consider the ultimate target or focal point of the movement. As I discussed previously, this is key to differentiating between contentious politics and private

[2] Divestment is the sale of investments because of ethical motivations. Disinvestment is the severing of business and financial ties to South Africa. In this chapter, businesses disinvest when they cut ties to South Africa, while universities divest when they sell some or all of their securities in companies that have not disinvested (Kibbe 1989; Knight 1990).

politics and is important to arguments about scale shift. The subject of this chapter is a case of how protest can be directed at an intermediary entity (in this case, the university) in an attempt to influence corporate behavior and policies regarding an issue core to principles of corporate social responsibility. Of course, the ultimate target of this campaign was the government of South Africa, thus, we can consider activism around divestment to be contentious politics despite the fact that the proximate targets (college, universities, and corporations) were not states. This case shows again how anticorporate activism often has many focal points or targets, including a governmental one. And, the case illustrates my points raised in earlier chapters about how activists, for a variety of reasons, shift scales (at least with respect to these focal points or targets), thus moving between private and contentious politics.

Before examining data which will speak directly to the issue of *if* and *how* student protest mattered to university divestment decisions, it is worth discussing the multiple and conflicting pressures that colleges and universities faced regarding the divestment issue during the 1980s. In the language used in Chapter 2, these pressures are part of the broader *opportunity structure* in which universities were located. In other words, these pressures likely impacted university and college decisions independently and in conjunction with one another in an interactive fashion. I have organized this discussion into two sections, one describing the pressures on universities to maintain their investments in South Africa in the wake of student pressure to divest, the other section describing the pressures (especially from the student movement) on the university to divest.

Pressures on the University to Retain South African Investments

Universities found themselves faced with several different kinds of pressures to keep their South African investments. These ranged from arguments about the expected role of universities as politically neutral entities, to pure financial arguments, to beliefs about the positive effects of U.S. business in South Africa. The strongest set of arguments against university divestment, however, was related to the actual and the perceived costs of divestment measures to the university. These arguments resonate with the discussion in Chapter 1 about the evolution of ideas of corporate social responsibility and whether or not a "business case" could be made for divesting. As such, this debate focused on how divesting would affect a university's overall stock portfolio and how much divestment would cost the university.

To argue for or against a business case for divesting, it is important to understand the costs to a portfolio that divestment incurred – something that entails understanding the type of businesses that had investments in South Africa during the 1970s and 1980s. Essentially, the typical business with South African investments was large, successful, and generally appealing to potential investors because of its relatively low risk (Hauck 1985). Businesses that had South African ties were mainly large, multinational firms and equities of these firms accounted for about one-third of the market value of all U.S. securities during this time period (Hauck 1985). To totally divest meant to eliminate thirty of the top fifty stocks from *Standard and Poor's* and to exclude basically all of *Standard and Poor's* firms doing business in electrical equipment, machinery, automobiles, hospital supplies, chemicals, soft drinks, and pharmaceuticals (Hauck 1985). On average, the return on South African investments was about twice as high as that of investments in other foreign countries (Williams-Slope 1971) and South African investments were considered by most to be low-risk, steady performers (Hauck 1985). Obviously, then, it was financially disadvantageous to disinvest from firms with South African operations during this period, both because of the fact that these stocks performed well and because so many companies had investments in South Africa.

In contrast to the large and low-risk firms that had ties to South Africa, South African-free securities were much smaller and not as well known. Investors could potentially spend a great deal of money researching these securities and producing new information on South African-free investments. Further, because South African-free securities were lesser known, they were subject to much higher risk, which generally leads to higher transaction and administration costs (Wagner et al. 1984).

Most experts at the time concluded that divestment would be costly to universities, especially those with larger portfolios (Rottenberg 1986). Transaction costs, including commissions to brokers and dealers, fees, and transfer taxes, were estimated to be between 1.5% to 6.0% of the value of stocks sold (Hauck 1985; Kibbe 1989). A study conducted for Michigan State University cautioned that while it was possible to construct a South African–free portfolio for smaller funds, the costs of doing so for larger funds would be far too great (Hauck 1985). This conclusion was echoed by others who argued that while the costs of divestment in the 1980s for small portfolio funds were actually quite low, for larger funds, divesting had a more substantial negative impact (Wagner et al. 1984). In addition to transaction costs, the increased investment risk of smaller, lesser-known companies was substantial enough to cause most portfolio managers pause.[3]

There is significant evidence to suggest that, from a strict financial standpoint, divestment may not have been especially wise. One financial study conducted at the time *explicitly* recommended that colleges and universities refuse to divest, arguing that a South African-free portfolio was simply of lesser quality and more volatile than a more diverse portfolio (Meidinger Asset Planning Service 1983). The veracity of such claims was the subject of much debate, but most experts agreed that there were costs of divestment and that these were especially high for large investment funds (Hauck 1985; Rottenberg 1986; Kibbe 1989; Jackson 1992).

The direct costs of divestment were accompanied by a number of *indirect* costs associated with divestment. One of these was the very real risk that corporate donors would cease giving cash, stock, and equipment to universities should they divest (Hauck 1985). Another indirect cost of divestment was the negative reaction from alumni, many of whom issued statements to colleges and universities threatening to stop donating should the university divest from South Africa.[4] Negative alumni reaction to both the issue of South African divestment and to the broader student movement was exemplified by the event at Yale University in 1988, when an enraged alumnus (Dr. Elwood D. Bracey), visiting campus for a thirty-year class reunion, burned down the shantytown that was erected on that campus in protest of Yale's investments in South Africa.

In addition to the direct and indirect financial costs of divestment, there are four other reasons that opponents of divestment frequently

---

[3] This discussion has focused on the costs of divestment to the college and university. A related question is how much disinvestment would cost corporations. On this point, Meznar, Nigh, and Kwok (1994) and Wright and Ferris (1997) find that withdrawing from South Africa led to sharp declines in stock performance, suggesting that this was also not a particularly wise strategy from a strict financial point of view. But note that Posinkoff (1997) and Kumar, Lamb, and Wokutch (2002) both find that the effects of disinvestment from South Africa depended on *when* the company pulled out. Those that pulled out later were less penalized than those who did so early. In fact, Posnikoff (1997) argues that the announcement of divestment was associated with positive returns to stock price for those that did so later.

[4] On the more general point of the need for colleges and universities to attend to alumni concerns, see Simon et al. (1972).

gave, all of which hinged on the expected role of the university. The first and most common of these was the argument that discussion of corporate responsibility should not be taken on by the university, an argument based on Friedman's (1970) discussion of corporate social responsibility (see Chapter 1). The purpose of a university, many claimed, is to produce competent and skilled leaders, *not* to debate issues of investment, divestment, disinvestment, and corporate responsibility (Simon et al. 1972). Hence, any debate surrounding the issue of divestment was viewed as an improper use of resources and one that hindered the proper functioning of the university. Moreover, some critics claimed that members of educational institutions make poor collective decisions on moral and social issues. In this view, a community of scholars is not a politically intelligent entity, thus questions of moral and social investment issues should not be approached by such people (Simon et al. 1972).

A second and fairly pervasive antidivestment argument hinged on the notion that adopting value-laden policies is incongruent with educational institutions' expected principles of political neutrality (Simon et al. 1972; Rottenberg 1986). Here, the position a university adopts with regard to investment decisions should protect the "conditions and atmosphere required for fostering academic work – particularly including conditions for the maintenance of academic freedom, which is … the right of scholars to pursue knowledge freely" (Simon et al. 1972: 70). By this line of reasoning, adopting moral and social investment positions caused universities and colleges to jeopardize their intended commitment to maintaining 'middle-ground' positions on social and political issues (Simon et al. 1972).

A third argument made by opponents was the belief that the presence and expansion of U.S. business in South Africa served as a modernizing force in that country and actually improved living conditions for all South African citizens (Rottenberg 1986; Marzullo 1987; Sethi 1987; Wilking 1987). These opponents recommended that U.S. firms maintain their positions in South Africa with the condition that all business be conducted morally and with goals of corporate social responsibility. By this reasoning, divesting of South African-related securities was more harmful than it was good. Derek Bok, then president of Harvard University, argued at the time that one of his main reasons for maintaining his university's South African investments was that divestment would harm black South Africans, as they would lose the protection of the Sullivan Principles, which ensured that adopting companies worked to end discrimination against South African blacks in the workplace (Harris 1986).[5]

Such opponents argued that U.S. businesses that withdrew from South Africa also withdrew whatever leverage they may have had against the South African government. They argued that by maintaining ties, businesses were able to exert pressure where it was needed most. Many believed that the social impact of U.S. investment in South Africa was an overall improvement of not only labor conditions, but also housing, healthcare, education, and legal assistance to black South Africans. Hence, many argued that businesses should keep their ties to South Africa in an effort to influence the government and improve the living conditions therein (Sethi 1987; Wilking 1987; *Cornell Chronicle* 1988). Similarly, an article published in *The Washington Post* argued that the South African "economy is its most effective engine of social transformation, compelling whites to grant blacks precisely the training and education, the livelihood and personal rewards, the choices of where to live and work, the associations and organizations, the sense of their own power and community, that apartheid would deny them" *Washington Post* 1985: A22). Businesses in South Africa were seen by many as a positive and moral force for good in a country that desperately needed help (*Cornell Chronicle* 1988). In fact, most published polls of black South African laborers indicated that they did not want U.S. companies to leave South Africa as this would mean fewer jobs and declining economic conditions (*Cornell Chronicle* 1988).

Finally, the fourth case made by opponents of divestment maintained that divestment was not an effective means of causing businesses to change. Because universities do not possess enough stock in any one company

[5] The Sullivan Principles (also referred to as The Statement of Principles) are probably the first example of voluntary codes of conduct that businesses adopted. They were seven principles that urged businesses in South Africa to implement fair employment practices and helped to advance the position of black and nonwhite employees of the companies that adopted them. Implemented in 1977 and modified in 1984, these principles included a call for desegregation of the workplace, equal pay for comparable work, equal and fair employment practices, management and supervisory training programs for disadvantaged groups, improving the quality of life outside of the workplace, and working to eliminate discriminatory laws in the broader national context. Reverend Leon Sullivan, the author of the principles, hired an accounting firm (Arthur D. Little) to help assess whether or not a given signatory was actually complying with the principles and to eventually issue grades to companies based on their success in compliance with the principles. Thus, the Sullivan Principles have been called the "first large-scale experiment in independent monitoring" of corporations (Seidman 2007: 60) and, as such, are an important precursor to the more recent wave of monitoring companies that is discussed in Chapter 5 (see also Bartley 2007).

to lower the market price, selling stock is rarely an effective means of exerting influence on the practices of a firm (Bok 1982). Generally, a business would not disinvest simply because one, or even several, of its investors threatened to divest. Although there was some evidence that corporate disinvestment might pressure the South African government to end apartheid (Schwartzman and Taylor 1999; Seidman 2007), it was clear that corporate decisions to disinvest were rarely, if ever, based on universities divesting of their stock (Rottenberg 1986). In this view, the university's actions had very little impact on the political situation in South Africa because their actions did not actually matter much to corporations (Sethi 1987; Rottenberg 1986).

Derek Bok (1982) captured the arguments of opponents of divestment in his claim that divesting seriously jeopardized the intended function of the university and that divestiture opened "the trustees to the risk of liability while costing the university substantial sums of money and exposing it to all the burdens and hazards of using investment decisions as a weapon to influence corporate behavior" (Bok 1982: 292-293). Moreover, adopting policies of divestment to quell student protests or to bend to social and environmental pressures was seen by Bok and others as a shortsighted measure on the part of the university.

Given the prevailing array of arguments *against* divestment, it seems reasonable to also discuss the pressures in *favor* of divestment that universities simultaneously faced. These, of course, came from the university's major constituencies (students and faculty members) but they also came from the broader society in the form of negative opinions regarding the South African system of apartheid, the U.S. government, and from the country of South Africa. Thus, these pressures came both from within the university itself but also from the larger context in which the university is embedded, exemplifying again my arguments in Chapter 2 about the nested structure of opportunities in which colleges and universities operate.

Pressures on the University to Divest of South African Investments

Conflicting with these strong pressures on the university to retain their South African holdings were many powerful signals promoting divestiture. Clearly, one of the greatest prodivestment pressures was the increasing rate of student protest across the country. Most readers remember the shantytown protests, but sit-ins, blockades, hunger strikes, rallies, and marches were also common as students used both demonstrative and informative tactics to broadcast the issue of apartheid (Rottenberg 1986; Vellela 1988; Loeb 1994; Massie 1997; Soule 1997). Whether or not the student movement actually mattered to university divestment decisions is the subject of this chapter, but it is worth noting that, at the time, there was the *perception* that university divestment was (at least in part) driven by student activism (see review in Soule 1999; Massie 1997).

Many students and faculty members at colleges and universities across the country viewed divestment as the only morally right measure to take and, as such, they exerted pressure on the administrations of their universities to divest (Soule 2001). Students accused their universities of "preserving the power structure" of the administration and failing to divest as a means of maintaining status quo politics (Wurf 1986: 3). Student activists in the mid-1980s believed that they had a "moral advantage" in that it was easy to "gain support for the notion that apartheid is wrong" (Williams et al. 1985: 61). The protests surrounding the issues of divestment and South Africa were of varied types and occurred all over the United States. It was impossible for college and university administrations to ignore the movement, even if there were no dramatic events on their own campuses (Soule 2001).

What most Americans will remember about this era of student protest were the shantytowns (or shanties) that appeared on campuses across the country. Shantytowns were makeshift shacks, constructed of miscellaneous building materials (e.g., wood, plastic, cardboard, tar paper, and metal), which were built to encourage administrators to divest of their South African-related securities. In many cases, students lived in the shanties, which worried universities and colleges because of the potential for physical harm to the student activists. From UCLA to Middlebury College, the University of Tennessee to New York University, the shantytown tactic diffused across college campuses (Soule 1997). At many universities, students had been fighting for divestment for years, but did not mobilize mass student support until the shantytowns were built.

The shantytown tactic evolved from the familiar tactic of the sit-in, which has been used on campuses in the United States since the civil rights movement. The evolution began at Columbia University in March 1985, when students met to call for divestment of South African-related stocks and bonds (Hirsch 1990; Massie 1997). Much to their surprise, the building (Hamilton Hall) in which the meeting was scheduled was too small to accommodate the growing number of concerned students. Determined not to discourage activism, the leaders turned this meeting into a "sit-out," where at least 300 students sat outside and conducted a peaceful protest meeting on the steps of the building. The blockade lasted almost two weeks, culminating in a speech by Reverend Jesse Jackson, which drew another 5,000 people (Loeb 1994). The Columbia event was highly publicized and the issue of divestment captured the attention of students across the country.

Following the "sit-out," the tactic began to evolve further. Princeton activists staged a "camp-out," which was quite similar to the Columbia event and was followed by additional "camp-outs" at the University of California at Santa Cruz and the University of Iowa. Finally, students at Harvard University held a "sleep-in" at the library and, shortly thereafter, students at Princeton built a "teach-in center," which they dubbed "Princetown, South Africa" (Adams 1985). The sit-out, camp-out, teach-in center, and sleep-in marked the beginning of the evolution of the shantytown, the first of which appeared in the spring of 1985 at Cornell University. Within eighteen months, the tactic had spread to numerous other colleges and universities.

The shantytowns were a visible reminder to campus communities that their institutions had investments in companies and banks with ties to South Africa. They were an embarrassment to universities and, as one might imagine, universities often attempted to repress this form of expression. For example, at Cornell University, the administration ordered campus police to remove the shantytown – something that occurred again and again each time students rebuilt it. Broader campus communities often tried to repress the shantytowns, too. For example, in December 1985, conservative students at Dartmouth College destroyed the shantytowns while activists slept inside and, as mentioned previously, an angry alumnus of Yale burned down the shanties on that campus. As I noted in Chapter 3, as is sometimes the case with repression, events such as these seemed to have fanned the flames of the movement, rather than extinguished it.

In addition to the shantytowns and broader divestment movement, a second set of pressures on the university had to do with the fact that the American public was well aware of the South African situation and, as will be discussed shortly, was concerned with it. There was much rhetoric at the time about the absolute immorality of the South African system of apartheid, and these arguments had a firm grasp of reality in South Africa. On average in 1986, 130 black South Africans were killed each month

(*Anti-Apartheid Act of* 1986 *Hearings* 1986: 53). The majority of black South Africans in 1988 were unemployed and more than 7 million were denied citizenship (*Anti-Apartheid Act Amendments* 1988). To be a black South African meant to live in constant fear of police brutality and of being forcibly removed from one's home (*Anti-Apartheid Act Amendments* 1988). In fact, the situation in South Africa led the United Nations to deem apartheid a crime against humanity (Friedman 1978).

The objective situation in South Africa was well publicized in the United States as well. Videotapes of mass demonstrations at funeral processions of black South Africans killed in events of political unrest and photographs of segregated public facilities served as painful reminders of conditions in the not-so-distant past of the United States. A count of news articles indexed in the *Reader's Guide to Periodical Literature* shows that in the 1985 volume, there were 333 articles on "Race Relations in South Africa." In the (nearly) two-year period spanning March 1978 through February 1980, there were only 75 articles on the "Race Question in South Africa." Moreover, around the time of the Sharpeville Massacre in 1960, there were 80 articles indexed by the *Reader's Guide* (March 1959 through February 1961). These figures indicate that race relations in South Africa captured the media's attention in the mid-1980s, even more so than around the time of the Sharpeville Massacre. If we examine the yearly counts of articles indexed in the *Reader's Guide* covering *any* topic having to do with South Africa, we reach a similar conclusion. The number of articles on South Africa rose to unprecedented highs in 1985 and 1986, with 349 appearing in 1985 and 447 appearing in 1986. These figures can be compared to those of years prior to 1984 when fewer than 100 articles were indexed per year.[6] Thus, colleges and universities faced with student activism around the divestment issue needed to contend with the broader American public, which was well-attuned to the problems in South Africa, in part because of the dramatic increases in media attention to the country. In short, the issue had become newsworthy, something McAdam (1996) and others point to as essential for social movements (see also Gamson 2004).

---

[6] An examination of the *Television News Index and Abstracts* shows a similar trend as these from the *Reader's Guide to Periodical Literature*. In 1985, there were 784 network news segments on "unrest/race riots in South Africa," "apartheid/discrimination in South Africa," and the "state of emergency in South Africa." In 1979, there were only nine network news segments "discrimination in South Africa" and "unrest in South Africa" (Soule 2001).

On top of the awareness of the situation in South Africa, there is also evidence that the American public was appalled by it. Thus, a third set of prodivestment pressures that educational institutions needed to consider were the beliefs and opinions of the larger society (Lewis 1984). Since the student protests of the 1960s, the boundaries between the university and the larger society have dissolved as the university has learned that it must be attuned to public opinion and listen to its constituent groups (Frey 1977). The beliefs and opinions of the public might be thought of in terms of the broader cultural opportunity structure, as described in Chapter 2.[7] In a 1977 Harris poll, 46% of Americans said that the U.S. government should pressure U.S. *corporations* to pull out of South Africa to end apartheid. By 1986, 56% believed that the U.S. government should pressure South Africa to end apartheid (Culverson 1996). As well, the public appeared to support protest against apartheid and South Africa. For example, a *Washington Post*-ABC News poll conducted in 1985 showed that of the people who knew about protests against South Africa, 70% supported such actions (Sussman 1985; see also Culverson 1996).

A fourth set of prodivestment pressures came from the U.S. Congress, which adopted several pieces of antiapartheid legislation in the mid-1980s. These pressures may be thought of as part of the broader political and legal opportunity structures, as described in Chapter 2. First, Representative William Gray introduced the Anti-Apartheid Act of 1985, which enforced sanctions on imports and exports from South Africa and called for the prohibition of loans to the South African government. Second, there was the Comprehensive Anti-Apartheid Act of 1986, which prohibited loans to and new investments in South Africa, and it called for the release of political prisoners in that country. A third piece of U.S. legislation was the 1988 Anti-Apartheid Amendments to the 1986 law, which extended the ban of all loans to South African business and to the government and prohibited any new investment in South Africa. These pieces of legislation were clearly important exogenous pressures on colleges and universities from the broader legal opportunity structure. On top of these federal legal pressures, some states also passed antiapartheid legislation, serving as a further set of pressures that colleges and universities faced.

---

[7] For general discussion of the effect of public opinion on policy and how we can consider public opinion to be part of the political opportunity structure, see Soule and Olzak (2004). For a general discussion of how international norms of racial equality were an important factor determining foreign policy on apartheid, see Klotz (1995).

By 1987, twenty-one states and sixty-eight cities had adopted some kind of divestment policy (Lansing and Kuruvilla 1988). And, some states passed laws that directly impacted universities. For example, Michigan passed a law in 1982 that required all higher educational institutions to divest from South Africa (Rottenberg 1986).

A final set of pressures toward divestment came from prominent black leaders in South Africa. In his testimony on the Anti-Apartheid Act of 1986 (1986:198), Representative William Gray highlights the thoughts of several prominent black leaders:

Archbishop Desmond Tutu, Reverend Allan Bosak, and other countless black leaders have pleaded with us not to make too much of their suffering. Apartheid has made suffering a way of life for them. If we want to help, they say, do whatever must be done to remove apartheid. That, they say, will end their suffering. Hesitating to do what we can because of concern for them rings, quite frankly, hollow in their ears.

Similarly, a letter published in the *Anti-Apartheid Act of* 1986 *Hearings* from the United Methodist Church of Zimbabwe documents the killing of several South African church organizers in South Africa. The letter compared the South African regime to those of Hitler and Idi Amin and remarked that apartheid is "extremely evil" and makes the "most terrible mockery [of] democracy" (1986: 283). Prominent church, political, and trade union leaders in South Africa helped publicize the situation in South Africa and called for international action. This call fell upon receptive ears at colleges and universities in the United States, and as a consequence served to heighten the political and moral debates at these institutions.

In sum, educational institutions faced these countervailing pressures about the appropriate stance on the divestment issue and they faced a great deal of uncertainty as they sifted through these arguments for and against divestiture. Divestment was costly to be sure, but many educational institutions decided to divest, despite the likely costs to their portfolios. The next section of this chapter assesses the extent to which student activism in the form of the shantytown had an impact on universities' decisions.

Analysis of University Divestment

In an attempt to understand the extent to which student activism impacted university decisions regarding divestment, this section describes an analysis of the effect of one form of student activism – building shantytowns at colleges and universities – on the decision to divest. (Please refer to Appendices C and D for data sources and analysis details.)

University response to the divestment issue included a variety of different kinds of policies, which might usefully be placed into two main categories: *total* and *partial* divestment. Some universities opted for *total divestment* from all South African-related stocks and bonds. We might think of this policy response as the ultimate form of divestment, one that was certainly a strong statement by the university. While this proved to be very difficult to monitor in the end, many colleges and universities claimed to do this and activists usually called for total divestment, believing that only total divestment would have the desired effect on corporations.

A second policy response by universities was to *partially divest* of South African-related securities, which was accomplished in a variety of different ways. For example, one strategy was to prohibit investment in any South African-*owned* companies, rather than in any business conducting business in South Africa. Or, a university could divest of companies that conducted the *majority* of their business in South Africa. Others required that all companies represented in their portfolio sign the Sullivan Principles, or that the companies prove that they have actually implemented the principles. Some universities opted to prohibit investment in companies that sold directly to the South African government or that made loans to the government. Finally, other universities said they would effectively screen all companies in their portfolio on a case-by-case basis and disinvest from those thought to be particularly offensive. All of these strategies may usefully be categorized as partial divestment because they call for doing something less than fully or totally divesting of South African securities.

To get at these two main types of policy responses to the divestment issue, I use data on divestment policies of colleges and universities (see Appendix C for sources). According to these sources, between 1977 and 1990 a total of 167 institutions divested; 80 colleges and universities totally divested and 87 partially divested during this period. Figure 4.1 shows divesting trends of U.S. colleges and universities over time.

In order to conduct the analysis herein, I compare these divesting colleges and universities against the population of four-year, nonspecialty, nonprofessional, nondenominational colleges and universities in the United States that had some investment in South Africa.[8] There were

---

[8] Examples of specialty and professional institutions that are excluded in these analyses are chiropractic colleges, podiatry schools, professional schools, theological seminaries,

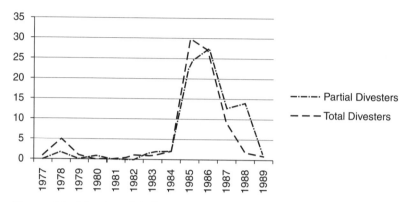

Figure 4.1 Number of Colleges and Universities Divesting, 1977–1989.

899 such educational institutions in the United States during the period of this study. Given this, about 18.5% adopted some kind of divestment policy between 1977 and 1989.

The central question of this chapter is whether or not student activism in the form of shantytown protests increased college and university divestment. A shantytown event is defined as the erection of a shantytown in protest of the university's economic involvement in firms with ties to South Africa. Often professing broader claims such as the problem of international human rights violations, the shantytown events coded here involved the clear statement of the necessity of university divestment.[9] Figure 4.2 shows the yearly number of shantytowns for this period (noting that the first one was in 1985); in all, there were forty-three shantytowns in the 1977–1989 period.

A second question addressed in this chapter is whether or not financial considerations played a large role in the divestment decision. As discussed earlier, studies conducted by the IRRC and by several independent financial analysts during the mid-1980s indicate that divestment was least advantageous for universities with large stock portfolios due to the

---

rabbinical institutes, and vocational training programs. In all, there were roughly 3,300 colleges, universities, and branch campuses in the United States in the mid-1980s.

[9] Shantytowns were a highly visible form of protest and often evoked a repressive response from the university administration and broader campus communities, as discussed earlier. In several cases a shantytown was disassembled by either the university administration or counterprotesters. Often these shantytowns were rebuilt. I have not considered the rebuilding of a shanty a new event. Rather, I only consider the first shantytown event on a campus in the following analysis.

The Effect of Protest on University Divestment

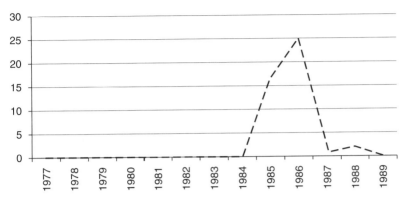

Figure 4.2   Number of Shantytowns in the United States, 1977–1989.

greater transaction costs associated with divestment and the greater costs of researching new investments. If this was the case, we ought to see that colleges and universities with larger stock portfolios were less likely to divest.

In addition to measures of student activism and financial considerations, the analysis that follows includes a number of variables in an attempt to measure differences in the rate of divestment policy adoption between different kinds of colleges and universities. First, I include a measure of the relative strengths or prestige of each of the 899 colleges and universities, under the assumption that more prestigious institutions may be more likely to divest because of concerns with image or because of reputation management.

Previous research indicates that larger colleges and universities had a higher probability of divesting (Kibbe 1989), thus I include the enrollment size of a university as a measure of the size of the institution. I also consider the effect of the size of the African American student population on the rate of divestment.

I also control for the type of college or university based on the Carnegie Foundation's classification. I include dummy variables for three of the four categories of institutions: liberal arts, comprehensive, doctoral granting, and research, leaving comprehensive institutions out of the models for reference (Boyer 1987).

Finally, I include a measure of whether or not the college or university had an African/African-American/black studies program or department (hereafter, "black studies department"). These programs often served

95

Table 4.1. *University and College Divestment in the United States, 1977–1989*

	Total Divestment (N=80)	Partial Divestment (N=87)
Enrollment (log)	1.011* (.474)	.351 (.300)
African American Enrollment (log)	.489** (.164)	.032 (.140)
Portfolio Size (log)	.096 (.109)	.344*** (.048)
Black Studies	1.857** (.543)	.171 (.520)
Prestige	1.831** (.563)	2.175*** (.534)
Shantytown Protest	−1.260 (.930)	1.343* (.703)
Liberal Arts	4.456*** (1.088)	.722 (.595)
Doctoral Granting	.501 (.651)	−.874 (.802)
Research	.479 (1.191)	−.247 (.729)
Constant	−25.067*** (3.827)	−13.580*** (2.743)
Log Likelihood	−424.295	−466.813

$^* p < .05, ^{**} p < .01, ^{***} p < .001$

the important function of educating the university and the surrounding communities about the issues of apartheid, which may have led to more salient environmental pressures on the university to divest. As well, the presence of a black studies program or department might serve as an indicator of an important internal characteristic of the movement. That is, these may be indicative of an important movement resource: indigenous organizational strength of both students and faculty. Such preexisting networks, as I noted in Chapter 2, are often used to mobilize activists.

Table 4.1 presents the results of two regression models used to test the arguments above. The first model (column 1) examines the effect of a shantytown protest on the adoption of a *total divestment policy*, while the second model (column 2) examines the effect of a shantytown on the adoption of a *partial divestment policy*. The most striking finding reported in Table 4.1 is that the effect of shantytowns on university divestment depends on whether or not we are interested in full or partial divestment strategies. If we model *full divestment*, we see (column 1) that shantytowns did not matter (controlling for other university characteristics) to divestment decisions.[10]

If we were to stop here as I have done in my previous work (e.g., Soule 1999; 2001), we would conclude that student protest (in the form of

[10] This finding replicates that which I have presented elsewhere (Soule 1995; 1999).

shantytowns) did not matter to university decisions and that, instead, the process was driven by other factors. In particular, we would conclude that the size of the African American student population, prestige of the university, type of institution (especially liberal arts) and whether or not the university had a black studies program were more important.

It is important to note that when we examine policies of *partial divestment*, one of the chief predictors of this strategy of divestment *is* the presence of a shantytown. That is, when considering the strategy of partial divestment, student protest did, in fact, matter to college and university decisions. However, contrary to the analysis of total divestment, neither the size of the black student body nor the presence of a black studies program or department mattered, nor were liberal arts institutions more likely to divest. However, the size of the university's portfolio *did* matter to partial divestment policies, with larger portfolios associated with the adoption of partial divestment policies. As was the case with full divestment, prestigious institutions were more likely to partially divest.

Thus, the models in Table 4.1 show some very clear and interesting differences with respect to the processes driving total and partial divestment. The analysis indicates that full divestment policies were driven by the presence of a black studies program on campus and the size of the African American student population, with liberal arts institutions more likely to adopt total divestment policies.

But, partial divestment policies appear to have been driven by somewhat different factors. Importantly, the size of the institution's portfolio increased the probability that the institution would adopt a partial divestment policy, suggesting that institutions with very large portfolios may have divested partially to appease students and the general public, while attempting to keep the costs associated with divestment (outlined earlier) low. Also important to partial divestment policies was the presence of a shantytown. An example here is Harvard, which had one of the largest portfolios and an active student movement, including a shantytown. Harvard resisted divesting, yet eventually agreed to do so selectively or partially, reportedly because of student protest (Kibbe 1989).

These findings indicate that there were two quite different processes driving these divestment strategies. Those opting for full divestment were driven by local constituencies and a possible history of activism on the part of African Americans and Africans, as indicated by the presence of a black studies department and a higher enrollment of black students. Those opting for partial divestment, instead, were driven by portfolio concerns.

Also important to partial divestment was the presence of a shantytown, suggesting that partial divestment may have been a strategy used to quell students, while not incurring the ultimate costs of total divestment.

These findings also raise the important question of whether or not partial divestment was merely some kind of symbolic measure taken by colleges and universities to assuage students and, perhaps, to maintain legitimacy in the eyes of their peers. Fineman and Clarke (1996: 721) note that overall, protesters must be dealt with – sometimes "cosmetically." My findings raise the possibility that partial divestment was a type of cosmetic policy, one that could be done without incurring the full costs, but one nonetheless that would signal to students that they were doing something about the divestment issue.

Assessing the Consequences of the Student Divestment Movement

Reflecting on the impacts of shantytowns on university divestment leads me back to my observations in Chapter 2 about *scale shift* (McAdam, Tarrow, and Tilly 2001; McAdam and Tarrow 2005; Tarrow 2005). Recall that I argued that one of the most important elements of the concept of scale shift is the insight that activists often target multiple systems of authority, some of which are private, others of which are governmental. In this case, the student divestment movement targeted universities and thus can be thought of as private politics. And, moving up the scale but still remaining in the realm of private politics, we see that activists also targeted corporations, as corporations were the entities that university divestment was alleged to *really* impact. Finally, if we move up the scale in terms of what the ultimate target really was – the South African government – we should also think of this case as one of contentious politics.

All of this means that to *really* assess whether or not the student divestment movement mattered, we need to consider the multiple, nested levels of these targets or focal points. The next three sections of this chapter discuss the impacts of the movement on each of these targets in turn.

Did the Student Movement Matter to University Divestment?

The analysis presented in this chapter shows that certain kinds of university divestment policies were, in fact, impacted by the presence of a student movement. In particular, universities appear to have responded to shantytowns by adopting *partial* divestment policies; however, *full* divestment policies were driven by entirely different factors, most notably a higher proportion of black students and the presence of black studies programs or departments.

Another important factor that is not tested in the previous analysis is the effect of the broader antiapartheid movement on college and university decisions. That is, while the presence of a shantytown may only have led to partial divestment policies, the broader movement may have had some impact on both partial and total divestment. On this point, I believe that there must be some support, although it would be difficult to test. Scholars of state policy outcomes, as discussed in Chapter 2, repeatedly point to the importance of public opinion to policy change. In fact, this may be thought of as an important part of the cultural opportunity structure. The discussion in this chapter highlights the fact that the U.S. public was well aware of the issue of apartheid and that there was an active movement directed at cities, states, pensions, banks, and corporations to divest of South African holdings that existed alongside the student divestment movement (Massie 1997). It is hard to believe that colleges and universities were unaware of this broader movement, given the media attention it garnered and the support of the broader public, as described above. Thus, an overall exogenous force behind university divestment may very well have been the broader antiapartheid and divestment movement, although this is difficult to assess empirically.

Did University Divestment Matter to Business?

But, did businesses care about university divestment? Was this considered a threat to their financial picture? Unfortunately, this is also not easy to assess. However, it is clear that, when compared to large pension and mutual funds, university portfolios were small potatoes to most of these corporations (Rottenberg 1986; Sethi 1987).[11] Thus, it would be difficult

---

[11] In 1982, the market value of *all* college and university funds was $24.4 billion, of which $20 billion was held by private institutions (Rottenberg 1986). Compared to large pension funds for nonuniversity employees (another target of the divestment movement), this amount was trivial, thus, some have puzzled about why college and university endowment portfolios were targeted at all by this movement (Rottenberg 1986). The answer seems to lie in the fact that universities and colleges were seen by activists as easier

to argue that university divestment mattered a great deal to most targeted companies. On top of this, the act of divesting simply means that the shares of stock sold are available to other investors, either individuals or institutions. The targeted company, then, is not directly part of the transaction of divestment.

This all said, it is also critical to note that while university investments may have been small potatoes to these corporations, they were very visible potatoes, garnering a great deal of media attention to both student activism and university response. This raises the important issue of the indirect costs of protest to a corporation's reputation or image (King and Soule 2007). Scholars of organizations note that the reputation of a firm is a kind of intangible asset that can be used to create shareholder value (Fombrun 1990; Fombrun and Shanley 1990; Roberts and Dowling 2002). Many scholars have confirmed that there are financial benefits associated with a good reputation (Formbrun and Shanley 1990; Herremans, Akathaporn, and McInnes 1993; Landon and Smith 1997; Roberts and Dowling 2002). It is possible that university divestment from certain companies could have damaged the reputation of a firm, leading to a decline in reputation or image and, perhaps, a decline in value. Thus, while I cannot measure this directly, there is ample evidence from the extant literature on business image and reputation to suggest that the media attention to university divestment of a certain company could lead this company to then disinvest in South Africa to maintain a positive reputation (despite the fact that university investments, when compared to other, much larger entities, were really quite small).

Did the Movement Matter to South Africa?

Finally, the ultimate target was, of course, South Africa. Did the anti-apartheid movement have any impact on South Africa? In the best analysis of this question to date, Schwartzman and Taylor (1999) present evidence that several characteristics of the domestic labor market in South Africa were important to the end of apartheid, but they also conclude that

---

targets, in that faculty and administrators may have been sympathetic to the claims of the movement. As well, universities and colleges receive a great deal of media attention, thus may have been targeted strategically to garner more press coverage. Finally, in line with my discussion of the effect of repression on target choice (Chapter 3), perhaps students chose universities over other targets because they thought they would be less likely to be repressed or repressed heavily by choosing in this manner.

international financial pressure in the form of boycotts of both foreign loans and corporate investment was critical to the end of apartheid. Because the South African economy was so dependent on foreign investment, the international movement against such investments had a profound effect on the political economy of South Africa.

This conclusion is also reached by Knight (1990), who reports that between 1985 and 1990, 200 U.S. businesses disinvested from South Africa and that between 1982 and 1988, U.S. direct investment in South Africa declined from $2.3 billion to $1.3 billion (see also Battersby 1988).[12] These losses, argues Knight, were an important factor in the demise of apartheid. Knight (1990) also provides the example of the gold mining industry in South Africa. This industry was developed with foreign capital and gold was historically 40% of South Africa's exports, thus, the gold mining industry was critically important to the economy of South Africa. During the period between 1970 and 1987, gold production in South Africa declined drastically in response to U.S. and U.K. companies' withdrawals from the country (Knight 1990).[13]

Aside from the effect of corporate disinvestment on the end of apartheid, it is reasonable to ask if corporate social responsibility had any effect on the lives of nonwhite South Africans (outside of ending apartheid, of course). It is very difficult to assess this question reliably, as there was no consistent way of checking reports by corporations on what they were doing to implement the Sullivan Principles. As mentioned in an earlier footnote, the accounting firm of Arthur D. Little eventually issued a grading system of Sullivan signatories' implementation, however, the basis of this grading system was never made public (Seidman 2007). But, these issues aside, in the wake of the Sullivan Principles, the percentage of supervisory positions held by nonwhites in South Africa increased, suggesting that pressures from signatories had an effect on how business was conducted in South Africa (Seidman 2007). As well, Seidman (2007) notes that community groups in South Africa clearly benefited from corporate donations, which reportedly amounted to $15 million in the 1977–1985 period.[14] These donations were used to help build schools, housing, and hospitals, thus arguably aided the South African population.

---

[12] To be fair, many of these retained contract, licensing, distribution, trademark, or franchise agreements with companies in South Africa.

[13] See also Love (1988).

[14] Lansing and Kuruvilla (1988) put this figure at $38 million.

On this point, Lansing and Kuruvilla (1988) also argue that the Sullivan Principles were actually quite successful in effecting change in South Africa. In 1986, 240 U.S. firms operated in South Africa, employing about 100,000 black South Africans. While this may have not been an enormous number, given the size of the black South African population, it is important to note that in addition to their commitment to equal pay (per the Sullivan Principles), these companies also invested in communities and supported education, healthcare, and housing initiatives. Thus, there is also some evidence that corporate social responsibility can positively impact the lives of those in the broader community.

Another way to ask the question of whether or not corporate social responsibility helped in the case of South Africa is to ask the flipside of this question about whether the Sullivan Principles mattered. That is, we should also ask if sanctions and corporate divestment *hurt* black South Africans? On this point, Lansing and Kuruvilla (1988) argue that sanctions were disastrous for black South Africans, causing a loss of jobs and a decline in GDP, alongside the loss of community support from Sullivan signatories. Moreover, these authors note that when a foreign company pulled out of South Africa, they typically did not sell their businesses to black South Africans; rather these were purchased by white South Africans who, in many cases, immediately discontinued the Sullivan Principles. Thus, there is evidence to suggest that the Sullivan Principles, as an early attempt at a corporate code of conduct and monitoring system, were effective and that divestment, at least in the short term, was harmful to black South Africans (despite any pressures it may have placed on the ruling government to end apartheid, as described previously).

Summary and Conclusion

This chapter has provided an empirical analysis of the effect of student activism on university decisions regarding divesting from South Africa. As such, we can think of this as a case of activism directed at the policies of an organization, but we must also realize that this movement was about the policies of an intermediary target (the university) designed to ultimately impact the policies of a foreign state.

The findings indicate that universities responded to student activism by adopting partial divestment policies and that partial divestment policies may have been a strategy used by universities with larger stock portfolios to buffer against the sizable costs of total or full divestment. Full divestment seems to have been driven more by the size of the black student population and black studies departments, and less by student activism and financial concerns related to the size of the portfolio.

But, did divestment matter to companies with South African ties and to South Africans, more generally? I've attempted to address these issues in this chapter. The bulk of the evidence suggests that corporate divestment did help bring down apartheid. However, it may also have had the unintended consequence of decreasing the number and quality of jobs for black South Africans and decreasing the social services provided by companies for their employees' families and communities.

The case of the student divestment movement in the United States was used to illustrate my earlier points about the multiple levels that anticorporate movements and contentious politics surrounding corporate issues target. In this case, we saw that a somewhat localized movement based on U.S. campuses actually had multiple targets. And, commensurate with my earlier arguments about scale shift, we can see how this localized movement, much like a butterfly flapping its wings, can have profound effects at a more systemic level.

5

Private and Contentious Politics in the Post-1990 Era

Thus far in this book I have examined anticorporate activism that occurred in the United States between 1960 and 1990. From this examination, I have emphasized two key dimensions that should be considered when attempting to understand the causes and consequences of anticorporate activism. First, in Chapter 3, I described the importance of examining and understanding the claims expressed by anticorporate activists. By looking carefully at anticorporate activism as reported in the *New York Times*, I found that most protests initiated by anticorporate activists over this thirty-one-year period articulated claims that fell into one of the following three categories: *antiproduct*, *antipolicy*, and *negligence*. While in many cases activists articulated multiple claims, in general I was able to locate a *primary* claim that fell into one of these three categories in each report of public protest events that I examined.

Second, in Chapters 2 and 3 I noted the importance of identifying what the *target* or *focal point* of a given anticorporate protest event is, noting that oftentimes anticorporate activism is directed at both corporations and the government. This led me to charge that it is critical for scholars of organizations and movements to move beyond their focus on "private politics" and "contentious politics" respectively and recognize that anticorporate activism is sometimes a hybrid of the two. Recall that private politics is the term used by organizations scholars for the class of politics that occurs without any state intervention, activity, or targeting. And, contentious politics is the term used by social movement scholars to refer to instances of activism in which one party (typically the focal point) is the state.

The purpose of this chapter is to illustrate that these two dimensions (issue and target) are important to our understanding of more recent

Table 5.1. *The Targets and Issues of Anticorporate Activism: Case Illustrations from the Post-1990 Period*

	Antiproduct	Antipolicy	Negligence
Private Politics: Target Corporations	The Greenpeace anti-GMO Campaign against Gerber Baby Food	The United Students against Sweatshops Campaign against Nike	The Amnesty International and Students of Bhopal Campaign against Dow Chemical
Contentious Politics: Target Corporations and State Authorities	The Earth Island Institute Campaign against StarKist for Dolphin-Safe Tuna	The Free Burma Coalition's Campaign against Pepsi and Other Multinational Companies	Laborers International Union of North America's Campaign against Corporate Home Builders

anticorporate protest events – that is, those which took place after 1990. To this end, I have crossclassified these two dimensions and have chosen six examples from the post-1990 era on which to focus. These cases are shown in Table 5.1.

These cases are meant to be illustrative and not definitive, but I have attempted to choose cases that fit (fairly) neatly into each cell of Table 5.1. In each case, I also attempt to describe the extent to which the given protest event or campaign has been successful at achieving its stated goals. In Chapter 2, I noted that scholars of social movements have a great deal of difficulty assessing whether or not social movements have their desired effects on their targets. To make solid claims about the effect of a movement on a given corporate outcome, one must show that the movement was a precursor to the outcome and one should make a reasonable attempt to control for rival and spurious causes of the outcome in question. Given this, in most of these examples, I am not able to establish ultimate causality of the movement on an outcome. However, in many cases I am able to provide some evidence of some kind of outcome. Thus, I hope to show that in most of these cases, activists have had some effect, even if that impact appears to be not precisely what the movement intended.

In each case I also discuss some of the facets of the movement and its environment that impacted the outcomes of mobilization, drawing on my discussion of "internal" and "external" factors in Chapter 2. Thus, I identify characteristics of the movement *and* its external environment (e.g., the political, industry, and corporate opportunity structures), which likely impacted the attainment of outcomes.

The ultimate goal of this chapter is to illuminate the points raised in previous chapters, while providing the reader with some illustrations of anti-corporate activism in the post-1990 period. I begin my discussion with the three examples of *private politics* shown in Table 5.1 (first row), one directed at a policy, one at a product, and one at an instance of corporate negligence. Following this, I shift to a discussion of the three illustrations of *contentious politics* shown in Table 5.1 (second row) – once again, one directed at a policy, one at a product, and one at an instance of corporate negligence.

The Anti–Gerber Baby Food Campaign

The first illustration is about a protest campaign targeting a corporation because a product that the company produced was deemed substandard and possibly harmful. In the late 1990s, as part of a wider movement against genetically modified organisms (GMOs), Greenpeace launched a campaign against the largest baby food producer in the United States, Gerber, because of its use of genetically modified (GM) grains in its cereal products for babies. I classify this as *private politics* because while it is true that the broader GM movement sometimes targets governments, this particular campaign was directed solely at Gerber.

Background of the Controversy

In 1999, an employee of Greenpeace purchased several Gerber baby food products in New York City and sent them to Britain to be tested for the presence of pesticides and GM ingredients. The lab found that while the jarred baby food was free of GM ingredients, Gerber's dry cereal tested positive for GM corn and soy (Lagnado 1999). Perhaps even more damning than the presence of the GM grain, the cereal also tested positive for Monsanto's notorious weed killer, Roundup. Greenpeace immediately notified Gerber Products in Michigan of these findings and a report was sent to executives at Novartis, the company that then owned Gerber (Lagnado 1999).[1]

---

[1] Novartis bought Gerber in 1994 and sold it in 2007. Gerber's U.S. sales were around $700 million annually at the time and they had an additional $300 million in sales abroad (Lagnado 1999). In 2006, baby food was roughly a $3.6 billion a year business (McKay 2006).

The Movement

Following their notification of Gerber and Novartis of these results, Greenpeace initiated a letter-writing campaign directed at the company that encouraged consumers to express their dissatisfaction with the use of GM products and their outrage at the company for allowing herbicides to be used on grains that would be fed to babies. They also held several news conferences in the New York area during this period to publicize their findings (Lagnado 1999).

One interesting question about this campaign has to do with why Greenpeace would choose Gerber when it could have chosen any number of different food processors – including those that produce processed foods that are consumed by a much larger segment of the population than just infants and small children. To understand this, it is essential to think about which collective action frames might work in the U.S. context and how these frames may differ in other national contexts. Generally, the anti-GM movement has been strong in Europe, but has gained much less traction in the United States (Marwick 2000). Europeans view GM crops as suspicious for many reasons, chief among them a fear of U.S. control over seeds for food crops, should GM seeds become globally dominant (Marwick 2000). Therefore, for the movement to gain momentum in the United States, it was necessary to develop a deeply resonant frame and a target to match. Framing the issue as not only possibly harmful, but harmful to largely defenseless human beings (i.e., babies) was a critical step in the direction of bringing attention to the movement and the issue. This frame likely also tapped into the collective guilt of American parents for purchasing jarred baby food (rather than preparing the food in the laborious, yet "traditional," manner).

As well, targeting the baby food company with perhaps the greatest name recognition in the United States was a critical facet of the strategy of the campaign. Since 1928, when Dorothy Gerber began selling cans of strained peas, carrots, prunes, and beef vegetable soup, Americans have been familiar with Gerber baby products and their labels with the sketch of a smiling baby (McKay 2006). Aside from name recognition, Gerber is the oldest commercial baby food maker and at the time of the Greenpeace campaign, Gerber controlled nearly 70% of the market.

Finally, it is important to note that Gerber had also been in the proverbial "hot seat" (or high chair, as the case may be) in the years leading up to the GM campaign. In 1996, Gerber sold 149 different products for babies and added sugar to 52 of them and modified food starch to 42 of them, while they also added salt to their products for toddlers. These additives had been criticized by consumers for quite some time, who contrasted Gerber's products with similar ones produced by Beech-Nut and Heinz, both of whom had better records on the sugar, salt, and starch issues.[2] The Center for Science in the Public Interest filed a petition with the Federal Trade Commission in 1996, challenging that Gerber's additions of sugar, modified food starch, and salt made its baby foods far less nutritious than those produced by other baby-food makers. The petition also argued that Gerber used misleading and false advertising, such as its slogan: "Nutritionally, you can't buy a better baby food than Gerber." Thus, Gerber had already been the target of a campaign that asserted that its products were inferior to competitors' and possibly harmful to babies. This earlier campaign was probably still on consumers' minds when the anti-GM campaign began, a fact that likely made Gerber more inclined to respond and respond aggressively to Greenpeace's campaign.

Was the Anti-Gerber Campaign Successful?

Novartis, a company that had plenty of contact with Greenpeace activists in Europe, advised Gerber to act aggressively to deal with the GM problem (Lagnado 1999). In response to this directive, the CEO of Gerber Products' North American Consumer Health Division announced that the company was dropping suppliers who used genetic engineering in their corn and soybean production (Lagnado 1999). They also announced that they would begin substituting organically grown corn and soy flour in their baby products. While these ingredients account for less than 2% of Gerber's products, it was an important signal to the public that they were not only willing to listen to Greenpeace, but they were willing to go above and beyond the group's specific demands. Gerber also began consulting with a pool of non-Greenpeace environmentalists and consumer groups concerned about the long-term effects of genetically modified foods.[3]

Thus, the movement was heralded as successful in part because of the strategy of choosing a company with such great name recognition and

---

[2] In contrast, natural and organic producers (e.g., Earth's Best and Growing Healthy) used none of these in their baby food products during this controversy (Burros 1996).

[3] In the current era of anticorporate activism, such partnerships or collaboration between companies and activists are becoming more and more commonplace (e.g., Argenti 2004; Berger, Cunningham, and Drumwright 2004; Hoffman 2009).

such a large share of the market, but also because Greenpeace was very clever with its choice of a collective action frame. These factors, of course, are part of the internal characteristics of the movement, as I described in Chapter 2.

But on top of these internal characteristics of the movement, external characteristics (and especially the industry and corporate opportunity structures) were also important. For instance, the campaign against Gerber was successful because it resonated with an earlier boycott of Nestlé initiated by the U.S.-based Infant Formula Action Coalition (INFACT). INFACT was formed in response to growing concern over the marketing practices of infant formula in lesser-developed nations in the 1970s. INFACT, in concert with other movement organizations, argued that there were several reasons why infant formula should not be marketed to parents in lesser-developed countries. First, powdered infant formula must be mixed with water and much of the water in these countries is contaminated, leading vulnerable babies to contract water-borne diseases. Second, because of the extreme poverty of many of these nations, parents often diluted the infant formula to make it last longer, causing their children to receive less than adequate nutrition. Third, the movement argued that breast feeding is much healthier for babies, thus, should be practiced whenever possible. Finally, INFACT and other organizations noted that Nestlé was using unethical marketing strategies of infant formula, such as using sales people dressed as nurses to hand out samples of the formula to women with infants. INFACT's boycott lasted for about six years, from 1977 to 1983. The organization called off the boycott once it had brokered a deal with Nestlé in which the company would no longer use deceptive means to market its products and would also promote breast feeding (Meyer 2007).

When thinking about the success of private politics and anticorporate activism, it is useful to think about how both the corporate and industry opportunity structures facilitate the attainment of goals. In this case, the earlier boycott of Nestlé served as an important facet of the industry opportunity structure. The long-lasting and well-publicized boycott of Nestlé likely made Novartis more interested in settling the Gerber controversy quickly and quietly. As well, at the more proximate level of the corporate opportunity structure, Gerber's earlier problems with critics charging that its baby food had too much added sugar, starch, and salt not only made the company a strategic target for Greenpeace, but also conditioned the company's response to the campaign. Thus, when thinking about private politics, it is important to consider the ways in which the multilayered, nested external environment in which the corporation is embedded simultaneously serves as a target of the movement and as a facilitator of the outcomes sought.

Epilogue

In August 2001, Greenpeace received test results from a lab in Hong Kong that showed alarmingly high levels of GM soy beans in Gerber foods sold in the Philippines. A press conference was held in Manila at the same time that Greenpeace activists protested in front of Novartis headquarters in Basel, Switzerland. They blocked the main entrance to the building, holding puppets of babies with signs reading "Novartis/ Gerber, keep your promise!" Obviously a major concern is the double standard of providing GM-free products in Europe and the United States, while selling similar products containing GM ingredients in other nations. Thus, while Greenpeace's original campaign was resolved beyond what the activists sought, the issue has reared its head again in subsequent years.

Nike and the Antisweatshop Movement

The next illustration is another of private politics, but here the claims were about a policy rather than a product. Specifically, this is the case of the United Students Against Sweatshops' (USAS) campaign against Nike for its policy of contracting with factories that had substandard working conditions. I have classified this as private politics because the campaign did not go beyond the corporate level in any significant way.

Background of Controversy

In May and June 1997, *Doonesbury* cartoonist Gary Trudeau depicted an encounter of an American woman, Kim, traveling in Vietnam and meeting her second cousin, an employee at one of the factories with which Nike then contracted. When Kim asks her about how she is being treated at the factory, Do Trang replies (through a translator) that she is not paid enough to eat three meals each day, that she suffers from fatigue and headaches, is abused physically and verbally, and gets only one bathroom break each day. In the comic strip, Kim returns to America and embarks on an

Internet boycott of Nike and contemplates picketing Phil Knight's (the cofounder and chairman of Nike) home and workplace.

What was the issue that Trudeau helped make so famous with his award-winning cartoon? Nike routinely contracted production of their apparel to factories in various Asian countries, where products could be made remarkably cheaper than in the United States.[4] Despite the fact that other apparel companies also contracted production with factories in Asia, Nike was targeted by activists and the media earlier and more vehemently than other apparel companies. In part, this was because of its large market share and because of its name recognition that was fostered through the company's award-winning advertisement campaigns (Carty 2002). But on top of these reasons, Nike was guilty of violating its own "Code of Conduct," which it had established in 1992 after it was criticized for its unfair labor practices in Asian countries.[5] And, Nike was arguably guilty of behaving in a manner inconsistent with the image that the company had tried very hard to cultivate: that of a socially responsible corporation seeking to improve the lives of factory workers in foreign countries.[6]

Later in 1997, two fairly damning reports about Nike's labor policies in Southeast Asia were released to the media. The first report was one of Nike's own factory-monitoring reports, which was released to the *New York Times*. Of particular embarrassment to Nike was the disclosure of the fact that Nike factory workers in the Tae Kwang Vina factory in Vietnam had been exposed to the dangerous chemical, Toluene, at levels far surpassing the Vietnamese legal limit (Connor 2001; Knight and Greenberg

---

[4] Just how much cheaper could sports shoes be made abroad? Some reports indicated that workers were paid $.20 per hour of work, substantially less than the minimum wage in the United States. Another way to think of this is that shoes that sold for more than $125 in the United States were made by workers earning less than $2 each day.

[5] Nike's initial "Code of Conduct" required all contractors to sign a Memorandum of Understanding requiring them to abide by all local government regulations on health and safety, to not use forced labor, and to not discriminate. It also required contractors to behave responsibly with respect to environmental issues and to follow equal opportunity practices.

[6] For example, in 1994, Nike hired Ernst and Young to audit the factories with which it contracted in an effort to show that it was paying attention to the working conditions in these factories. As well, in 1996 it established its own Labor Practices Department, which was supposed to ensure that its subcontractors provided good and safe working conditions. These actions were designed to signal to the broader public that Nike was behaving in a progressive and socially responsible manner.

2002).[7] The second report was one picked up by Reuters, which alleged that a Nike factory had forced fifty-six Vietnamese workers to run around the factory grounds until a dozen of them fainted and were taken to the hospital for medical attention (Vietnam Labor Watch 1997).

These reports and Trudeau's depiction of Nike in his comic strip likely did not come as much of a surprise to Jeffrey Ballinger of Press for Change who had been studying labor violations in Nike factories in Indonesia since the late 1980s (Ballinger 2001; Greenberg and Knight 2004). And, for people who at the time were paying attention to the labor conditions in the overseas factories of garment companies, the reports also did not come as much of a surprise. In fact, Nike itself had been the subject of several negative reports on factory working conditions before 1997.[8] Perhaps the most damning of these was the October *CBS News: 48 Hours* special on the company's practices in Asian countries, which uncovered the severe exploitation of workers that was taking place in Nike's factories. For example, at that time, employees worked six days a week and were paid about twenty cents an hour.[9] As well, the program alleged that workers were physically and sexually abused by their superiors, including the practice of taping workers' mouths shut for talking during working hours.

The Movement

The damaging reports about Nike in 1996 and 1997 drew widespread public attention to the activities of multinational companies and the conditions of the factories with which they routinely contracted (especially those involved in apparel).[10] And, the controversy led human and labor

---

[7] Toluene is a solvent that has been linked to a host of physical problems including damage to the central nervous system, liver, and kidneys, as well as miscarriage and skin and eye irritation (Connor 2001). Note that this is the same substance that was the subject of the suit against W. L. Gore and Associates discussed in Chapter 1.

[8] For example, in 1996 alone, *Life* magazine documented the use of child labor in Pakistan in the production of Nike soccer balls, the *New York Times* ran a story on union busting by Nike shoe contractors in Indonesia, and the *Washington Post* ran an article on the military "boot camp" style management of Chinese shoe factories producing shoes for Nike and other companies (Vietnam Labor Watch 1997; Connor 2001).

[9] "48 Hours Transcript-Boycott Nike." *48 Hours*. CBS News. October 17, 1996. www .saigon.com/~nike/48hrfmt.htm, accessed May 28, 2008.

[10] These reports also came on the heels of a number of well-publicized raids of sweatshops in California (Collins 2003; Greenberg and Knight 2004). For example, in 1996, the U.S. Labor Department raided a sweatshop in El Monte, California, and members of the

rights organizations to criticize the increasingly routine exploitation of cheap labor by large multinational corporations.[11] The "antisweatshop" movement was borne out of this rising controversy and is made up of a number of organizations in the United States and other Western industrialized nations, which are linked through the Internet. They work together to disseminate information about factories, as well as information for citizens wishing to organize grassroots campaigns against multinational corporations. Organizations promoting the antisweatshop movement work to raise consumer and investor awareness of sweatshop labor by making explicit the connection between purchasing decisions and the material conditions to which workers are subject (Carty 2002).

While the broader antisweatshop movement has coordinated many different campaigns following the Nike controversy, antisweatshop campaigns took off following the negative publicity about Nike's contracts with factories abroad. These campaigns coined terms such as "swooshtika" (a play on the company's "swoosh" logo) and organizations like Boycott Nike attempted nationwide boycotts of the company's products and called for public protests at Niketown stores across the country.[12]

But it is perhaps student activism, which was thought to be moribund since the 1980s when students mobilized around the divestment issue discussed in Chapter 4, that readers will remember most clearly. In 1998, the United Students Against Sweatshops (USAS) was formed (Featherstone 2002). This organization coordinated over 180 campus groups, which began the process of negotiating codes of conduct with university administrators (Ballinger 2001).[13] Students affiliated with USAS used direct action tactics, such as demonstrations and sweatshop

---

National Labor Committee exposed Kathy Lee Gifford's line of clothing as being made by sweatshop labor. The coincidence of the U.S. sweatshop raids helped bolster attention to Nike and other American companies contracting with factories abroad.

[11] It is reasonable to ask why organized activism against Nike and other multinational companies arose in the mid-1990s, when it is clear that the use of foreign labor predates such concern about it. With increasing communication facilitated by the Internet, information about working conditions in foreign factories was more easily diffused to the rest of the world (Carty 2002). As well, with the Internet, activists throughout the world have been able to mobilize transnational advocacy networks more easily, thus facilitating the development of transnational social movements (Keck and Sikkink 1998; Carty 2002).

[12] Between 1997 and 2000, there were nearly fifty Niketown protests across the country, some of which became violent (Emerson 2001). As well, in 1997, Global Exchange coordinated eighty-four protests at Nike stores in twelve countries (Shaw 1999).

[13] The campaign made extensive use of the Internet to mobilize people and because students had free and easy access to the Internet, they became an integral part of the movement

fashion shows, to gain media and public attention with the hope of enhancing their bargaining position with universities (Greenberg and Knight 2004).

Between 1999 and 2000, college and university campuses experienced significant student protest regarding the sweatshop issue; most of these campus campaigns were coordinated through the USAS (Kreider 2005). These began on January 29, 1999, when twenty Duke University students sat in the lobby of the university president's office for thirty-one hours before winning a compromise agreement on a "sweat-free campus."[14] Seven days later Georgetown students sat in for eighty-five hours, and three days after Georgetown, Madison students sat in for ninety-seven hours (Kreider 2005). In April of 1999, University of Arizona students set a new record with a 225 hour sit-in, which won full disclosure, a living wage, women's rights, and half the seats on a newly formed taskforce (Kreider 2005). That spring, significant occupations of administrators' offices were also held at the University of North Carolina and the University of Michigan (Featherstone 2002).

In 2000, the campaign continued with student-led occupations at Michigan, Tulane, SUNY Albany, the University of Pennsylvania, Oregon, Purdue, Macalester, Kentucky, and Iowa (Featherstone 2002; Kreider 2005). Many of these events were repressed by campus police and the administration, but at Tulane (after the university attempted to get the names of the activists) students moved their protest outdoors and "camped out," a tactic reminiscent of the shantytowns used by divestment activists in the 1980s, as described in Chapter 4.

In 2002, anti-Nike activists scored a decisive victory by reaching a settlement with Nike in the case *Kasky v. Nike* in which Nike was sued for its deceptive public relations campaign that included advertisements alleging that they had improved their sweatshop policy (Baue 2003). The settlement charged that over the next three years, Nike would donate $1.5 million to the Fair Labor Association (FLA), an industry-sponsored nonprofit organization promoting adherence to international

---

(Carty 2002). As we will see later in this chapter, like the Free Burma Coalition, this use of Internet resources was important to the success of the movement.

[14] The university signed on to the Collegiate Licensing Company's (CLC) code of conduct, which was considered to be weaker than other options. Nonetheless, the university's actions were seen as a good example to set for other USAS campaigns nationwide (Kreider 2005).

labor standards and improved working conditions throughout the globe (Baue 2003).[15]

Such outsider strategies (e.g., protest, boycotts, lawsuits) were accompanied by the actions of some investment companies that opted to use the power of corporate "insiders" to effect change at Nike. Essentially, these investment companies (some of whom had promoted investment in South African-free portfolios in the 1980s) sought investments in companies that were taking an active role in eradicating sweatshops and/or that would allow inspections by human rights groups. These investment groups were instrumental in increasing pressure on Nike to change its labor policy on Asia (Galvin 1996). Thus, the anti-Nike campaign illustrates my earlier points about the multipronged repertoire of anticorporate activists.

So, what exactly were the antisweatshop activists so incensed about? At the start of the antisweatshop campaign, insider and outsider activists largely focused their attention on human rights violations in factories with which major multinational corporations, like Nike, contracted. These included hazardous and stressful working conditions, forced overtime, long working hours, abusive management, and (of course) below subsistence wages (Ballinger 2001; Knight and Greenberg 2001).

Activists made explicit demands on Nike over the course of the campaign (Connor 2001), which included paying a living wage and improving working conditions, of course. But, they also demanded that Nike protect workers who wish to speak out about factory conditions, allow regular, transparent, and independent factory monitoring, and that unionization be allowed in factories with which Nike contracted (Connor 2001; Clean Clothes Campaign 2000).

It seems reasonable to ask why it was that Nike became emblematic of multinational corporations using sweatshop labor, when it is abundantly clear that many other apparel companies were just as guilty (some of which, as noted previously, even used sweatshop labor within the United States). Baron (2003b) and Friedman (1999) identify a number of factors that make companies vulnerable to activism and many of these seem to fit the Nike case.

First, as noted before, Nike had grown rapidly over the course of the 1980s and early 1990s such that it was the largest company in its market segment (Baron 2003b; Collins 2003). Related to its financial success and because of its aggressive advertisement campaigns, Nike had become a

---

[15] As I discuss later in this chapter, Nike became a charter member of the FLA in 1996.

"household name" in the United States and abroad (Collins 2003). Name recognition has been shown to increase a company's vulnerability to activism (Friedman 1999), as described earlier in this chapter with respect to Gerber.

Second, Nike had cleverly integrated a positive stance on social issues into its image as a brand and a company. For example, the company promoted female participation in sports and bolstered funding for school and youth sports (Knight and Greenberg 2002). Nike's own company website, Nikebiz.com, was designed to communicate the stance and role the company takes on several social issues, labor practices included (Knight and Greenberg 2002). Thus, Nike's use of sweatshop labor in the developing world was juxtaposed against this carefully constructed and positive corporate image.

Third, it is important to note that consumers had alternatives and this also made Nike vulnerable. While Nike was the largest manufacturer of sports shoes, there were other acceptable brands that consumers could purchase. Thus, the public could easily, and without much sacrifice, become involved in the boycott against Nike (Friedman 1999).

Finally, another facet that makes companies susceptible to being targeted by activists is the negative externalities they produce (Baron 2003b). In the case of Nike, it was clear that the company was in fact guilty of violating its own code of conduct by using factories that paid below a living wage, provided questionably safe working conditions, sometimes hired children, and had been accused of abusing workers. Thus, it was easy for consumers to view Nike as hypocritical, as well as unethical and socially irresponsible.

Was the Anti-Nike Campaign Successful?

One thing that is clear with the Nike campaign is that the company made a big tactical mistake initially by rejecting activists' allegations and denying that they were doing anything wrong (Baron 2003b). Nike argued that it did not *own* any factories (which was true) and that by contracting with factories abroad (regardless of their policies and practices), they were providing much-needed jobs in lesser-developed nations (Baron 2003b). Phil Knight pointed to the growth experiences in Japan, Taiwan, and South Korea, noting that these countries transitioned from largely low-wage economies to countries with high per capita incomes via the same route.

Despite this early defense by Nike, the antisweatshop campaign has been heralded as a success (Baron 2003b).[16] Perhaps a first and early indicator that Nike was listening to activists was in 1996, when the company became a charter member of the FLA. The FLA emerged out of the Apparel Industry Partnership (AIP), which was headed by the Clinton administration, and was a group of interested parties, including apparel and footwear companies, human-rights groups, the National Consumers Association, and organized-labor groups, that came together to work out a common, voluntary code of corporate conduct aimed at the eventual elimination of domestic and foreign sweatshops (Greenberg and Knight 2004). The FLA was formed to monitor factories and assess the implementation of the code of conduct, which had provisions for prohibiting child labor and for keeping the work week under sixty hours (Gereffi et al. 2001; Baron 2003b). Nike's membership in the FLA hinted at the company's willingness to listen to what its critics were beginning to publicize and may thus be thought of as an element of the corporate opportunity structure. However, critics might charge that if Nike were *really* listening to activists, they would have also more directly supported the Workers Rights Consortium (WRC), which is an organization supported by the AFL-CIO and Union of Needletrades, Industrial, and Textiles Employees (UNITE), and which was founded by students, college administrators, and labor activists.[17] The WRC advocates for a living wage for garment workers, independent unions, unannounced factory investigations, and full disclosure of factory conditions (Gereffi et al. 2001). As such, the WRC goes beyond the FLA and, as a result, is often considered a more radical alternative (Gereffi et al. 2001).[18]

---

[16] Using event study methodology, Rock (2003) shows that the public disclosure of a firm's use of sweatshop labor is associated with a decline in stock price of the firm. Assuming that firms pay attention to factors impacting their stock price, this hints at a mechanism for why companies respond to private and contentious politics.

[17] Note that support for the WRC comes from universities, colleges, and some high schools, but that no firms actually participate in the WRC (Baron 2003). Also note that the FLA and WRC are not the only monitoring organizations in the global apparel industry (see discussion in Bartley 2007 and O'Rourke 2003). On the differences between the FLA and WRC, see Broad (2002) and Chang and Carroll (2008).

[18] Additionally, the WRC works to monitor factories directly in a systematic way and it connects solidarity groups in consuming countries with workers producing specific apparel items (Ballinger 2001). Note that the WRC does monitor Nike factories worldwide. See their website for reports on Nike factories between 2001 and 2007 (http://www.workersrights.org, accessed May 28, 2008).

A second indicator that Nike listened to activists was its formation of the Global Alliance for Workers and Communities. Formed in partnership with Mattel and the International Youth Foundation, the goal of this organization is to build schools and establish health clinics in worker communities (Knight and Greenberg 2002). The organization also published reports on factory conditions, though critics continue to view the organization's reports as failing to represent the reality of the grievances experienced by workers (Ballinger 2001). That said, one report (published in 2001) *did* document labor abuses similar to those of the early 1990s in Indonesian factories (Ballinger 2001; Gereffi et al. 2001).

A third indicator that Nike listened to activists was its program (announced in 1998) to replace petroleum-based solvents with water-based compounds in its production processes. Efforts such as these reduce the toxicity of chemicals used in the production of apparel, thus improving the safety of the factories as well as reducing the effects of dangerous chemicals on the environment. Related, Nike also pledged to insure that its footwear plants met U.S. air quality standards (Baron 2003b).

Also indicative that Nike listened to activists was its 1998 announcement that it would allow monitoring of its factories worldwide and would retain PriceWaterhouseCoopers and Ernst & Young to do the monitoring. However, critics charged that PriceWaterhouseCoopers' reports demonstrated a promanagement bias, overlooked violations in health and safety standards, ignored problems over freedom of association and collective bargaining, and failed to report problems related to unfair wages and long hours (Greenhouse 2000). Nonetheless, by agreeing to independent monitoring of its factories, Nike clearly showed a willingness to listen to its critics and respond in some very real ways.

A final indication that Nike listened to activists was its 2004 Corporate Responsibility Report, which admitted to countless abuses in contract factories abroad. On the same day the report was released, Nike also disclosed the location of every one of its over 700 factories, something activists had been struggling to obtain for over a decade.

Thus, several factors point to the fact that Nike, while initially reluctant to do anything about the sweatshop issue, did come to the table and did respond to many of the activists' demands. In this case, it was clear that the activists had their desired impact on their universities and that the broader movement against Nike led the company to make important changes.

Epilogue

One of the lasting effects of the antisweatshop campaign directed against Nike is that the WRC and FLA both continue to investigate factories used by apparel and shoe corporations and both organizations make some or all of their reports available on their websites. As well, other similar monitoring organizations have sprung up in the apparel industry, and in many other industries, too (Gereffi et al. 2001; O'Rourke 2003; Bartley 2007). The kind of information that these associations produce is invaluable for individuals who are making purchasing decisions, but also for those individuals and organizations interested in developing "sweat-free" stock portfolios. These systems can potentially bring new information to the table, thus offering up the potential to improve global supply chains (O'Rourke 2003).

There has, however, been some debate in recent years about whether or not monitoring of factories has had the desired long-term effect of improving working conditions and enforcing labor rights in these factories. A recent study examined over 800 of Nike's suppliers in 51 different countries and concluded that monitoring has only a small effect on improving working conditions (Locke, Qin, and Brause 2006). The same study suggests that to improve working conditions in these factories, efforts must be directed at eliminating the root causes of the poor conditions. Similarly, critics of nongovernmental attempts at regulation warn that these could potentially privatize regulation, which could lead to corruption as well as cut off traditional governmental regulatory systems (O'Rourke 2003). Thus, while we might be tempted to view monitoring and certification by nongovernmental entities as a positive outcome of the antisweatshop campaign against Nike, we might be well advised to pay attention to *who* is doing the monitoring, where their loyalties lie, and what their interests are.[19]

---

[19] Another lasting effect of the USAS campaign is that many apparel companies have adopted voluntary codes of conduct and/or signed on to the UN Global Compact (discussed in Chapter 1). That said, as hinted at in Chapter 4, the verdict is far from in on the question of whether or not voluntary codes of conduct actually have any effect on the business practices and the quality of life in areas in which the factories are located (Seidman 2003; 2007). Mandle (2000) suggests that one shortcoming of the USAS strategy was the extreme focus on codes of conduct when, in fact, factory workers would have been better off had their rights been strengthened via unionization. Widener (2007) offers a similar conclusion with respect to oil companies in Ecuador.

The Anti–Union Carbide/Dow Chemical Movement

On December 3, 1984, thirty-five to forty tons of poisonous gas leaked from a pesticide factory in Bhopal, India, killing thousands of people. There is some debate about just how many people died in this disaster: Early on, the Indian government claimed that 1,430 people died, but in 1991 they increased this estimate to 3,800 (Browning 1993; Sengupta 2008). However, Amnesty International reports that at least 7,000 people died within days of the accident and an additional 15,000 have died in subsequent years from their exposure to the gas. They also claim that an additional 100,000 suffer from chronic and debilitating illnesses as a result of exposure to the gas (Amnesty International 2002).[20] Finally, because the ground water and soil surrounding the (now abandoned) pesticide plant is allegedly contaminated, residents of Bhopal suffer from higher than average rates of many different kinds of ailments such as respiratory issues, birth defects, and a wide range of neurological problems (Sengupta 2008).

In the wake of this accident, which most agree is one of the worst industrial accidents on record, an international movement formed in an attempt to get compensation for the families of those killed and for those who were injured as a result of arguably lax safety standards at the Bhopal plant. The movement, which is still active at the time of this writing, has largely been driven by Amnesty International and Students for Bhopal, but Greenpeace and several other organizations (e.g., International Campaign for Justice in Bhopal, Justice for Bhopal) have also mobilized on behalf of the victims. In the post-1990 era, the subject of this chapter, the movement may be classified as *private politics* because it focuses most squarely on targeting Dow Chemical, the corporation that acquired the Union Carbide Company (UCC) and which many argue is now liable for compensation to the victims and clean up of the site in Bhopal.[21] Thus, this third case is an illustration of private politics around corporate negligence.

---

[20] Sengupta (2008) estimates this figure to be much higher – 500,000. The bulk of the poisonous gas that was leaked in the 1984 accident was methyl isocyanate (MIC), a compound used in making pesticides (and in particular, Sevin). Not much is known about the health effects of MIC, but it is clear that survivors of the disaster suffer from respiratory ailments, eye problems, cleft palates, gastrointestinal issues, and neurological disorders (Sengupta 2008).

[21] Browning (1993) charges that the Indian government was also at fault for meddling in the process by which citizens of Bhopal could make claims on the UCC and early on the Students of Bhopal organization tried to get the Indian government to recognize the

Background

UCC built the Bhopal plant in the 1970s in an effort to cease importing pesticides from abroad and it chose Bhopal because of its centrality in India, proximity to a rail station, sufficient energy sources, and its ample supply of labor (Weir 1987). The safety systems at the plant were far from adequate and others (e.g., Weir 1987; Cassells 1993) document the long list of errors (some of which were human, but most of which had to do with inadequate safety measures at the plant) that led up to the catastrophe. Nonetheless, the UCC claimed that the accident was a direct result of a disgruntled worker who sabotaged the plant, and not due to its own lax safety standards.

Students of Bhopal, however, argue that such claims were fabricated to cover up UCC's responsibility for the accident. They have called this an instance of "corporate crime," charging that UCC deliberately installed unproven and lax safety systems at the plant, despite routinely using far better safety systems in their U.S. plants.[22] The Students of Bhopal website also lists (and appears to provide citations for legitimate sources on) several more minor gas leaks and accidents at the plant, occurring in the three-year period leading up to the December 1984 accident. As well, they claim that the company's own safety reports warned of problems with both the safety system and with lack of proper training of employees.

The Movement

As I noted previously, Dow bought the UCC in 2001 and has since become the target of a movement on behalf of the victims and survivors of the 1984 Bhopal gas leak. However, the company claims that because they did not own or operate the Bhopal factory in 1984, they are not responsible for compensation of victims or the cleanup of the site.

Many Indians and international activists do not agree, making Bhopal a difficult public relations issue for Dow (Kripalani 2008). Since 2001, activists have been targeting Dow directly for their refusal to do anything

claims of the victims of Bhopal. Nonetheless, because the focus here is on the post-1990 period, I classify this as a case of private politics, but I do recognize that in the early stages of this movement, activists also targeted the state (thus, this case may also be classified as contentious politics).

[22] http://www.studentsforbhopal.org/WhatHappened.htm#KeyFacts, accessed June 10, 2008.

about the cleanup. For example, in December of 2001, Greenpeace activists and Bhopal survivors collected contaminated groundwater in Bhopal and delivered it to Dow offices in many countries. They labeled the bottles, "Refreshingly Toxic Bhopal Water."[23] In 2002, hundreds of survivors and sympathizers organized the "Hit Dow with a Broom" campaign, which involved marching on the Dow headquarters in Mumbai carrying brooms and also sending brooms to Dow offices in the United States. In 2003, students from the University of Michigan traveled to the homes of Dow executives (for instance, then CEO William Stavropoulos) and presented them with contaminated water from Bhopal in hopes of encouraging Dow to help clean up the site (Edwards 2003). Also in that year members of the International Campaign for Justice in Bhopal organized hunger strikes in conjunction with Dow's annual shareholder meeting. In 2005, Greenpeace activists protested at the World Economic Forum in Davos about Dow's refusal to pay compensation to victims and their refusal to help with the clean up of the area. At this protest event, activists dressed up as skeletons and lay in the streets outside of the Forum.[24] And, in 2007, Amnesty International and other groups protested a visit by the Dow CEO, Anthony Liveris, to the Kelley School of Business at Indiana University.[25]

Like many of the anticorporate events that I have profiled in this book, activists use both insider and outsider tactics when targeting Dow. In addition to these outsider tactics, they have also filed at least four separate shareholder resolutions regarding Bhopal between 2004 and 2007. For example, in 2006, Amnesty International and several other groups filed a resolution asking Dow to provide information on what the company is doing to address specific health, environmental, and social concerns of Bhopal survivors.[26] More recently, in May 2008, another resolution was introduced that charged that Dow has not yet disclosed the potential liabilities of Bhopal (Kripalani 2008).

Was the Movement Successful?

When we try to assess the outcomes of this movement, we must first note that the corporate targets of the movement have changed over time

[23] http://archive.greenpeace.org/toxics/html/content/toxic_crime.html, accessed June 10, 2008.
[24] http://www.edie.net/news/news_story.asp?id=9459&channel=0, accessed June 10, 2008.
[25] http://www.indiana.edu/~aid/?q=node/41, accessed June 10, 2008.
[26] http://www.proxyinformation.com/toxics/dowbhopalres.html, accessed June 10, 2008.

because of the acquisition of UCC by Dow Chemical. I raised this issue briefly in Chapter 2, noting that one of the thorny issues in assessing the outcomes of anticorporate activism is that corporate targets often change via mergers and acquisitions. On the one hand, activists claim that an acquiring company should assume the liabilities of an acquired company. On the other hand, acquiring companies (such as Dow in this case) claim that they should not be held responsible for the past misdeeds of a company that they now own (or with which they have merged). Dow, while publicly sympathetic to the victims and survivors of Bhopal, has been steadfast in its position that because they did not own UCC when the Bhopal gas leak occurred in 1984, they cannot be held responsible for the aftermath of the disaster.[27]

That said, we can say that in the years following the leak, UCC settled out of court for $470 million dollars (Cassels 1993). These funds were paid to the government of India, which as a result of the Bhopal Gas Leak Disaster Act of 1985, was appointed to represent victims making claims on the UCC. Despite this settlement, which was thought to be far too low to actually cover the costs of treatment and compensation for the victims of the leak, it has taken years for the Indian government to pay out the settlement.[28] Moreover, as I noted previously, many argue that Dow must now help pay for the cleanup of the old plant, which is alleged to still be leaking hazardous chemicals into the groundwater around Bhopal.

It is still too early to assess whether or not Dow will do anything about cleaning up Bhopal or assisting the victims. At the time of this writing, however, Dow continues to assume no responsibility for the disaster. Their website has the following quotation from a spokesperson, Bob Questra, for the company:

We understand the anger and hurt. But Dow does not and cannot acknowledge responsibility. If we did, not only would we be required to expend many billions of dollars on cleanup and compensation – much worse, the public could then point to Dow as a precedent in other big cases. 'They took responsibility; why can't you?' Amoco, BP, Shell, and Exxon all have ongoing problems that would just get much worse. We are unable to set this precedent for ourselves and the industry, much as we would like to see the issue resolved in a humane and satisfying way.[29]

---

[27] http://www.amnestyusa.org/business/AmnestyResponse.pdf, accessed June 11, 2008.
[28] Many argue that the amount was based on estimates of numbers injured and killed that were far too low and that it did not include adequate compensation for people disabled from the accident who would need long-term care (*Lancet* 1989).
[29] http://www.dowethics.com/r/about/corp/bhopal.htm, accessed June 11, 2008.

Nonetheless, the company *has* signed on to the "Responsible Care" initiative, which is a set of suggested (but voluntary) guidelines and principles for chemical companies designed to reduce the chances of industrial accidents. Like other kinds of voluntary initiatives and codes of conduct described earlier in this chapter with respect to sweatshops, it is unclear whether or not these have any practical implications, but Dow's actions do represent a change in the corporate opportunity structure that might, in fact, lead them to do more on the Bhopal issue. And, they have also established a website on ethics and corporate social responsibility, with special sections on Bhopal. Thus, we might conclude that Dow is making some modest steps in the right direction regarding Bhopal, but is clearly faced with a dilemma regarding its responsibilities for UCC's past malfeasance.[30]

Thus far, I have talked about three examples of private politics directed at corporations – one around a policy, one around a product, and one about alleged negligence of a company. In all of these cases, activists directly targeted the corporation rather than targeting some state institution. And, in all cases, activists used a multipronged approach, drawing on many types of tactics and strategies. I turn now to a discussion of three examples of anticorporate activism in which activists, in addition to targeting a corporation, also target some level of the state. That is, I turn now to three cases of contentious politics.

The Dolphin-Safe Tuna Controversy

The fourth illustration is that of the Dolphin-Safe Tuna campaign, a case of contentious politics, in that the target of the movement moved up the scale from the private (e.g., tuna companies) to the state. In April 1990, H.J. Heinz (then owner of StarKist), announced that within three months, it would ensure that all of its tuna was "dolphin safe." This action was immediately followed by the company's two main competitors, Bumble Bee and Chicken of the Sea. By the end of the year, the U.S. federal government followed suit and passed legislation ensuring that all tuna sold in the United States would be dolphin safe. These apparent legislative and corporate victories followed many years of protest, lawsuits, public

---

[30] The Dow controversy shows little sign of abating. In July of 2008, Indian villagers torched the construction site of a Dow plant in western India, charging fears of another Bhopal.

education, and boycotts designed to force the tuna industry to alter its way of catching tuna so as not to inadvertently capture and harm dolphins. And, as many know, in the years following them, these victories have been subjected to multiple attacks from business interests in the United States and abroad.

Background of the Controversy

Most tuna fish consumed in the United States comes from the Eastern Tropical Pacific (ETP), which is the area between San Diego (California), Chile, and Hawaii.[31] People catching tuna have noted for years that dolphins like to swim above yellowfin tuna in this area and this knowledge has historically been used by fishing boat operators to locate good tuna-fishing locations. Prior to the 1950s, most people working in the tuna industry fished with methods that did not harm these dolphins. Basically, they used rods and lines that were lowered beneath the swimming herd of dolphins. However, it was soon discovered that the use of "purse seine" netting, which involved using nets that worked like bags or purses to capture fish, could increase the tuna catch.[32] Of course, an unintended consequence of this new method of tuna fishing was that the dolphins swimming above the tuna were also caught in the nets. As the method improved over the years, more and more dolphins were drowned and/or caught in the winches used to pull the "purses" up on to the decks of boats. Marine biologists estimate that by the end of the 1960s, between 250,000 and 500,000 dolphins were killed each year in these nets (Danaher and Mark 2003).

In 1972, Congress passed the Marine Mammal Protection Act (MMPA), which among other things, provided funds for developing ways to reduce the number of dolphin deaths that were occurring as a by-product of tuna fishing. The MMPA required tuna fishers to reach a "zero-mortality rate" for dolphins within two years (Körber 1998). The effect of this law was a decrease in the number of dolphin deaths such that by 1977 the official estimate for the United States was around 25,000 (Danaher and Mark 2003). While this fell short of the intended zero-mortality rate

---

[31] My discussion of this controversy relies on Danaher and Mark's (2003) account of the history of the Dolphin-Safe Tuna Movement.

[32] Purse seine nets are large (roughly a mile long and six hundred feet deep). Essentially, the nets were used to encircle tuna (and collateral dolphins) and then lines pulled the "purses" closed at the bottom (Teisl, Roe, and Hicks 2002).

that the MMPA sought, it was obviously far better than the figures from the previous decade.

In 1976, the National Marine Fisheries Service (NMFS) provided incentives for the fishing industry to adopt new technologies that would reduce the number of dolphin casualties (Körber 1998). As well, the NMFS required that MMPA "observers" be present on tuna boats to both ensure compliance with the law and to tally any dolphin deaths. Both the MMPA and the actions by the NMFS were heralded by some conservationists as progress in the fight to end dolphin mortality.

However, by the early 1980s, as part of the general trend in deregulation that was set in motion by the Reagan administration, funding for the MMPA was scaled back dramatically and the "zero-mortality rate" goal was changed to an allowable kill of 20,500 dolphins each year. And as part of the funding cuts, there was a dramatic reduction in the number of MMPA observers who were sent along on fishing trips (Körber 1998).

On top of these cutbacks, in the 1980s there was an increase in the number of foreign tuna ships working in the ETP who were not subject to U.S. environmental laws and, allegedly, killed about four times as many dolphins as U.S. ships did.[33] These two combined forces, deregulation and the increase in non-U.S.-owned tuna ships, led to dramatic increases in the killing of dolphins by the tuna industry in the 1980s.

But, by 1988, there was potentially good news for both U.S.-run fishing boats and dolphins: The MMPA was amended to ensure that foreign fishing fleets also demonstrate that they were using dolphin-safe fishing practices. This was accomplished through an initial 1984 amendment, which allowed embargoes on tuna from countries that did not use dolphin-safe tuna fishing practices and then through an additional 1988 amendment, which strengthened the 1984 amendment (Körber 1998). However, the history of this controversy shows that these amendments were never properly enforced, and in fact, this led to the legal basis for a later embargo of tuna imported from Mexico (Körber 1998). It was around this time that the organized social movement around the dolphin-safe tuna controversy really gathered steam.

[33] In the 1960s, virtually all tuna ships working in the ETP were from the United States, but by 1986, only about 30% of them were. But note that many of these were once U.S. ships, which simply reflagged themselves under a foreign fleet to evade the MMPA regulations (Danaher and Mark 2003).

The Movement

While groups such as Greenpeace and the Environmental Defense Fund had been active in getting the MMPA passed in 1972 and the Humane Society had launched an earlier boycott of tuna (*New York Times* 1977), by the 1980s most of these groups had retreated from the Dolphin-Safe Tuna issue, charging that the Reagan administration was so unfriendly to environmental causes, that the issue was no longer worth pursuing (Danaher and Mark 2003). But, in the late 1980s, the Earth Island Institute entered the picture and a concerted social movement was launched. The Earth Island Institute attempted in the mid-1980s to raise public awareness through its journal, the *Earth Island Journal*. But, like many issues, despite the fact that the estimated number of dolphin deaths was alarmingly high, the issue had not yet achieved the "stickiness" necessary to sustain a social movement (Heath and Heath 2007). All of that changed in 1988 when Sam LaBudde became aware of the dolphin deaths and was able to get a position on a tuna trawler called the *Maria Luisa*. Armed with a camera, LaBudde captured incredibly graphic footage of dolphin killings, which the Earth Island Institute used to make a short video depicting dolphins being crushed by ships and drowning in nets en masse (Danaher and Mark 2003).

The Institute launched a three-pronged approach centered on the remarkable footage that LaBudde had captured. Their approach quite nicely illustrates my earlier points about shifting the scale of contention by simultaneously targeting multiple entities, only some of which are state actors. First, they used LaBudde's film to encourage Congress to tighten the existing rules on allowable dolphin deaths as part of their reauthorization of the MMPA (Girdner 1988). Lobbying Congress was an important step for the institute, and one that environmental groups increasingly took in the 1980s (Olzak and Soule 2009).

Second, they launched a series of lawsuits designed to get the government to actually enforce the MMPA and its later amendments. Most importantly, along with the Marine Mammal Fund, the Institute filed suit in federal court against the Commerce Department and the NMFS for not enforcing the MMPA. The outcome of this lawsuit was that the Commerce Department was forced to impose an embargo on tuna from Mexico and several other countries, which I discuss in more depth later.

These first two parts of the Earth Island Institute's strategy would clearly be classified as contentious politics in that the object or focal point of the claims made by this group was the state and its policies. However, the movement spearheaded by Earth Island Institute did not stop at the state, instead choosing to move down the scale of contention to corporations, which were also culprits in the dolphin deaths, thus this is also an example of private politics.

Specifically, the third prong of the movement's strategy involved targeting U.S. corporations marketing tuna, noting that the MMPA's failure to protect dolphins necessitated holding corporations responsible for the unnecessary deaths of dolphins. Thus, the Earth Island Institute went after the three largest tuna marketers in the United States: StarKist, Bumble Bee, and Chicken of the Sea. This third prong of their strategy made perfect sense given that at the time, the United States was one of the largest consumers of tuna and these three companies represented about 75% of all tuna consumed in the United States (Danaher and Mark 2003).

The first kind of action that the Institute, along with other environmental groups, launched was a national boycott of tuna (Girdner 1988; Wilkens 1989; Green 2000). To do this, in 1988, they released LaBudde's film to media outlets, including the major television networks. The broadcasting of the horrific images immediately galvanized the American public and threatened to do immediate harm to the image of corporations marketing tuna. The boycott was taken up by school children, who took advantage of the Earth Island Institute's educational and activist materials to press their schools to stop serving tuna in cafeterias, many of which responded favorably by taking tuna off menus and out of their larders (George 1990; Howe 1990).

Secondly, some environmental groups, such as Earth Liberation Front, organized events using direct action tactics, such as sabotage of tuna boats (Freeman 2000) and protest demonstrations, like the 200 person protest at the Embarcadero in San Francisco in June 1989 (Richmond 1989). At this event, protesters chanted and held signs in an effort to educate the public about the dolphin-safe tuna controversy.

Was the Dolphin-Safe Tuna Campaign Successful?

Most observers consider the dolphin-safe tuna campaign to have been, by and large, successful. The strategies employed by the Earth Island Institute combined targeting the government and corporations with multiple tactical forms and were fairly effective. In 1989, the Dolphin Protection Consumer Act, which would require that tuna caught with purse seine nets be labeled as such, was introduced into Congress by Barbara Boxer. While this act was being debated, some grocery stores (e.g., Thom's Natural Foods, Other Avenues Food Store) refused to stock tuna. Also at this time, H. J. Heinz conducted surveys of consumers showing very high consumer awareness of the dolphin issue. And, Earth Island Institute was planning "National Dolphin Day," a day of protest outside of H. J. Heinz offices in sixty cities, a fact that worried executives at H. J. Heinz, who were already being branded as "dolphin killers." In an attempt to preempt these protests, H. J. Heinz announced that it would begin to take steps to assure that all of their tuna would be dolphin safe. Within a day, the two other major tuna marketers followed suit. On the heels of these concessions, Congress passed the Dolphin Protection Consumer Information Act (1990), which established conditions for protecting dolphins and provided labeling standards for tuna products that are sold in, or exported from, the United States. In 1990, the Earth Island Institute successfully instituted a tuna embargo against tuna imported from Mexico, Ecuador, Venezuela, and Vanuatu. This followed their aforementioned suit against the U.S. government for not enforcing the MMPA.

It is critical to note that one of the biggest factors leading to the success of this campaign was the fact that the Heinz Company recognized that negative images and a bad reputation can directly impact a company's bottom line. Because Heinz recognized the fact that StarKist was about to be implicated in the slaughter of creatures that were successfully framed as highly evolved mammals able to communicate and because they vowed publicly to do something to stop the senseless slaughter, other companies had to follow suit. To this day, all three of the big tuna companies maintain their commitment to dolphin-safe tuna. For example, StarKist advertises the fact that the company is committed to protecting dolphins and that it will not purchase any tuna caught in association with dolphins. As well, the company notes on its website that it was the first American company to make the pledge to buy only dolphin-safe tuna (http://www.starkist.com/template.asp?section=faqs.html March 6, 2008).[34]

Of course other ways to gauge the effectiveness of a campaign might be to ask whether or not consumers modified their behavior in response to the dolphin-safe tuna controversy and whether or not dolphin-safe tuna captured a larger portion of the market. On these dimensions, the

---

[34] The websites of the other two tuna companies, Bumble Bee and Chicken of the Sea, include similar pledges about dolphin-safe tuna.

evidence is somewhat mixed. Early studies (e.g., Wallstrom and Wessels 1994) seemed to show that while there was an initial negative market reaction to the exposure of the killing of dolphins, the subsequent controversy and labeling of tuna as "dolphin safe" did not affect consumers' behavior. However, using data collected by A. C. Nielsen Marketing Research Company on grocery store items scanned at cash registers from 1988 to 1995, Tiesl, Roe, and Hicks (2002) show that over this period, consumers' behavior was in fact affected by media attention to the controversy. Over this time period, canned tuna sales declined, however, the introduction of dolphin-safe tuna labels slowed this decline considerably, suggesting first that the controversy led consumers to be squeamish about eating tuna, but that when tuna was deemed to be dolphin free, consumers resumed eating it.

In reflecting on what makes a movement successful, I noted in Chapter 2 that movements' use of collective action framing, an internal factor, is essential. A leading scholar of the success of consumer boycotts, Monroe Friedman, notes that the tuna boycott worked because it was cognitively simple and emotionally compelling, two characteristics of frames that help them to resonate (Green 2000).

Related to the discussion is the notion of how an idea or social movement frame "sticks." Heath and Heath (2007) point to a number of elements that give ideas, more generally, "stickiness" or, in the terms of framing scholars, resonance. Many of these elements are seen in the dolphin-safe tuna campaign and help us to understand why this campaign was so successful. First, there was a clear *emotional dimension* to the campaign. Not only did the Earth Island Institute successfully convey the fact that dolphins are mammals and are highly evolved, but they also played on the fact that generations of Americans had grown up watching dolphins perform on television or live at places like Sea World. As well, Americans had fallen in love with movie portrayals of dolphins such as *Flipper*.

Second, the campaign was framed in a *simple* manner in that it was made clear that killing dolphins was simply not necessary, because the dolphin deaths only occurred in the Eastern Tropical Pacific where dolphins swam in the seas above the yellowfin tuna. As well, the technology to stop the killings was simple. That is, it was the technological advances in nets and fishing apparatuses that caused the problems, thus it was clear that there was existing technology that could be used instead (i.e., older methods of fishing). In other words, by broadcasting to consumers the simple fact that tuna could be caught elsewhere and/or with other fishing methods without harming dolphins, the issues surrounding the dolphin-safe tuna campaign were stated in very concrete and unambiguous terms.

Third, the entire issue was made very *credible* by the LaBudde film, which was released to the national media. Because the film was fairly unambiguous (and graphic), Americans issued credibility to the issue right away. On this dimension, celebrities also helped. For example, George C. Scott narrated a Discovery Channel special on the issue and actors such as Danny Glover made reference to the campaign in their films.

Finally, aside from the clever and resonant framing of the issue, which served to make it "sticky," the campaign drew on multiple tactical forms in targeting companies. Activists picketed grocery store chains, instituted a boycott of the three main tuna marketers, organized press conferences, sent information to teachers and school children about the issue, and protested outside of the September 1988 shareholders' meeting of H. J. Heinz, the owner of StarKist.

Epilogue

As I noted earlier, when the initial wave of dolphin-safe tuna legislation was passed, tuna packers in the United States responded by purchasing more tuna from foreign tuna fleets, leading to an increase in foreign fishing vessels, while the American fleet began to decline. This trend continued throughout the 1980s and early 1990s, with the Mexican fleet growing rapidly. As might be expected, the 1990 tuna embargo hurt the Mexican tuna industry, which had grown to be one of the largest in the Eastern Pacific. In response, in 1991 the Mexican government filed a complaint with the General Agreement on Tariffs and Trade (GATT), which was an international treaty set up after World War II to promote free trade and is the precursor to the World Trade Organization (WTO). The GATT panel that met in 1991 to discuss the complaint ruled that the United States cannot regulate what foreign producers do. This certainly was a defeat for the Earth Island Institute and other organizations that had joined the dolphin-safe tuna issue. And, it represents the first stage of a counterattack against environmentalists concerned with the dolphin-safe tuna issue.

In 1995, Mexico threatened the United States with additional complaints to the WTO, unless the United States agreed to call off the tuna embargo and give up the labeling of "dolphin-safe tuna." This led, eventually, to the introduction of a bill that would reverse years of protective legislation by allowing tuna fishing boats to use purse seine nets, so long as observers from the U.S. Commerce Department could determine that there were no dolphins at risk. Some environmental groups believed this would be sufficient, but Earth Island Institute and others did not. Eventually, the original "Dolphin Death Bill' (as it was dubbed in 1995) was defeated in the Senate; however, another version of the bill was passed in 1997. This version maintained the "dolphin-safe tuna" labeling.

In 2003, the Bush administration's Commerce Department further relaxed the standards such that tuna caught by encircling methods and purse seine nets could be labeled dolphin safe (Marquis 2003). The Earth Island Institute and other environmental groups immediately filed an injunction, charging that the Commerce Department had not based its ruling on its own scientific findings regarding the ills of purse seine nets, but had instead bent to the political will of the Bush administration and pressures from Mexico (Kay 2003). In 2004, the issue was provisionally settled when Judge Thelton Henderson (a judge who had ruled in favor of dolphins in the past) ruled that the Commerce Department had ignored its own scientists' evidence showing that the nets in question were, in fact, responsible for dolphin deaths. In 2007, an appeals court upheld this ruling, further noting that the Bush administration had used undue influence over Commerce Secretary Donald Evans, citing a letter written to him by then Secretary of State Colin Powell, urging him to relax the labeling standards (Egelko 2007). Thus, at the time of this writing, tuna sold in the United States remains dolphin safe.

The Free Burma Campaign

The fifth example is another that illustrates contentious politics in that anticorporate activism moved up the scale from targeting corporations (specifically, a corporate policy), to targeting policies of city and state governments, with the ultimate goal of impacting the policies of a foreign state. This is the case of the Free Burma Campaign launched in the United States in the mid-1990s.

Background

Burma is a small country located between India, Thailand, and China that has a long history of oppression of its citizens. The most recent military junta to rule Burma took over in 1962 and ruled the country with an iron fist, cracking down on any glimmers of student or worker activism. The Burma Socialist Program Party (BSPP), over the next twenty-six years, spent most of the country's resources quelling ethnic guerilla groups, driving the country's economy to near shambles.

In 1988, the police killed a student during a dispute in a tea shop in Rangoon/Yangon (Danaher and Mark 2003). When the military government ignored requests from other students to investigate the killing, the students (joined by workers and Buddhist monks) staged a series of nonviolent demonstrations. In August of 1988, the demonstrations began to grow and, as a result, the military junta responded with force, killing several hundred peaceful demonstrators. Despite the escalation of repression, the demonstrations continued throughout August and September. However, on September 18, 1988, the military repression escalated, resulting in the loss of at least 3,000 lives (Marlay and Ulmet 2001: 115). Prior to this demonstration, the military government had announced the State Law and Order Restoration Committee (SLORC) in an effort to publicize its intention to reinstate order in the country. Between 1988 and 1990, demonstrations continued and some estimate that SLORC killed over 10,000 Burmese citizens during this period because of their participation in antistate demonstrations (Danaher and Mark 2003).

The 1988–1990 demonstrations paved the way for multiparty legislative elections in 1990, in which the opposition party, the National League for Democracy (NLD) led by Aung San Suu Kyi, won 83% of parliamentary seats. Despite this landslide victory, the military junta refused to give up their power and declared the elections null. They instead placed Aung San Suu Kyi under house arrest and jailed many of her supporters, some of whom had been elected to Parliament during the 1990 elections.

The Burmese government has been accused of numerous human rights violations as documented by Marlay and Ulmet (2001) and White (2004) including: no freedom of assembly, physical surveillance, wire-tapping and censorship of mail/Internet, lack of workers' rights, no freedom of press, restricted freedom of religion, persecution of political opponents, no independent judiciary, degrading conditions of prisons and torture of prisoners, extrajudicial killings, ethnic cleansing and deliberate creation of refugees, brutal and arbitrary treatment of tribal groups, forced relocations, and slavery. White (2004) also notes that the military government routinely forces children into combat, and estimates that 70,000 child soldiers have been conscripted for unpaid combat. She also notes that soldiers routinely enter villages to recruit laborers, take land, and rape and murder citizens (2004: 50).

In addition to these human rights abuses, the country of Burma is characterized by widespread poverty caused largely by the military rule, which has forced citizens to leave farms to serve in the military (White 2004). Burma is one of the poorest countries in the world and its health-care services are substandard (Danaher and Mark 2003). Compared to other Southeast Asian countries, Burma is near the bottom with regard to levels of education, healthcare, and protein consumption (UNICEF 2002: 50) and it is estimated that 40% of Burmese children are malnour-ished (Danaher and Mark 2003). As well, many accounts of labor in Burma point to the widespread use of child labor and to the fact that employers in Burma are not required to follow any health and safety standards nor are they required to provide benefits, sick leave, or maternity leave (White 2004).

The Movement

Following the SLORC crackdown in 1990, there was a brief flurry of stu-dent activism in the United States designed to educate the public about what was going on in that country (Danaher and Mark 2003). Most of this activity was centered at a few colleges in northern California, where several student refugees from Burma had relocated.

In 1995, SLORC released Aung San Suu Kyi from house arrest, under the assumption that the prodemocracy forces were not strong enough to stage more demonstrations. Her release garnered a great deal of media attention and brought the focus of many student activists back to Burma, as did the release of the film *Beyond Rangoon*. In particular, a Burmese graduate student called Zarni, who had collaborated on this film, became quite interested in launching an international movement against Burma, knowing full well that the military government of Burma would not allow the movement to form from within the country. Zarni, along with two other Burmese exiles, tapped into the Student Environmental Action Council (SEAC), which offered them a vast network of student activists across the country. While SEAC activists were primarily concerned about the environmental devastation of Burma, they were also sympathetic to claims about human rights violations therein.

In September of 1995, Zarni launched a website devoted to a new group called the Free Burma Coalition (FBC). At this time, the Internet was still in its infancy and, in reality, at the time the FBC was not much more than the website that Zarni launched. In fact, some scholars of Internet activism claim that this is one of the first Internet-driven social movements (Danaher and Mark 2003). The website provided information and, importantly, activist materials, which were used by student groups all over the country. As well, it connected these activist groups and allowed them to communicate easily and without cost, something that was new to student activism. By October 25th of 1995, over seventy campuses were able to participate in the "International Day of Action to Free Burma," in large part because of the rapid dissemination of information provided by the FBC website.

Zarni's use of the Internet to coordinate students and disseminate information and materials is an example of an internal characteristic of a social movement that impacts the consequences of the movement. In this case, we might consider this as an important resource – both in terms of the skills needed to use the Internet in this way, as well as simple access to it.

Was the FBC Successful?

The central goal of the FBC, of course, was to support the prodemocracy movement in Burma and, seeing the similarities between the issues in Burma and the earlier antiapartheid movement discussed in Chapter 4, students rapidly seized on the strategy of targeting corporations, arguing that it was immoral for any corporation to do business with governments that were known to be abusive.

One of the first targets of the campaign was PepsiCo, which had been criticized for entering into a joint venture with a Burmese businessman with ties to the military government. While PepsiCo was obviously not the only, nor the worst, offending business, it was an important strategic choice for students, as Pepsi (and its subsidiaries, like Taco Bell, KFC, and Pizza Hut) was (and still is) a visible corporate presence on college and university campuses. As was the case above with Nike, Gerber, and StarKist, visibility of a company can make it more vulnerable to activism. Thus, Pepsi was an important strategic choice on the part of the FBC.

Students across the United States staged sit-ins, pickets, and boycotts of Pepsi products on their campuses and, eventually, in 1996, Harvard University denied a contract to PepsiCo after the Harvard students launched a letter-writing campaign urging the university to sever ties to Pepsi. Within a month, Stanford University students were successful at denying Taco Bell a place at their student union. These prominent victories worked. In April of 1996, Pepsi announced that it would pull out of Burma, just a few weeks before a planned demonstration at Pepsi's annual shareholder meeting.[35]

Following the PepsiCo decision, the FBC realized that it needed to become more efficient if it was going to be able to encourage the myriad other companies doing business in Burma to divest. Focusing on each company individually was resource intensive and could take a long time. As such, they settled on the related strategy of encouraging cities to pass *selective purchasing* laws. Essentially, selective purchasing laws use the power of a government's purse to affect the bottom lines of corporations by refusing to do business with companies with ties to, in this case, Burma. In 1995, before the birth of the FBC, at least two U.S. cities (Berkeley, California, and Madison, Wisconsin) had passed selective purchasing laws, and after the upsurge in student activism, several other cities passed similar laws (e.g., Santa Monica, Ann Arbor, San Francisco, and Oakland). Then, in 1996, the state of Massachusetts passed a law stating that it would levy a 10% penalty on bids from businesses with ties to Burma.[36]

By October 1996, Apple Computer completely pulled out of Burma, allegedly because the selective purchasing law in Massachusetts was costing it so much money. Within a month, Hewlett Packard followed suit, and then Motorola did, charging that the San Francisco selective purchasing law would cause that company to lose $40 million. Essentially, the selective purchasing laws were doing precisely what activists hoped; that is, they were making it economically unfeasible for corporations to maintain ties to Burma. Between 1996 and 2002, sixty-eight U.S. firms severed their ties to Burma (IRRC 2002).

Finally, another estimate of success of the movement is the 1997 Executive Order (13047) signed by then President Clinton. This order banned most new U.S. investments in Burma, citing the human rights abuses in that country as well as the fact that Burma was financing its military through production and trafficking of opium and heroin (Hadar

[35] While this was certainly a victory, the FBC maintained its boycott of Pepsi, charging that the company was maintaining a franchise agreement in Burma (Danaher and Mark 2003). In 1997, PepsiCo pulled out of Burma completely.

[36] The FBC was not as successful at getting the states of California, Connecticut, and Texas to pass selective purchasing laws (Danaher and Mark 2003). But, it was successful at getting many other cities to pass laws in the 1995–1998 period.

1998).[37] In 2003, the Burmese Freedom and Democracy Act was signed into law; this act (and an accompanying executive order) prohibits the importation of Burmese goods to the United States and prohibits U.S. persons from providing financial services to Burma.

When thinking about the success of the FBC, it is important to reflect on my points in Chapter 2 about how we must consider the internal characteristics of a movement and how these impact its ability to achieve its stated goals. In this discussion, I noted that one of the key determinants of a movement's impact has to do with the resources it is able to mobilize. It is important to note that Zarni and the FBC were able to use the Internet to rapidly mobilize students on campuses throughout the country – and, as I noted previously, this was one of the first movements to use this important resource. As well, they were able to use the preexisting networks of SEAC. Thus, in this case, we see how important the resources of the FBC were to its eventual success.

Epilogue

As we saw with some of the legislation passed in the wake of the dolphin-safe tuna mobilization discussed previously, selective purchasing laws were also challenged by the WTO. Specifically, in 1997, the European Union (backed by Japan) requested a WTO consultation on the Massachusetts law, arguing that the law violated a 1994 government procurement agreement between the United States and Europe (Danaher and Mark 2003). Specifically, the EU suggested that the Massachusetts law violated the WTO's rules on not allowing "political" criteria in awarding government contracts. Oddly enough, the WTO never ruled on this challenge (Danaher and Mark 2003).

But, following this, a business consortium of nearly 600 U.S. companies called the National Foreign Trade Council (NFTC), filed suit in federal court challenging that the Massachusetts law was not constitutional. Treating the Massachusetts law as a test case, the NFTC argued that the law infringed on the federal government's exclusive right to the foreign policy domain (Danaher and Mark 2003). In the end, the court ruled in favor of the NFTC in 1997, dealing a blow to the FBC. The case was then brought to the First Circuit Court of Appeals, which upheld this decision

---

[37] However, U.S. firms that had investments prior to 1997 have been allowed to maintain investments there.

in 1999. Finally, Massachusetts appealed again and the Supreme Court agreed to hear the case in March 2000. Unfortunately for the FBC, the Supreme Court ruled in favor of the NFTC in 2000 (Danaher and Mark 2003). Nonetheless, despite this blow, it is clear that the FBC was able to galvanize support for the issue – support which led many companies to pull out of Burma.

Laborers International Union of North America and the Antiforeclosure Prevention Act Movement

The final illustration in this chapter is that of a movement directed at both the state and corporations around an issue framed largely in terms of alleged corporate negligence. This case is that of the movement that arose in the Spring of 2008 as the U.S. House of Representatives was considering the Senate Foreclosure Prevention Act of 2008 (S. 2636), though its roots are much deeper as I will describe. Critics of the bill (as originally drafted) charged that it would do more to help corporate homebuilders than it would to help homeowners who were (and currently still are) struggling to make their mortgage payments. Such critics took to the streets to protest corporate malfeasance, introduced shareholder resolutions, and lobbied Congress as they considered this bill. Thus, this case is an example of contentious politics in that the activists clearly wanted to prevent the state from enacting this particular piece of legislation (or at least prevent the state from enacting it as it was originally written), but it also targeted corporate homebuilders.

Background

The factors leading up to the U.S. mortgage crisis of 2008 are complex and I do not intend to do them justice herein. Instead, I will sketch the very broad contours of what happened in the United States in an effort to provide some context for the genesis of this type of anticorporate activism. The crisis began in 2006, when the U.S. housing bubble began to burst and housing values in many areas of the country began to decline. Because of the availability of "subprime" mortgages, which are those made to high-risk borrowers, and of adjustable rate mortgages (ARMs), many homeowners were not able to make their monthly mortgage payments and began to fall behind. Foreclosure rates skyrocketed (and, at the time of this writing, continue to do so). For example, in February 2008, foreclosure rates increased 60% over the February 2007 figures (Rooney 2008) and during February 2008, nearly 224,000 homes were foreclosed (Rooney 2008). While certain states (e.g., Arizona, California, Florida, Nevada) were especially hard hit by foreclosures, other states have suffered, too (Rooney 2008). Between January and August 2008 alone, there were over 2.5 million homes foreclosed in the United States (Streitfeld 2008). In the first quarter of 2008, the rate of new foreclosures reached nearly one percent, which was the highest it has been since the Mortgage Bankers Association began tracking it (Armour 2008). And, finally, in May 2008, the delinquency rate, which is defined as those who are at least thirty days behind in their mortgage payment, was 6.356%, another record (Armour 2008).

Part of the problem, of course, is that so-called predatory loans (e.g., subprime and ARMs) were made to people who believed that they would be able to refinance their loans after a short period. And, in fact, this was the case through the late 1990s and early 2000s. As housing prices increased during this period, Americans routinely refinanced their homes to get lower interest rates and/or they took out second mortgages based on their equity in their current homes.[38] But, as housing values began to decline in 2006, refinancing loans became much more difficult than it was just a few years earlier. As the higher rates of ARMs began to kick in as rates were reset, people simply could not meet their mortgage payments (Armour 2008).

One of the main factors contributing to the decline of home prices is an oversupply of housing driven, at least in part, by the conscious strategy of corporate homebuilders who gambled that people would have the financing options open to buy them.[39] The glut of homes on the market, including those that have been foreclosed recently, is driving down home prices as banks slash prices to unload foreclosed homes (Armour 2008). But on top of the excess in housing stock, some of the

[38] Some also criticize banks for their aggressive marketing of "home equity" loans, which removed the stigma associated with what these were formerly known as – "second mortgages" (Story 2008).

[39] A particularly striking example is Merced, California where in 2008 there were thousands of foreclosed homes on the market driving down the prices of real estate. In 2008, three-quarters of the existing homes sold in this city were foreclosures (Streitfeld 2008). This over supply of homes was fueled by corporate homebuilders who built close to 5,000 new homes that they planned to sell for over $500,000 each without paying attention to the fact that the city of around 80,000 had very few people who could afford such homes (Streitfeld 2008).

corporate homebuilders also routinely offered their own financing and many charge that they pushed predatory loans on unsuspecting buyers (LiUNA 2008).

In early 2008, the Senate introduced and passed a bill designed to help families struggling with foreclosure and communities hit hard by high rates of foreclosure. However, social movement organizations such as Laborers International Union of North America (LiUNA) and Citizens for Tax Justice objected vehemently to the Senate bill, charging that, as it was originally written, it would have done more to help corporate homebuilders than families and communities. Specifically, the original bill would have allowed corporate homebuilders (e.g., Lennar, Pulte, Toll Brothers, KB Home) to count current year losses against previous years' gains on their taxes.

In this case illustration, I focus primarily on LiUNA's actions, as they were at the forefront of this movement. The union charged that the mortgage crisis was, at least in part, fueled by the negligence of corporate homebuilders who for many years continued to build housing units on the speculation that people would be able to buy them and, as noted previously, pushed predatory loans through their own financing mechanisms. LiUNA argued that one of the most significant reasons they were against the act was that, "Corporate homebuilders are seeking a handout for a crisis they recklessly helped create" (LiUNA 2008).

The Movement

Mobilization around the mortgage crisis used several different tactics and strategies, all of which framed the mortgage crisis as an issue of corporate negligence and/or downright malfeasance. LiUNA's website and their written materials clearly charged that some of the main factors feeding the mortgage crisis were negligence and greed of corporate homebuilders who, despite warnings from economists, continued to buy land and build houses on speculation at the same time they also pushed their own subprime loans on unknowing homebuyers (LiUNA 2008).

The first strategy of the movement drew on the *outsider* status (with respect to corporate homebuilders) of one of its key organizations, namely LiUNA, and involved protest events that directly targeted corporations. For example, on May 6, 2008, LiUNA organized a protest event in Washington, DC, at the Capitol Hilton where housing industry lobbyists were staying. Protesters dressed up in pink pig costumes and held signs reading, "Corporate Homebuilders Stop Foreclosing on our American Dream" and "No Pigs at the Trough. Stop Corporate Welfare." This event was part of a series of similar events held across the country in April and May 2008 known as the "Pigs at the Trough Tour" (Schor 2008). These events targeted corporate homebuilders directly and thus might be classified as private politics.

LiUNA also produced documentation designed to encourage citizens to contact their Congresspeople to express opinions about legislation, such as the Foreclosure Prevention Act, designed to ameliorate the mortgage crisis. Specifically, they encouraged people to tell Congress to remove any aid to corporate homebuilders, while preserving aid to homeowners and communities. Thus, in many ways, we might also view this example of anticorporate activism as contentious politics, given that they also targeted the government.

But, LiUNA also used tactics that draw on its *insider* status at some corporations. Namely, because LiUNA holds shares in many financial institutions through its pension fund, the union was able to use its insider status to file shareholder resolutions at several financial services and mortgage companies (e.g., Lehman Brothers, Washington Mutual, and Bear Stearns). The resolutions required that these companies provide full disclosure on what kinds of mortgages were bought and sold so that shareholders could assess risk better.

Thus, this case illustration provides an example of a movement that targeted both corporations and the government around issues related to negligence or malfeasance on the part of the corporations. And, as noted earlier, the movement (like so many others described in this book) used both insider and outsider tactics.

Was LiUNA Successful?

As we know now, the mortgage crisis and its ripple effects throughout the United States and global economies are far from over, but it does appear that Congress was influenced by the movement. At the end of July 2008, Congress passed a housing bill that would benefit homeowners but, importantly, they rejected the part of the bill that would have allowed corporate homebuilders to carry their current losses against their past-year gains. This was the major goal of LiUNA, who certainly did not object to help for individuals and families struggling to make their mortgage payments.

Part of the success of the movement is that it took a multipronged approach similar in many ways to that of the Dolphin-Safe Tuna campaign described earlier. Like this earlier campaign, LiUNA drew on their insider status and filed shareholder resolutions, but they also mobilized protest events and letter-writing campaigns. And they targeted corporations directly as well as the state.

But, it is also important to note that the political and economic climate of 2008 was an important facilitator of the movement and its success. The mortgage crisis was (and still is) big news and at the time of this writing, Americans remain panicked about it (and the economy more broadly). In this crisis, large corporations (homebuilders and lenders alike) are being portrayed in a negative light, often as opportunistic predators taking advantage of hapless consumers. Thus, the stage was set for this movement to have real effects and, apparently, it did. Time will tell, of course, whether this movement will actually change corporate homebuilders, but for now it is clear that they were able to effect change in Congress.

Summary and Conclusion

This chapter discussed six examples of anticorporate activism in the post-1990 era that mobilized around issues of policy, products, and corporate negligence. Some of these cases should be classified as private politics while others are better categorized as contentious politics. It seems reasonable to step back now and ask what these cases teach us about anticorporate activism more broadly.

One theme that emerges from these illustrations, and which I introduced in Chapter 2, is that when we consider this class of social movement activism, that is, that which is directed at corporations, we must straddle the line between organizations scholars and social movement scholars and draw insight from both. Organizations scholars have primarily focused on private politics; that is politics that do not involve the government and are instead between private parties. While some organizations scholars look at the politics related to the regulation of corporations (e.g., Schneiberg and Soule 2005), most have focused on movements that target corporations. At the same time, contentious politics scholars have been more interested in examining the class of activity that involves some unit of governance, typically the nation state (however increasingly contentious politics study how transnational governance institutions are targeted). This has led social movement scholars to gloss over the fact (shown in Chapter 3) that historically movements have targeted *corporations*, sometimes in concert with targeting the government, sometimes solely. The cases that I describe in this chapter illustrate these themes.

I chose these particular examples to fit as neatly as possible into the typology introduced at the start of this chapter and they are meant to illustrate this typology, but are not meant to be the definitive word on these cases. However, over the course of researching these cases, I found that most do not fit as neatly as I had thought at the outset. For example, the case of the movement against Dow Chemical because of the Bhopal disaster had such deep, historic roots that, while current activism against Dow Chemical seems to be clearly a case of private politics, historically there have been instances of contentious politics directed against the Indian government. Or, when we consider the movement against Gerber for its use of GM grains (another case of private politics), and if we consider the broader anti-GM movement, we soon realize that the broader movement may be a case of contentious politics in that it often targets state authorities alongside corporations.

These observations underscore my earlier points from Chapter 2 about the importance of scale shift to anticorporate activism. While it is clearly not the case that *all* anticorporate protest events and campaigns target governments alongside corporations, a lot of events do choose multiple focal points. In the 1960–1990 period described in Chapter 3, nearly 18% of the anticorporate events also targeted the government in some fashion, and in many years, this was much higher.

In addition to the importance of scale shift, it is also important to consider the issue of moving targets (as also discussed in Chapter 2), as the case of the movement against Dow for the Bhopal disaster illustrates. When a company acquires another, is it liable for the acquired company's past negligence? What do activists do with respect to their corporate targets when two companies merge? In Chapter 2, I noted that the issue of moving targets is one that complicates research on anticorporate activism and the case of Dow is likely just one of many such cases.

The illustrations in this chapter also show that the issues identified at anticorporate protest events in the 1960–1990 period are also prevalent in the post-1990 period. The antipolicy, antiproduct, and antinegligence issues that I described in Chapter 3 are still important to activists and citizens alike. These issues, as I noted in Chapter 3, are part and parcel to the concept of corporate social responsibility and, if we think deeply about these issues, we might also connect them to my discussion in Chapter 1 of the broader issues about which anticorporate activists mobilize. That is, negligence, creation of harmful products, and certain corporate policies may be thought of as the consequences of the growth in corporations and the inability or unwillingness of the state to intervene on behalf of citizens. And, of course, we can think of all of these issues as part of the broader concept of corporate social responsibility described in Chapter 1.

Another theme that emerges from my discussion of these six cases is the way in which anticorporate activists employ a multipronged approach, drawing on an extensive toolkit of different tactics, to effect change in their targets. We see again and again that protest is accompanied by shareholder activism and other tactics, such as the boycott. Thus, when we think about the differences in efficacy between insider and outsider activism, it is critical to note that smart activists straddle this line, drawing on both simultaneously or sequentially.

Finally, in each of the cases discussed earlier, I have tried to assess whether or not the social movement in question has been successful in achieving change at the corporate and/or state level. In so doing, I have noted that the internal characteristics of the movement (such as the stickiness of the frame it deploys, the strategic choice of targeting certain corporations, and the resources it mobilizes) are clearly important. But, I have also noted the importance of the multilevel opportunity structure (e.g., the corporate, industry, and political opportunity structures as depicted in Figure 2.1 in Chapter 2) in which the movement is embedded. The main conclusion that we can draw here is much like that drawn in other chapters. That is, corporations can and do listen to activists. While they may not acquiesce to all claims made on them by activists, they do change. Thus, we can think of social movements and anticorporate activists as important engines driving corporate innovation with respect to issues of corporate social responsibility.

6

Conclusion

I began this book by noting that anticorporate sentiment and distrust of corporations in the United States date much further back than the current era – an era that has been hailed by scholars, corporate leaders, and activists alike as one of increasing levels of private politics directed at corporations. I suggested a gentle corrective to this characterization by arguing that what we may in fact be seeing is a transformation in the way that those dissatisfied with corporations attempt to effect change therein. With the decline in organized labor and the erosion of the regulatory system in the United States, critics of corporations seem to have adopted another strategy to influence corporations. Rather than focusing on *indirectly* targeting corporations via organized labor and/or government regulation, they now also *directly* target corporations, thereby circumventing these older channels of influence. They do this as outsiders to the corporation via protest, boycotts, and other means, but they sometimes also do this as insiders to the corporation via various forms of shareholder activism. Thus, at the outset of this book, my hope was to encourage researchers to view anticorporate activism through a broader historical lens and to think about the way in which early events of anticorporate activism are similar to those occurring in the second half of the twentieth century and to those occurring today.

It is now important to reflect on several general themes that emerged from my empirical analyses presented in Chapters 3, 4, and 5 and from my discussion in Chapter 2 of how social movement and organizational theories can shed light on the question of the outcomes of anticorporate activism more broadly. Following this discussion, I will conclude this chapter with some suggestions for future research in this area.

Key Themes Emerging from this Book

Private and Contentious Politics

Perhaps the first important theme to emerge from my analysis has to do with how we should classify anticorporate activism. I noted that scholars in several different disciplines are interested in this phenomenon and have brought their own disciplinary leanings to the fore. Social scientists in business schools are interested in this phenomenon for practical reasons related to understanding organizational innovation and strategy and because of a general interest in business ethics. Organizations scholars are interested in the phenomenon because of the potential for activism to shape organizations, markets, and industries and because activism shapes the general processes of institutionalization and entrepreneurship. And, sociologists and political scientists are interested in anticorporate activism as an important class of social movement and collective action.

But how do we classify anticorporate activism and what disciplinary tools are appropriate to use to understand it? Sociologists and political scientists note that anticorporate activism is *contentious politics* because it is often directed at state focal points well beyond the confines of any given corporation. For example, in some cases activists target the corporation as a means of exerting leverage over a state, as we saw in Chapter 4 when activists hoped to speed the demise of the South African system of apartheid via targeting American companies doing business therein and it was also the case in Chapter 5, when similar processes were at work in the case of Burma. But, sometimes anticorporate activists target the government *before* targeting corporations in hopes of influencing change in the latter indirectly, as discussed in Chapter 5, when activists hoped that changes to legislation protecting marine life would put a stop to the killing of dolphins in the tuna fishing industry. And, of course, anticorporate activists sometimes challenge the state and corporations *simultaneously*. This was discussed in relation to some of the civil rights activism described in Chapter 3, wherein activists sat in at lunch counters at the same time as they were challenging the state to encourage the passage of key civil rights legislation. Thus, scholars of contentious politics are not wrong when they say that anticorporate activism is a form of contentious politics because in many cases the state is involved – in most cases as an additional focal point or target beyond the corporation.

Conclusion

But much of anticorporate activism really has little to do with targeting the state and, as such, is better characterized (as organizational scholars do) as *private politics*. Many of the events described in Chapters 3 and 5 were directed solely at corporations, with little attention paid to the state. For example, the anti-Gerber and anti-Nike campaigns discussed in Chapter 5 were directed at corporations for their perceived wrongdoings, as were some of the events discussed in Chapter 3, such as those directed at toy manufacturers for producing violent and sexist toys. In such cases, it might have been plausible for activists to direct their grievances at the state, but they did not do so, instead focusing directly on corporations. Thus, if we were to define our subject of study as involving struggles between private actors and some state authority (e.g., contentious politics), such events would fall out of our area of inquiry.

The reality is that we must recognize that anticorporate activism can be classified as both private and contentious politics depending on the focal point(s) of the given event or campaign. As I noted throughout this book, the targets of anticorporate activism are multifaceted and exist at multiple levels and it is critical that we acknowledge this in the study of anticorporate activism. In so doing, we will be better able to classify this phenomenon and not exclude cases simply because of the blinders inherent in our own definitions.

Therefore, as scholars of anticorporate activism, we must be attentive to both of these literatures – that is, the literature on contentious politics and that on private politics. They are both essential to understanding the factors that facilitate anticorporate activism, to understanding how and why some anticorporate activists shift scales with regard to their focal points, and to ultimately understanding why only some instances of anticorporate activism achieve the stated goals, while others appear to fall on deaf corporate ears. Without both of these literatures, I argue, we risk losing a full understanding of the phenomenon.

The Embedded Nature of Opportunity and Outcomes of Anticorporate Activism

A second key theme to emerge from my analysis has to do with the outcomes of anticorporate activism and how these outcomes are impacted by both the characteristics of the social movement itself (e.g., what I referred to as *internal factors*) and by the broader opportunity structure in which the movement is embedded (e.g., what I referred to as *external factors*).

On the internal side, the cases described in this book revealed that the resources mobilized by a given movement (a characteristic of the social movement itself) were essential to its ability to achieve its stated goals. For example, when I discussed the Free Burma Coalition (FBC) and its successful campaign against Pepsi, I noted that the FBC cleverly used Internet resources provided by the University of Wisconsin and drew on the preexisting organizational structure of the Student Environmental Action Council (SEAC) to rapidly mobilize students all over the country. This is an example of how movement resources (here, computer skills and access to both the Internet and to an existing student movement network) can be critical to the outcome of the movement.

We also saw that the tactics used by activists (another internal factor) can be important to the outcomes attained. On this point, I emphasized repeatedly that anticorporate activists draw on a wide range of tactics when targeting organizations. I noted that sometimes activists draw on their status as insiders to the corporation (e.g., shareholder activism), while at other times they draw on their outsider status (e.g., protest). I discuss these differences in more detail later, but the important point for now is that tactical choice is another characteristic of a movement that can influence its effectiveness.

Like tactics, the strategic choices (another internal factor) made by a movement are certainly important to its ability to obtain its stated goals. One trend that I uncovered in many of the cases described in this book is that companies with a large market share, a great deal of name recognition, and evidence of behaving in a hypocritical fashion seem to be more likely to be chosen as targets by anticorporate activists. We saw this in my discussion of Nike, Gerber, and StarKist in Chapter 5, but we also saw this in my discussion of Polaroid and Dow in Chapter 1 and Kodak in Chapter 3. Essentially, the visibility of a company can make it vulnerable to anticorporate activism, as can suspected hypocrisy, such as when a favorably perceived company does something that is counter to its positive image.

Finally, we also saw that the collective action frames deployed by a social movement are critical to its achievement of desired outcomes. I related this idea to the idea of "stickiness;" that is, successful frames are those that, like good ideas, *stick*. They stick because they resonate with emotions, because they are familiar, and because they are perceived of as credible. For example, when Greenpeace chose to frame its anti-GMO concerns in terms of what it is that we feed infants, it was drawing on an extant frame used in an earlier campaign against Nestlé. But, Greenpeace also chose a frame that resonated deeply because of the emotions related to child rearing and the perception of infants as defenseless and in need of protection. And, because Greenpeace conducted scientific tests on Gerber products, their claims were made to appear more credible. In essence, this frame "stuck" and, in the end, worked remarkably well in this given campaign and national context.

But, importantly, part of the reason that the Greenpeace campaign against Gerber was so successful is beyond anything that the movement organization itself did. We must not ignore the fact that the corporate opportunity structure of the company was already open to the claims of the movement, having recently been targeted by other groups for its use of sugar, starch, and salt in its products. As well, because the broader baby food industry had been targeted before in the Nestlé boycott, the broader industry opportunity structure was also likely facilitative of the movement and the outcomes it sought. Thus, the Greenpeace campaign was not only successful because of its frames and choice of target, but also because the corporate and industry opportunity structures were already primed for its success.

This discussion illustrates some of the *external factors* that impact movement outcomes – another major point that I raised throughout this book. And, just as the corporate and industry opportunity structures are part of the broader external environment in which anticorporate activists operate, so too are the broader legal and political opportunity structures, which themselves exist at multiple levels, including the increasingly important transnational levels. In my discussion of the student antiapartheid movement (Chapter 4), I described the multiple levels of opportunity in which these activists were operating, noting the importance of the larger, external, multilevel environment to the attainment of this movement's goals. For example, I noted the importance of city and state antiapartheid legislation, the importance of public opinion on, and media attention to, the issue of apartheid, as well as the various transnational pressures from the activities of other countries and of transnational bodies.

Shifting Scales and Moving Targets

A third key theme to emerge from this book has to do with the targets of anticorporate activism and is related to the embedded nature of opportunity discussed in the previous section. We might reflect on my earlier Figure 2.1, which I have reproduced here in Figure 6.1 with some modification to represent the *targets* of anticorporate activism. In Chapter 2 (and previously), I noted that anticorporate actors are embedded (and their outcomes influenced by) a nested, multilevel opportunity structure. But, just as these levels of opportunity impact the day-to-day business of activism and the probability of eventual attainment of activists' stated goals, these levels *also* represent distinct focal points that anticorporate activists may target. This point is recognized by scholars of contentious politics – that is, the opportunity structure represents not only conditions that may be more or less facilitative of social movements, but it also represents the targets of these same social movements. But, it is important for organizations scholars to recognize this, too, lest they ignore the more state-oriented instances of anticorporate activism. Of course, it is equally important for contentious politics scholars to consider the importance of substate targets, such as those that exist at the industry and corporate levels, lest they ignore activism directed purely at corporate or industry targets. All of these levels are depicted in Figure 6.1.

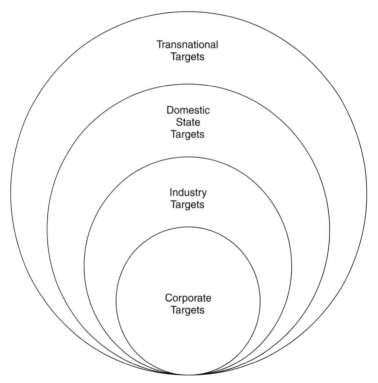

Figure 6.1   The Targets of Anticorporate Activism.

Conclusion

Looking at Figure 6.1 and considering my earlier distinction between private and contentious politics, we see that private politics typically target the corporate and sometimes industry level, while contentious politics typically target the state and transnational targets. But, my discussion in this book shows that activists often shift scales (or shift focal points) when targeting corporations, thus, they shift between private and contentious politics. At times they move up and down the levels depicted in Figure 6.1, such as when a movement strategically changes its focus. For example, when the Free Burma Coalition shifted from targeting Pepsi and other corporations to encouraging cities and states to pass selective purchasing agreements, they moved up the scale from targeting corporations to targeting multiple levels of the domestic opportunity structure.

But sometimes rather than moving up or down the scale in sequence, activists choose to target more than one level simultaneously. We saw this in my discussion of LiUNA's campaign against corporate homebuilders in which they protested large, corporate homebuilders, but at the same time they lobbied Congress to change important legislation around the mortgage crisis. We also saw this in my discussion of much of the civil rights activism in the early 1960s, for example, when activists sat in at lunch counters they were simultaneously challenging laws governing segregation *and* targeting businesses directly.

And, of course, sometimes activists use a focal point at one level to leverage concessions from another level, such as when student antiapartheid activists hoped to influence what corporations were doing by targeting their universities. Of course, the ultimate target of these events was the South African government, thus, student antiapartheid activists were targeting a very proximate focal point with the ultimate hope of influencing leverage over a very distant focal point.

Finally, another issue that arose in this book and is related to shifting scales is the fact that in some instances activists may stay at the same level, but focus on "moving targets." That is, because the boundaries around corporations are often in flux, it is not always crystal clear which company should be targeted over a given set of issues. We saw this most clearly in the case of Dow Chemical, which acquired Union Carbide and is now being targeted by activists in the hope of getting Dow to clean up the Bhopal plant that was the site of a deadly gas leak in 1984. But it is also the case in the current campaign against Chevron, which acquired Texaco and now is the target of a campaign to get the company to clean up spilled oil in Ecuador. Given the recent wave of mergers and acquisitions that I mentioned in

Chapter 1, we might expect this to be an increasingly prevalent issue – one that activists and corporations will be grappling with for quite some time. That is, are companies liable for the past sins of firms they acquire? On the one hand, activists argue that acquiring companies take on both assets and liabilities of companies that they acquire, and should be held responsible for what acquired companies have done in the past. But, on the other hand, corporations disagree, noting that they cannot be liable for something that they did not do or cause. This debate, I expect, will be playing itself out over the next several years as such cases come into the public eye.

The Tactical Repertoire of Anticorporate Activism

As touched on briefly earlier, another fairly prevalent theme to emerge from my analysis is that there is a wide and varied tactical repertoire available to critics of corporations who wish to do something that might change the corporation. Some of these tactics (e.g., protest, boycotts, and so on) draw explicitly on the *outsider* status of the critics, while some (e.g., shareholder resolutions, socially responsible investment) require that the critics are *insiders* (e.g., hold shares of stock) to the corporation. One of the key points that I made with respect to this large tactical repertoire is that protesters often, and perhaps increasingly, draw on *both* kinds of strategies – insider and outsider strategies – in a multipronged strategy designed to encourage corporations to change. For example, in 2004, we saw activists associated with PETA target Proctor and Gamble for testing its products on animals. These activists used protest (drawing on their outsider status), but they also introduced shareholder resolutions (drawing on their insider status as a shareholder of Proctor and Gamble). This multipronged approach was one that was shown to be prevalent throughout the post-1960 period in campaigns as distinct as the one waged against Kodak by FIGHT in the late 1960s around racial issues and the one currently being waged against Dow Chemical for the past sins of Union Carbide (which Dow acquired in 2001).

This theme – that is, the importance of focusing on the full reper-toire of tactics used by anticorporate activists – is important to scholars of anticorporate activism because there is often a tendency in this literature to focus solely on protest, or solely on boycotts, or solely on shareholder resolutions. This tendency is often driven by the availability of data, but may also be related to the chief concerns of the scholars conducting the research. My analysis suggests, however, that we should begin to focus instead on the entire set of tactics (i.e., the tactical repertoire) used by a given movement or movement organization before we can make comparative claims about the relative efficacy or inefficacy of a given movement in effecting change at the corporate level.

The Initiators of Anticorporate Activism and Their Complaints

I spent a great deal of time in this book, and in particular Chapter 3, describing *who* anticorporate protesters are and what claims they articulate (at least in the 1960–1990 period). One of the key points to emphasize here is that African Americans, workers, students, women, and resident groups were the most active anticorporate actors in the 1960–1990 period. While the proportion of anticorporate protest events initiated by each group varied over time, these groups were active and vocal critics of corporations throughout this entire thiry-one-year period.

This discussion should not imply that these were the only groups that targeted corporations; rather, my point was simply that these were the most prevalent. However, I wish to again emphasize my earlier point about thinking about the full repertoire of anticorporate activists. The data drawn on for this analysis, of course, came from news reports of *protest* events in the United States. While in many cases, the news reports mentioned protesters' use of additional tactics (e.g., shareholder activism), in this book I did not present a thorough analysis of other such insider tactics. If I had, I believe religious actors, for example, would have emerged as initiating a great many events, especially introducing shareholder resolutions. Thus, my discussion about the initiators of anticorporate activism should be qualified by the fact that this analysis refers primarily to protest and not to insider forms of activism (unless, of course, these were used in conjunction with protest and also reported in the newspaper).

With respect to the complaints of anticorporate activists, I was able to code nearly all protest events directed at business and corporate targets for a thirty-one-year period into three main issue areas: antipolicy, antiproduct, and antinegligence events. The largest share of the events in the 1960–1990 period were about some sort of corporate product or service (44%), but a fair share (41%) were about some corporate policy or some incident of corporate negligence (11%).[1] These three specific issue

---

[1] Of course, these kinds of complaints should be qualified as well, because these were the kinds of complaints articulated at public protest events. While I believe that shareholder

areas are all related to the broader issue of corporate social responsibility, as defined in Chapter 1. When we ask what critics of corporations are so incensed about, the broad answer is that they are angry at the growth of corporate power and greed and the unwillingness or inability of government institutions to do anything about this. The growth of corporate power, they argue, has led corporations to behave in ways that trod on the rights and quality of life of citizens; in sum, it has led them to behave irresponsibly with respect to their broader social environment, while trying to maximize benefits for their shareholders. This behavior manifests itself in negligence and malfeasance, the production of substandard or harmful products, and in exploitative policies and practices. Thus, when we look at the complaints of anticorporate activists in detail, we see that they are very much related to the broader idea of corporate social responsibility.

The Impact of Anticorporate Activism on Corporations

Finally, and perhaps most importantly at a substantive level, the key theme to emerge from this book is that social movements, contentious politics, and private politics can and do matter to corporations. We saw this in my discussion of the effects of protest on stock price, a case of protest mattering to financial performance. And, we saw this in my discussion of student antiapartheid activism, a case of protest mattering to university divestment policy. Finally, this was a major theme in my discussion of the examples drawn from the post-1990 period (described in Chapter 5). This is good news for activists, of course. But, it is also good news for corporations who can find that doing the right thing can actually make good business sense.

This message harkens back to some of the work of John Kenneth Galbraith, who in the 1950s argued that one of the key mechanisms for keeping corporate greed and power at bay is social activism. But, it goes beyond a mere call to activist arms. My message resonates with what I like to think of as an increasing willingness of both activists and corporations to talk to each other and to work together on issues of corporate social responsibility. We are currently seeing an increasing tendency of corporations to partner with activists or activist groups on issues of social

resolutions likely also can be classified as such, doing so was well beyond the goal of this book.

responsibility (Hoffman 2009). For example, Coca-Cola is collaborating with the World Wildlife Fund, a global environmental group that has been known to participate in protest and other social movement activities, on the issue of water conservation. And, Coca-Cola is also working with Greenpeace on issues related to carbon emissions from cola vending machines. Such collaborative efforts might be seen by cynics as attempts by corporations to obtain legitimacy by associating with social movement actors. Or, they may be criticized by activists accusing their comrades of "selling out," as I will discuss later. But, I prefer to see this as a positive trend that indicates that corporations often *want* to behave responsibly (for moral reasons or because they recognize that it is better for their bottom line) and are increasingly recognizing that the suggestions of activists can make good sense. Thus, while our gut reaction may be that of suspicion regarding these liaisons, I hope that we can be open minded about these collaborations – at least until we have a deeper understanding of the motives and outcomes of them. I take up this point in my discussion of suggestions for future research.

Some Suggestions for Future Research

The previous discussion highlights what I perceive to be the most important take-away points from this book. However, in the course of writing this book, I discovered many places where the empirical research and/or theorization on anticorporate activism are a bit thin. Thus, it seems reasonable to conclude with a brief discussion of my suggestions for future research on anticorporate activism.

Joint, Mediated, and Relative Impacts

When thinking about the outcomes or consequences of anticorporate activism, it is important to note that the character of the movement and the broader opportunity structure both impact the attainment of outcomes, as I describe throughout this book. However, it is equally important to consider the fact that sometimes these internal and external factors are only important in the presence or absence of each other. For example, perhaps the characteristics of a movement (e.g., frames used, resources mobilized, strategies and tactics used) *only* work to effect corporate change when the corporate opportunity structure is open or favorable. Or, perhaps the effects of the movement are amplified when the corporate opportunity structure is open or favorable. For example, it may be that shareholder resolutions only lead to change when corporate leaders are generally predisposed to the issue at hand anyway. Or, perhaps protest only causes change when the leaders of the corporation are divided on the issue or when there has been a recent change in key leadership positions. Or, maybe the effects of protest on the stock price of a given company are magnified when the industry opportunity structure is favorable because of previous, similar campaigns directed at other corporations in the same industry. The general point I wish to suggest here is that scholars of anticorporate activism begin to ask these sorts of questions. That is, we should begin to assess the relative and joint impacts of various factors on how corporations respond to activists' demands and complaints.

As well, we should also begin to think about how the various levels of opportunity described in Figure 6.1 might work together (or against one another). Perhaps when the domestic opportunity is closed, activists begin to target corporations directly because the state has proven unreceptive to their claims. This idea is certainly suggested by my finding (Chapter 3) that protest events targeting businesses were less likely than those targeting the state to be repressed. But is the same process at work when we consider protest events that target the transnational opportunity structure? Do they switch to this strategy because the domestic opportunity is closed? For example, did anticorporate activists flock to Seattle in November of 1999 to criticize the WTO because the U.S. government was not receptive to their claims? In general, we must begin to seriously think about how the various levels of opportunity mutually reinforce each other in some instances and work in opposition to one another in other instances.

Finally, the analysis of anticorporate activism should begin to more accurately assess the relative impact of various tactics on corporations. We should begin to assess, for example, the relative impact of shareholder actions, lawsuits, boycotts, and protest on corporate change. This suggestion stems from my earlier contention that we need to focus on the entire tactical repertoire of anticorporate activists, rather than on a single tactic in isolation. But, we should also ask which of these tactics has a larger net effect on various corporate outcomes of interest. For example, are certain tactics better at forcing corporate policy change, while others have bigger effects on stock price changes? Do some tactics work especially well when used to target corporations around certain issues? For example, are lawsuits better suited for the environmental issues (e.g., Eesley and Lenox

2006), while protest is better suited for labor and consumer issues (e.g., King and Soule 2007)?

In sum, we need to begin to think about which tactics work and under what circumstances. This information will be valuable to activists, but it will also be valuable to corporate leaders in that it might increase the efficiency with which they are able to respond to stakeholder claims.

The Relationships among Anticorporate Tactics

Related to thinking more broadly and creatively about when certain tactics might work to effect change at the corporate level, we should also begin to think about the relationships between different anticorporate tactics. In particular, we should begin to think about the sequencing of tactics and how some tactics may actually impact the emergence and success of others. For example, does protest affect the outcomes of shareholder resolutions? It could well be the case that shareholder resolutions are not able to gain much steam unless there is an existing protest campaign underway at the same time. We saw throughout this book that many of the protest campaigns described also involved shareholder forms of activism, however not all instances of shareholder activism are reinforced by a protest campaign. Thus, a logical question involves isolating the net impact of protest on the emergence and outcomes of shareholder resolutions.

Moreover, in addition to thinking about how tactics affect one another, we should also consider how tactics impact the various levels of opportunity structure, which then in turn can impact subsequent tactical deployment. For example, in the broader literature on protest tactics, it is well understood that tactical innovation is driven in part by repression (McAdam 1983). Here, protest drives state repression, which (as an element of the opportunity structure) in turn drives activists to experiment with innovative tactics. Related, in the broader literature on social movements, it is understood that protest can open up the opportunity structure for subsequent waves of protest (e.g., Soule, McAdam, McCarthy, and Su 1999). It is important that we begin to investigate whether or not similar processes are at work with anticorporate activism. For example, we should ask questions about whether or not shareholder activism opens up the corporate opportunity structure, making it more vulnerable to outsider tactics. Or, we can ask how protesters respond when they are met with repression. Do they retreat and then initiate a boycott? Do they shift scales and choose a different target and an entirely new set of tactics? In sum, there are many questions of this sort that we should be asking so that we can begin to understand the sequencing of, and relationships between, different anticorporate tactics and how these impact corporate outcomes.

Consequences of Activism on Anticorporate Movements and Activists

Throughout this book I have focused on the consequences that private and contentious politics have on corporate outcomes. However, in Chapter 2 I noted that activism also has outcomes at the movement and activist level, ranging from collective identity building and consciousness raising in the movement to repression of workplace activism. Analysis of all of these was beyond the scope of this book, however, I urge researchers to study these with respect to anticorporate activism. For example, we should begin to study employee networks systematically to understand how movement-level processes play out in movements within corporations. Or, we should begin to ask questions about how participation in movements within firms (e.g., tempered activism) affects employee trajectories at the targeted firm and beyond.

Related to these questions, I urge researchers to consider what some might refer to as "cooptation" of social movements by corporations. As I discussed earlier, scholars have noted the emergence of collaborations between corporations and the activists that have criticized them (e.g., Chasin 2001; Argenti 2004; Berger, Cunningham, and Drumwright 2004; Hoffman 2009). While some may view this as "selling out" on the part of activists, or as cooptation on the part of corporations, it is a phenomenon that is not fully understood. One of the earliest studies of the outcomes of social movements noted that cooptation is one important outcome of social movements (Gamson 1990); however, few studies of anticorporate activism have attempted to fully understand when such collaborations will occur. An exception is the work of Chasin (2001), who studies the evolution of the gay and lesbian niche market alongside the evolution of the gay and lesbian movement. Importantly for my purposes here, she demonstrates the way in which the movement impacted corporations via boycotts and protest, but then describes how corporations responded to the movement by making (sometimes hefty) donations to major gay and lesbian organizations. Through Chasin's work, which is somewhat critical of the gay and lesbian movement, we see that as the movement began to accept corporate funding, it was channeled into less confrontational (and perhaps less efficacious) tactics. Along these same lines, Jenkins and Ekert (1986) have also demonstrated that foundation and philanthropic funding defused some of the more confrontational tactics of the civil rights movement. My suggestion here is that we need similar studies on how corporate response to social movements can, in turn, alter the movement itself.

Activism, Corporate Financial Performance, Corporate Social Performance

Finally, the analysis presented in this book attempts to answer questions about how social activism (both private and contentious politics) matters to both corporate finances and corporate policies (one element of the broader concept of *corporate social performance*). For example, in Chapter 3 I described the results of a study that my collaborator, Brayden King, and I conducted. This study showed that anticorporate protest in the 1960–1990 period was associated with fairly striking declines in the stock price of targeted companies. And, in Chapter 4, I showed that student protest mattered to the divestment policies of their universities, in particular to the strategy of partial divestment. Finally, in Chapter 5, I described several cases in which various forms of anticorporate activism appeared to influence the policies of several corporations. Taken together, the main claims of this book are that anticorporate activism can impact corporate financial performance *and* it can impact corporate social performance.

But, this book has scarcely delved into the issue of how corporate social performance and corporate financial performance are related. Of course, the operating assumption of studies assessing the impact of activism on corporate financial performance is that financial performance matters to corporate leaders, thus, they will respond to activism preemptively, that is before their bottom line is impacted negatively. However, there is a need to really assess the relationship between financial and social performance empirically. Extant analyses (e.g., Waddock and Graves 1997; Margolis and Walsh 2001; Orlitzky, Schmidt, and Rynes 2003) find a positive but weak correlation between the two, but have failed to really disentangle the causal direction and the causal mechanisms at work. Moreover, this work has not yet begun to identify the scope conditions under which one of these (corporate social and financial performance) may lead to the other. And, these analyses have generally not yet attempted to add in *other* factors, such as how anticorporate activism matters to corporate social and financial performance. Thus, I call for research on this question – especially research that also attempts to include analyses of anticorporate activism.[2]

Summary and Conclusion

It is clear as we reflect on the goals of this book and what I was able to accomplish that there is still a lot of work yet to be done on the topic of anticorporate activism. It is my hope that my attempt to bring the contentious and private politics literatures together will be helpful to others conducting research in this area. As well, I hope that my suggestions for future research will stimulate more debate and further attempts at understanding how private and contentious politics matter to corporations. The good news is that there is a great deal of data and there are many cases to be analyzed and there appears to be a renewed scholarly interest in the topic. But, we must not forget that corporate leaders are also interested in this topic and, I believe, are more willing than they once were to assist scholars wishing to work on this topic. Just as we are seeing more and more collaboration between activists and corporations, I hope that we will see more and more collaboration between academics, activists, and corporations.

Thus, I conclude on a high note. We are finding that private and contentious politics matter to corporations and we are finding a greater willingness of corporate leaders to collaborate with activists and activists to respond in kind. The hope is that this will lead to an improvement in corporate records on corporate social responsibility and to real and substantial corporate change.

---

[2] I applaud the recent work by Baron and his colleagues (2008), which is beginning to do just this.

Appendix A

Description of Data Used in Chapter 3

The data used in Chapter 3 were collected from daily editions of the *New York Times* (*NYT*) as part of a larger research project initiated by myself along with Doug McAdam, John McCarthy, and Susan Olzak (see McAdam and Su 2002; Earl, Soule, and McCarthy 2003; Van Dyke, Soule, and Taylor 2004; Soule and Earl 2005; Earl and Soule 2006; King and Soule 2007; King, Soule, and Bentele 2007; Soule and King 2008; Larson and Soule 2009; Olzak and Soule 2009; and Soule and Davenport 2009 for descriptions of the larger project).

In 1997, armed with a team of National Science Foundation-funded research assistants, we launched the project with the ambitious goal of searching the daily editions of the *NYT* for any mention of any kind of collective protest taking place in the United States during this thirty-one-year period. In order to be included in our dataset, events had to meet several criteria: 1) more than one person had to participate in an event because our concern was with *collective* action and not individual acts of protest (e.g., self-immolation or uncoordinated hunger strikes); 2) participants must have articulated some claim, whether it be against some target, or in favor of some target (i.e., we exclude collective gatherings that did not explicitly articulate a claim, such as block parties, annual parades, outdoor concerts, and so on); and 3) the event must have happened in the public sphere (i.e., we exclude private meetings by social movement actors such as organizing and strategy sessions, but we do include events occurring inside of buildings so long as they were open to the public).[1]

---

[1] This means that we also exclude events involving institutionalized persons, such as prison or jail inmates or in-patient mentally ill individuals, because these were not open to the public. We also exclude labor-related events because the dynamics of these are likely substantially different from nonlabor protest events.

In the end, we coded extensive information on over 21,000 protest events. From this large dataset, I have selected those events that target businesses and corporations. Some of these events target additional entities (e.g., the state, educational institutions, medical facilities, and so on), however, to be included in my analysis in this chapter, the protest must have targeted some business interest. This includes 3,632 events, which form the backbone of this chapter, and is likely the most extensive dataset on antibusiness protest in existence today.

For the analysis described in the Epilogue to Chapter 3 and also in King and Soule (2007), from this dataset of antibusiness events we selected only those for which there was an *explicitly named* corporation for which we could also locate over-time financial information (342 events). This is a smaller subset of antibusiness events, yet it is important to note that it is a larger and more extensive set than has been used in any other, similar analysis.

Newspaper data on collective action events is one of the most frequently used forms of data in the field of social movements and we have learned a great deal from studies employing newspaper data (see Earl et al. 2004 for a review). In fact, McAdam and Su (2002: 704) note that the analysis of protest event data culled from newspapers is a "methodological staple" in social movement studies and that many of the "classical empirical works in the field" use newspaper data. Because of the popularity of newspaper data on protest, there have been many attempts to assess the potential biases associated with this source. In particular, studies have asserted that there are two main sources of bias in newspaper data: *selection bias* and *description bias*. Selection bias refers to the fact that not all protest events will be covered by a given newspaper and the possibility that what *is* covered is not a random sample of all events that took place and that selection bias may also vary over time (Mueller 1997). Description bias refers to the veracity of the coverage of events that are selected for coverage. In their extensive review of the literature, Earl et al. (2004) conclude that the type of event, location of event, and issue involved all impact the selection of events that will be covered, but that the "hard facts" of the event are generally accurately covered by newspapers.

Our data collection design attempted to deal with some of these potential biases of newspaper data. First, unlike many prior studies using newspapers as a source of data on collective action events, we did *not* use an index of the *NYT* to identify events nor did we sample days of the newspaper. Instead, we skimmed *daily* editions of the newspaper and identified *all* protest events that were reported therein.[2] This strategy reduces selection bias by not introducing further sources of selection (in this case, researcher induced or indexing procedure induced). Second, we only coded the "hard facts" of the events (e.g., tactics used, goals articulated, targets, organizations present, and policing), and not the "soft facts" (such as opinions on the issue of the event); this strategy reduced description bias.

As further evidence that this data source is comprehensive, at least on the anticorporate protest events described in the Epilogue to Chapter 3 and in King and Soule (2007), we searched for data on anticorporate events in both the *Wall Street Journal* and the *Washington Post* for six years (1964, 1968, 1974, 1978, 1984, and 1988). Searching these additional news sources for relevant keyword combinations (e.g., protest, activist, and demonstration) produced a small subset of the articles already found in our *New York Times* data. We found that the *Wall Street Journal* reported only 6% of the protest events covered by the *New York Times*. Moreover, we also found that only two protest events in these six years were reported by the *Wall Street Journal* but *not* by the *New York Times*. The *Washington Post* did a little better, and reported around 10% of all protests reported by the *New York Times* in these six years. And, we found no events reported in the *Washington Post* that were not also covered by the *New York Times*. The *Wall Street Journal* appears to have covered some of the issues that motivated protests but often initiated coverage following the actual protest event, while the *Washington Post* tended to cover protests involving court cases, but not protest events. Thus, I conclude that of these national newspapers, the *New York Times* provides the most comprehensive coverage of anticorporate protest events during this period.

---

[2] Research assistants then content coded these events, achieving intercoder reliability rates that were consistently at or above 90% agreement.

Appendix B

Modeling Technique Used in Chapter 3

In the analysis presented in Table 3.1 in Chapter 3, I model the effects of a set of variables on two different forms of police response to protest: police presence at an event and police use of violence and/or force at an event. Because my two dependent variables are dichotomous, I use logistic regression to model the effects of a set of independent variables on these outcomes. This allows me to model the likelihood of police presence and police force/violence, given a set of protest event characteristics. The models in Chapter 3 were estimated using logistic regression in Stata (Version 9.0). This model is nonlinear and expressed as:

$$P = \frac{\exp(x_j \beta)}{1 + \exp(x_j \beta)},$$

where P = the probability of a given police strategy (presence and force/violence), and x is the set of covariates for event $_j$, and β is the set of coefficients (including the constant). In the analysis, I cluster observations by year and present the robust standard errors (also referred to as the Huber/White or sandwich estimates), which allow for more conservative estimation of the models.

Appendix C

Sources of Data for Analysis in Chapter 4

Variable	Source
Campus Divestment Policy	Investor Research Responsibility Center (IRRC) and the American Committee on Africa (ACOA)
Presence of Shantytown on Campus	Lexis/Nexis Academic Universe, 42 Newspapers. See Soule (1997) for details.
Portfolio Size (logged): Approximated as one-half of the institution's endowment (Rottenberg 1986).	Higher Education General Information Survey (HEGIS): Financial Statistics of Institutions of Higher Learning.
Prestige Ranking	Gourman Report: A Rating of Undergraduate Programs in American and International Universities. This rating is the only longitudinal rating available for such a large number of universities and has been used in other social scientific research (e.g., Eckberg 1988). It is a continuous scale from 1 to 5 (5 being the highest prestige). It takes the following 14 criteria into account: control and organization of institution, total degrees conferred and educational programs offered, age or experience level of institution, qualifications of faculty, student records, difficulty of admission, size of student body, content of curriculum, teaching load, quality of administration, quality of non-departmental areas such as counseling and career placement, quality of physical plant, finances of institution, and the quality of the library.
Enrollment (Total and African American)	HEGIS
Black Studies Department	Peterson's Guides to Four Year Colleges
Institutional Type	Boyer (1987)

Appendix D

Modeling Technique Used in Chapter 4

In the analysis presented in Table 4.1 in Chapter 4, I model the effects of a set of variables on two divestment policy outcomes (partial vs. full), across the 899 colleges and universities in the study. Because my data are longitudinal in nature and my two dependent variables are dichotomous, I use discrete time event history analysis (Allison 1995). I array the data in a university by year matrix to estimate the likelihood that each of these two policy outcomes will take place in a given year at a particular university.

The models in Chapter 4 were estimated using cross-time logistic regression in Stata (Version 9.0). This model is nonlinear and expressed as:

$$P = \frac{\exp(x_j\beta)}{1 + \exp(x_j\beta)},$$

where P = the probability of adoption of a given divestment policy, and x is the set of covariates for university $_j$, and β is the set of coefficients (including the constant). The options available in Stata for logistic regression are particularly useful for this research design because they allow specification of within-group correlation structure for the university-level panels in my dataset. Because the data are pooled, cross-sectional, I run the risk of biased results due to unmeasured time-invariant heterogeneity within a university. Thus, to reduce this bias, I cluster observations by university, allowing me to assume that cases are independent across universities, but not necessarily within universities. By clustering observations by university, Stata calculates the robust standard errors (also referred to as the Huber/White or sandwich estimates), thus allowing for more conservative estimation of the models.

Bibliography

Africa Fund. 1987. "Divestment Action on South Africa by U.S. Colleges and Universities." Pamphlet. New York.

Amenta, Edwin and Jane D. Poulsen. 1996. "Social Politics in Context: The Institutional Politics Theory and State-Level U.S. Social Spending Policies at the End of the New Deal." *Social Forces* 75: 33–61.

Amenta, Edwin and Michael P. Young. 1999. "Making an Impact: Conceptual and Methodological Implications of the Collective Goods Criterion." Pp. 22–41 in *How Social Movements Matter* edited by Marc Giugni, Doug McAdam, and Charles Tilly. Minneapolis: University of Minnesota Press.

Amenta, Edwin, Bruce G. Carruthers, and Yvonne Zylan. 1992. "A Hero for the Aged? The Townsend Movement, the Political Mediation Model, and U.S. Old-Age Policy, 1934–1950." *American Journal of Sociology* 98: 308–39.

Amenta, Edwin, Kathleen Dunleavy, and Mary Bernstein. 1994. "Stolen Thunder? Huey Long's Share Our Wealth, Political Mediation, and the Second New Deal." *American Sociological Review* 59: 678–702.

Amnesty International. 2004. *Clouds of Injustice: Bhopal Disaster 20 Years On*. New York, NY: Amnesty International.

Anderson, Sarah and John Cavanagh. 2005. *Field Guide to the Global Economy*. New York: The New Press.

Andrews, Kenneth. 2001. "Social Movements and Policy Implementation: The Mississippi Civil Rights Movement and the War on Poverty, 1965–1971." *American Sociological Review* 66: 71–95.

Anti-Apartheid Act of 1986. *Ninety-ninth Congress*. Washington, DC: United States Government Printing Office.

Anti-Apartheid Act Amendments of 1988. Washington, DC: United States Government Printing Office.

Argenti, Paul A. 2004. "Collaborating with Activists: How Starbucks Works with NGOs." *California Management Review* 47(1): 91–116.

Armour, Stephanie. 2008. "Record Foreclosures Won't Ease Soon." *USA Today* June 6: B1.

Ashford, Susan J., Nancy P. Rothbard, Sandy Kristin Piderit, and Jane Dutton. 1998. "Out on a Limb: The Context and Impression Management in Selling Gender-Equity Issues." *Administrative Science Quarterly* 43(1): 23–57.

Ballinger, Jeff. 2001. "Nike's Voice Looms Large." *Social Policy* Fall: 34–37.

Barbaro, Michael. 2008. "Wal-Mart: The New Washington." *New York Times* February 3:WK3.

Baron, David P. 2001. "Private Politics, Corporate Social Responsibility and Integrated Strategy." *Journal of Economics and Management Strategy* 10:7–45.

2003a. *Business and Its Environment, Fourth Edition.* Upper Saddle River, NJ: Prentice Hall.

2003b. "Private Politics." *Journal of Economics and Management Strategy* 12:31–66.

Baron, David P. and Daniel Diermeier. 2007. "Strategic Activism and Nonmarket Strategy." *Journal of Economics and Management Strategy* 16(3):599–634.

Baron, David P., Maretno A. Harjoto, and Hoje Jo. 2008. "The Economics and Politics of Corporate Social Performance." Research Paper Number 1993, Stanford Graduate School of Business Research Paper Series. Stanford.

Bartley, Tim. 2007. "Institutional Emergence in an Era of Globalization: The Rise of Transnational Private Regulation of Labor and Environmental Conditions." *American Journal of Sociology* 113(2):297–351.

Battersby, John D. "Sanctions Squeeze South Africa." *New York Times* November 13:F1.

Baue, William. 2003. "The Implications of the Nike and Kasky Settlement on CSR Reporting." *Social Funds* September 18. (Available at http://www.socialfunds.com/news/article.cgi/1222.html; last accessed August 13, 2008).

Beck, Ulrich. 2000. *What is Globalization?* Cambridge, England: The Polity Press.

Beckles, Colin A. 1996. "Black Bookstores, Black Power, and the FBI: The Case of Drum and Spear." *Western Journal of Black Studies* 20:63–71.

Benford, Robert D. and David A. Snow. 2000. "Framing Processes and Social Movements: An Overview and Assessment." *Annual Review of Sociology* 26:611–639.

Benford, Robert D., Timothy B. Gongaware, and Danny L. Valadez. 2000. "Social Movements." Pp. 2717–2727 in *Encyclopedia of Sociology, Volume 4 (Second Edition)* edited by Edgar F. Borgatta and Rhonda J.V. Montgomery. New York: Macmillan Reference.

Bennett, W. Lance. 2003. "Communicating Global Activism: Strengths and Vulnerabilities of Networked Politics." *Information, Communication, and Society* 6(2):146–168.

Berger, Ida E., Peggy H. Cunningham, and Minette E. Drumwright. 2004. "Social Alliances: Company/Nonprofit Collaboration." *California Management Review* 47(1):58–90.

Blau, Eleanor. 1970. "Welfare Parents Seized at Macy's." *New York Times* November 6:39.

Bibliography

Bok, Derek. 1982. *Beyond the Ivory Tower: Social Responsibilities of the Modern University.* Cambridge, MA: Harvard University Press.

Bowen, Howard. 1953. *Social Responsibilities of the Businessman.* New York: Harper and Brothers.

Boyer, Ernest L. 1987. *A Classification of Institutions of Higher Education: A Carnegie Foundation Technical Report.* Princeton, NJ: The Carnegie Foundation for the Advancement of Teaching.

Briscoe, Forrest and Sean Safford. 2008. "The Nixon-in-China Effect: Activism, Imitation and the Institutionalization of Contentious Practices." *Administrative Science Quarterly* 53: 460–491.

Broad, Robin. 2002. *Global Backlash: Citizen Initiatives for a Just World Economy.* Lanham, MD: Rowman and Littlefield Publishers.

Browing, Jackson B. 1993. "Union Carbide: Disaster at Bhopal." *Jackson Browning Report – Union Carbide Corporation.*

Buhner, Rolf, Abdul Rasheed, Joseph Rosenstein, and Toru Yoshikawa. 1998. "Research on Corporate Governance: A Comparison of Germany, Japan, and the United States." Pp. 121–155 in *Advances in International Comparative Management Volume 12* edited by J. L. C. Cheng and R. B. Peterson. Stamford, CT: JAI Press.

Burros, Marian. 1996. "Eating Well." *New York Times* February 21:14.

Burstein, Paul. 1999. "Social Movements and Public Policy." Pp. 3–21 in *How Social Movements Matter* edited by Marc Giugni, Doug McAdam, and Charles Tilly. Minneapolis: University of Minnesota Press.

Cambell, Barbara. 1975. "11 Restaurants Accused of Bias." *New York Times* May 9: 71.

Carty, Victoria. 2002. "Technology and Counter-hegemonic Movements: The Case of Nike Corporation." *Social Movement Studies* 1(2):129–146.

Cassels, Jamie. 1993. *The Uncertain Promise of Law: Lessons From Bhopal.* Toronto, Canada: University of Toronto Press.

Chafe, William H. 1981. *Civilities and Civil Rights: Greensboro, North Carolina and the Black Struggle for Freedom.* New York: Oxford University Press.

Chang, Victoria and Glenn Carroll. 2008. "Monitoring Factories Around the Globe: The Fair Labor Association and the Worker Rights Consortium." Stanford Graduate School of Business Case SI-108, June 10, 2008.

Chasin, Alexandra. 2001. *Selling Out: The Gay and Lesbian Movement Goes to Market.* New York: Macmillan.

Chiang, Harriet. 1989. "Bay Area Stores Joining Tuna Boycott to Protest Dolphin Kill." *San Francisco Chronicle* March 28:2.

Clean Clothes Campaign. 2000. "Research into Nike's Global Alliance Assessment Study." *Clean Clothes Campaign* November 13. (Available at www.cleanclothes .org; last accessed May 28, 2008.)

Collins, Jane. 2003. *Threads: Gender, Labor, and Power in the Global Apparel Industry.* Chicago: University of Chicago Press.

Connor, Tim. 2001. *Still Waiting for Nike to do It: Nike's Labor Practices in the Three Years Since CEO Phil Knight's Speech to the National Press Club.* San Francisco: Global Exchange.

Cornell Chronicle. 1988. "Special Report on the Board of Trustees' Review of Cornell's Selective Divestment Policy." November 22:1–2.

Creed, W. E. Douglas and Maureen Scully. 2000. "Songs of Ourselves: Employees' Deployment of Social Identity in Workplace Encounters." *Journal of Management Inquiry* 9(4):391–412.

Cress, Daniel M. and David A. Snow. 1996. "Resources, Benefactors, and the Viability of Homeless SMOs." *American Sociological Review* 61: 1089–1109.

Cress, Daniel M. and David A. Snow. 2000 "The Outcomes of Homeless Mobilization: The Influence of Organization, Disruption, Political Mediation, and Framing." *American Journal of Sociology* 105: 1063–1104.

Creswell, Julie and Ben White. 2008. "The Guys From Government Sachs." *New York Times*, October 17:1.

Culverson, Donald R. 1996. "The Politics of the Anti-Apartheid Movement in the United States, 1969–1986." *Political Science Quarterly* 111(1): 127–149.

Cunningham, David. 2004. *There's Something Happening Here: The New Left, the Klan, and FBI Counterintelligence*. Berkeley: University of California Press.

Curtis, Charlotte. 1968. "Miss America Pageant Is Picketed by 100 Women." *New York Times* September 8:81.

d'Anjou, Leo. 1996. *Social Movements and Cultural Change: The First Abolition Campaign Revisited*. New York: Aldine de Gruyter.

Da Costa, Beatriz and Kavita Phillip. 2008. *Tactical Biopolitics: Art, Activism, and Technoscience*. Cambridge, MA: MIT Press.

Danaher, Kevin and Jason Mark. 2003. *Insurrection: Citizen Challenges to Corporate Power*. New York: Routledge Press.

Davenport, Christian. 1995. "Multi-dimensional Threat Perception and State Repression: An Inquiry into Why States Apply Negative Sanctions." *American Journal of Political Science* 39(3):683–713.

2007. "State Repression and Political Order." *Annual Review of Political Science* 10:1–23.

Davenport, Christian and Marci Eads. 2001. "Cued to Coerce or Coercing Cues? An Exploration of Dissident Rhetoric and its Relationship to Political Repression." *Mobilization* 6:151–171.

Davidson, Wallace N., Dan L. Worrell, and Abuzar El-Jelly. 1995. "Influencing Managers to Change Unpopular Corporate Behavior Through Boycotts and Divestitures." *Business and Society* 34:171–196.

Davies, Lawrence E. 1965. "Projected Oil Refinery Near Monterey Involves Californians in Conservation Battle." *New York Times* December 16: 55.

Davis, Gerald F. and Mayer N. Zald. 2005. "Social Change, Social Theory, and the Convergence of Movements and Organizations." Pp. 335–350 in *Social Movements and Organization Theory* edited by Gerald F. David, Doug McAdam, and Mayer N. Zald. New York: Cambridge University Press.

Davis, Gerald F. and Michael Useem. 2002. "Top Management, Company Directors, and Corporate Control." Pp. 233–259 in *Handbook of Strategy and Management* edited by Andrew Pettigrew, Howard Thomas, and Richard Whittington. London: Sage.

Denend, Lyn and Erica Plambeck. 2007. "Wal-Mart's Sustainability Strategy." Stanford Graduate School of Business Case Study OIT-71.

Deng, Fang. 1997. "Information Gaps and Unintended Outcomes of Social Movements: The 1989 Chinese Student Movement." *American Journal of Sociology* 102:1085–1112.

Della Porta, Donatella and Sidney Tarrow. 2005. *Transnational Protest & Global Activism*. Lanham, MD: Rowman & Littlefield Publishers, Inc.

Doh, Jonathan P. and Hildy Teegan. 2003. *Globalization and NGOs: Transforming Business, Government, and Society*. Westport, CT: Praeger.

Domhoff, G. William. 1976. *Who Rules America?* Englewood City, NJ: Prentice Hall.

Donaldson, Thomas and Lee E. Preston. 1995. "The Stakeholder Theory of the Corporation: Concepts, Evidence, and Implications." *Academy of Management Review* 20:65–91.

Dugger, Ronnie. 1987. "The Company as Target." *New York Times* September 20:SMA30.

Earl, Jennifer. 2000. "Methods, Movements, and Outcomes: Methodological Difficulties in the Study of Extra-Movement Outcomes." *Research in Social Movements, Conflicts, and Change* 22:3–25.

———. 2003. "Tanks, Tear Gas and Taxes: Toward a Theory of Movement Repression." *Sociological Theory* 21:44–68.

———. 2004. "The Cultural Consequences of Social Movements." Pp. 508–530 in *The Blackwell Companion to Social Movements* edited by David A. Snow, Sarah A. Soule, and Hanspeter Kriesi. Malden, MA: Blackwell Publishing.

Earl, Jennifer, Sarah A. Soule, and John D. McCarthy. 2003. "Protest Under Fire: Explaining the Policing of Protest." *American Sociological Review* 68: 581–606.

Earl, Jennifer, Andrew Martin, John D. McCarthy, and Sarah A. Soule. 2004. "Newspapers and Protest Event Analysis." *Annual Review of Sociology* 30:65–80.

Earl, Jennifer and Sarah A. Soule. 2006. "Seeing Blue: A Police-Centered Explanation of Protest Policing." *Mobilization* 11:145–164.

Eckberg, Douglas Lee. 1988. "The Physicians' Anti-Abortion Campaign and the Social Bases of Moral Reform Participation." *Social Forces* 67:378–97.

Economist. 2008. "Just Good Business." January 17. (Available at http://www.economist.com/specialreports/displaystory.cfm?story_id=E1_TDQJTDSS, last accessed March 25, 2009).

Economist Intelligence Unit. 2008. "Doing Good: Business and the Sustainability Challenge." (Available at http://a330.g.akamai.net/7/330/25828/20080208191823/graphics.eiu.com/upload/Sustainability_allsponsors.pdf, last accessed March 25, 2009).

Edelman, Lauren B. and Mark C. Suchman. 1997. "The Legal Environments of Organizations." *Annual Review of Sociology* 105:406–454.

Edgelko, Bob. 2007. "U.S. Court Rebuffs Bush on Tuna Ban: White House Chided for Trying to Loosen 'Dolphin-Safe' Rules." *San Francisco Chronicle*. April 28 (Available at http://www.sfgate.com/cgi-bin/article.cgi?file=/c/a/2007/04/28/MNGF2PHDCQ1.DTL, last accessed March 25, 2009).

Edwards, Victoria. 2003. "Students Protest Bhopal Disaster on Dow Executives' Doorsteps." *The Michigan Daily* December 4:1.

Eesley, Charles and Michael J. Lenox. 2006. "Firm Responses to Secondary Stakeholder Action." *Strategic Management Journal* 27:765–781.

Egan, Timothy. 1989. "Alaska Oil Cleanup Near End But Beaches Remain Fouled." *New York Times* September 10:1.

Elsbach, Kimberly D. and Robert I. Sutton. 1992. "Acquiring Organizational Legitimacy through Illegitimate Actions: A Marriage of Institutional and Impression Management Theories." *Academy of Management Journal* 35:699–738.

Emerson, Tony. 2001. "Swoosh Wars." *Newsweek* March 12:35.

Epstein, Marc and Karen Schnietz. 2002. "Measuring the Cost of Environmental and Labor Protest to Globalization: An Event Study of the Failed 1999 Seattle WTO Talks." *The International Trade Journal* 16(2):19.

Epstein, Barbara. 1991. *Political Protest and Cultural Revolution: Nonviolent and Direct Action in the 1970s and 1980s.* Berkeley: University of California Press.

Eyerman, Ron and Andrew Jamison. 1995. "Social Movements and Cultural Transformation: Popular Music in the 1960s." *Media, Culture, & Society* 17:449–468.

Featherstone, Liza. 2002. *Students Against Sweatshops.* London: Verso Publishers.

Fineman, Stephen and Ken Clarke. 1996. "Green Stakeholders: Industry Interpretations and Response." *Journal of Management Studies* 33(6): 715–730.

Fischhoff, Baruch, Alain Nadaï, and Ilya Fischoff. 2001. "Investing in Frankenfirms: Predicting Socially Unacceptable Risks." *Journal of Psychology and Financial Markets* 2(2):100–111.

Fombrun, Charles J. 1996. *Reputation: Realizing Value from the Corporate Image.* Boston: Harvard Business School Press.

Fombrun, Charles J. and Mark Shanley. 1990. "What's In a Name? Reputation Building and Corporate Strategy." *Academy of Management Journal* 33:233–258.

Fort, Timothy. 2001. *Ethics and Governance: Business as Mediating Institution.* New York: Oxford University Press.

Fraser, C. Gerald. 1967. "Boycott at Madison." *New York Times* October 20: 1.

Freeman, Stan. 2001. "Activists Say Ecoterrorism Not Helping Their Cause." *Sunday Republican of Springfield* February 4:2.

Friedman, Monroe. 1985. *Consumer Boycotts: Effecting Change Through the Marketplace and the Media.* New York: Routledge.

Friedman, Milton. 1970. "A Friedman Doctrine: The Social Responsibility of Business is to Increase Profits." *New York Times* September 13:SM17.

Friedman, Raymond A. and Kellina M. Craig. 2004. "Predicting Joining and Participating in Minority Employee Network Groups." *Industrial Relations* 43(4):793–816.

Friedman, Julian. 1978. *Basic Facts on the Republic of South Africa and the Policy of Apartheid.* United Nations Centre Against Apartheid, Department of Political and Security Council Affairs. New York.

Bibliography

Frooman, Jeffrey. 1999. "Stakeholder Influence Strategies." *The Academy of Management Review* 24(2):191–205.

Galbraith, John Kenneth. 1952. *American Capitalism: The Concept of Countervailing Power.* Boston: Houghton Mifflin.

Galvin, Kevin. 1996. "Investors Take a Stand Against Sweatshops." *The Associated Press* September 18 (Available at http://thunhan.net/~nike/ap-reject.htm, last accessed March 25, 2009).

Gamson, William A. and David S. Meyer. 1996. "Framing Political Opportunity." Pp. 291–311 in *Comparative Perspectives on Social Movements* edited by Doug McAdam, John D. McCarthy, and Mayer N. Zald. New York: Cambridge University Press.

Gamson, William. 1990. *The Strategy of Social Protest, Second Edition.* Belmont, CA: Wadsworth.

———. 2004. "Bystanders, Public Opinion, and the Media." Pp. 242–261 in *The Blackwell Companion to Social Movements* edited by David A. Snow, Sarah A. Soule, and Hanspeter Kriesi. Malden, MA: Blackwell Publishers.

Gamson, William A. and Andre Modigliani. 1989. "Media Discourse and Public Opinion of Nuclear Power: A Constructionist Approach." *American Journal of Sociology* 95:1–37.

———. 1998. "Social Movements and Cultural Change." Pp. 57–77 in *From Contention to Democracy* edited by Marco G. Giugni, Doug McAdam, and Charles Tilly. Lanham, MD: Rowman and Littlefield Publishers, Inc.

George, Mary. 1990. "Aurora Schools Boycott Tuna Fish: Students Win Protest Over Use of Fishing Nets." *Denver Post* January 10: 3.

Gereffi, Gary, Ronie Garcia-Johnson, and Erika Sasser. 2001. "The NGO-Industrial Complex." *Foreign Policy* July-August 125:56–65.

Gillham, Patrick F. and John A. Noakes. 2007. "More than a March in a Circle: Transgressive Protests and the Limits of Negotiated Management." *Mobilization* 12(4):341–357.

Girdner, Bill. 1988. "Groups Seek Tuna Boycott to Protest Dolphin Kills." *San Diego Evening Tribune* August 5: 14.

Giugni, Marco. 1998. "Was it Worth the Effort? The Outcomes and Consequences of Social Movements." *Annual Review of Sociology* 24: 371–393.

Giugni, Marco, Doug McAdam, and Charles Tilly. 1999. *How Social Movements Matter.* Minneapolis: University of Minnesota Press.

Goldstone, Jack A. and Doug McAdam. 2001. "Contention in Demographic and Life-Course Context." Pp. 195–221 in *Silence and Voice in the Study of Contentious Politics* edited by Ronald R. Aminzade, Jack A. Goldstone, Doug McAdam, Elizabeth J. Perry, William H. Sewell, Jr, Sidney Tarrow, and Charles Tilly. New York: Cambridge University Press.

Gourman, Jack. 1989. *The Gourman Report: A Rating of Undergraduate Programs in American and International Universities.* Princeton: National Education Standards.

Gourman, Jack. 1985. *The Gourman Report A Rating of Undergraduate Programs in American and International Universities.* Princeton: National Education Standards.

Green, Frank. 2000. "Making Their Point in Public: Protesters Target Firms, but Do Boycotts Work?" *San Diego Union Tribune* May 16:4.

Greenberg, Josh and Graham Knight. 2004. "Framing Sweatshops: Nike, Global Production, and the American News Media." *Communication and Critical/ Cultural Studies* 1(2):151–175.

Greenberg, Stan, Al Quinlan, and James Carville. 2007. "Finding Their Voice as The Agents of Change." Report issued by Democracy Corps. Washington, DC.

Greenhouse, Steven. 2000. "Report Says Global Accounting Firm Overlooks Factory Abuses." *New York Times* September 28 (Available at http://www.nytimes.com/2000/09/28/business/28SWEA.html, last accessed March 25, 2009).

Grossman, Richard and Ward Morehouse. 1996. "Minorities, the Poor & Ending Corporate Rule." *The Boycott Quarterly* Spring: 3.

Guillen, Mauro F. 2000. "Corporate Governance and Globalization: Is There Convergence across Countries?" Pp. 175–204 in *Advances in International Comparative Management Volume 13* edited by J. L. C. Cheng and R. B. Peterson. Stamford, CT: JAI Press.

Hadar, Leon T. 1998. "U.S. Sanctions Against Burma: A Failure on All Fronts." Cato Institute's *Trade Policy Analysis* No. 1, March 26 (Available at http://www.cato.org/pubs/trade/tpa-001.html, last accessed March 25, 2009).

Halebsky, Stephen. 2006. "Explaining the Outcomes of Antisuperstore Movements: A Comparative Analysis of Six Communities." *Mobilization* 11(4): 443–460.

Harris, Maria. 1986. "Bok's Empty Words." *Harvard Crimson* July 18: 1.

Hart, Stuart L. and Sanjay Sharma. 2004. "Engaging Fringe Stakeholders for Competitive Imagination." *Academy of Management Executive* 18(1): 7–18.

Hartman, Thomas. 2002. *Unequal Protection*. New York: Rodale Press.

Hauck, David. 1985. *The Impact of South African-Related Divestment on Equity Portfolio Performance*. Report by the Investor Responsibility Corporation's South Africa Review Service. Washington, DC.

Heath, Chip and Dan Heath. 2007. *Made to Stick: Why Some Ideas Survive and Others Die*. New York: Random House.

Heirich, Max. 1968. *The Beginning: Berkeley 1964*. New York: Columbia University Press.

Henry, David. 2002. "Mergers: Why Most Big Deals Don't Pay Off." *Business Week*, October 14:60.

Herremans, Irene M, Parporn Akathaporn, and Morris McInnes. 1993. "An Investigation of Corporate Social Responsibility, Reputation, and Economic Performance." *Accounting Organizations and Society* 18: 587–604.

Higher Education General Information Survey: Fall Enrollment and Compliance Report of Institutions of Higher Education (HEGIS XI). 1976–1977.

Higher Education General Information Survey: Fall Enrollment and Compliance Report of Institutions of Higher Education (HEGIS XV). 1980–1981.

Higher Education General Information Survey: Fall Enrollment and Compliance Report of Institutions of Higher Education (HEGIS XX). 1985–1986.

Bibliography

Higher Education General Information Survey: Financial Statistics of Institutions of Higher Learning (HEGIS XXI). 1985–1986.

Higher Education General Information Survey: Financial Statistics of Institutions of Higher Learning (HEGIS FY). 1980–1981.

Higher Education General Information Survey: Financial Statistics of Institutions of Higher Learning (HEGIS FY). 1976–1977.

Hinings, C. R. and Royston Greenwood. 2002. "Disconnects and Consequences in Organization Theory." *Administrative Science Quarterly* 47:411–421.

Hirsch, Eric L. 1990. "Sacrifice for the Cause: Group Processes, Recruitment, and Commitment in a Student Social Movement." *American Sociological Review* 55(2):243–254.

Hodson, Randy. 1996. "Dignity in the Workplace under Participative Management: Alienation and Freedom Revisited." *American Sociological Review* 61:719–738.

Hoffman, Andrew J. 2009. "Shades of Green." *Stanford Social Innovation Review* Spring: 40–49.

Howe, Robert F. 1990. "Tuna Gets Hook in Alexandria Schools After Students Object." *Washington Post* March 3: 24.

Ingrahman, Joseph C. 1965. "Physicians Picket Automobile Show." *New York Times* April 8:34.

Ingram, Paul and Hayagreeva Rao. 2004. "Store Wars: The Enactment and Repeal of Anti-Chain Store Legislation in America." *American Journal of Sociology* 110(2):446–487.

Investor Responsibility Research Center (IRRC). 1996–2002. *Multinational Business in Burma. Quarterly Publication.* Washington, DC.

Ivins, Molly. 1977. "Feminist Leaders Join Anti-Smut Campaign Despite Reservations." *New York Times* July 2:31

Jackson, John L. 1992. "The Symbolic Politics of Divestment: Protest Effectiveness on US College and University Campuses." Unpublished paper presented at the NEH Seminar Symposium. Ithaca, NY: Cornell University. August 12.

Jasper, James M. and Jane Paulsen. 1995. "Recruiting Strangers and Friends: Moral Shocks and Social Networks in Animal Rights and Animal Protest." *Social Problems* 42:493–512.

Jenkins, J. Craig and Charles Perrow. 1977. "Insurgency of the Powerless: Farm Worker Movements (1946–1972)." *American Sociological Review* 42:249–268.

Jenkins, J. Craig and Craig M. Ekert. 1986. "Channeling Black Insurgency: Elite Patronage and Professional Social Movement Organizations in the Development of the Black Movement." *American Sociological Review* 51:812–829.

Jensen, Michael. C. 1977. "ACLU Suit Says Honeywell Conspired with FBI." *New York Times* April 21:82.

Johnston, Hank and Bert Klandermans. 1995. *Social Movements and Culture.* Minneapolis: University of Minnesota Press.

Johnston, David Cay. 2007. *How the Wealthiest Americans Enrich Themselves at Government Expense (and Stick You With the Bill).* New York: Portfolio/Penguin Books.

175

Jones, Thomas M. 1995. "Instrumental Stakeholder Theory: A Synthesis of Ethics and Economics." *The Academy of Management Review* 20(2): 404–437.

Jones, Peter, Daphne Comfort, and David Hillier. 2006. "Anti-Corporate Retailer Campaigns on the Internet." *Journal of Retail and Distribution Management* 34(12): 882–891.

Jones, David R. 1964. "Negroes Picket General Motors." *New York Times* May 5: 30.

Jones, Theodore. 1965. "49 Arrested at Chase Building In Protest on South African Loans." *New York Times* March 20:11.

Kahn, Richard and Douglas Kellner. 2004. "New Media and Internet Activism: From the Battle of Seattle to Blogging." *New Media and Society* 6(1): 87–95.

2005. "Oppositional Politics and the Internet: A Critical and Reconstructive Approach." *Cultural Politics* 1(1):75–100.

Kay, Tamara. 2005. "Labor Transnationalism and Global Governance: The Impact of NAFTA on Transnational Labor Relationships in North America." *American Journal of Sociology* 111(3):715–758.

Kay, Jane. 2003. "Groups Protest Rules Change on 'Dolphin Safe' Label." *San Francisco Chronicle* February 12 (Available at http://www.commondreams .org/headlines03/0212-04.htm, last accessed March 25, 2009).

Keck, Margaret and Kathryn Sikkink. 1998. *Activists Beyond Borders: Advocacy Networks in International Politics.* Ithaca, NY: Cornell University Press.

Kerbo, Harold and L. Richard della Fave. 1979. "The Empirical Side of the Power Elites Debate: An Assessment and Critique of Recent Research." *The Sociological Quarterly* 20(1):5–22.

Khagram, Sanjeev, James V. Riker, and Kathryn Sikkink. 2002. "From Santiago to Seattle: Transnational Advocacy Groups Restructuring World Politics." Pp. 3–23 in *Restructuring World Politics: Transnational Social Movements, Networks, and Norms* edited by Sanjeev Khagram, James V. Riker, and Kathryn Sikkink. Minneapolis: University of Minnesota Press.

Kibbe, Jennifer. 1989. *Divestment on Campuses: Issues and Implementation.* Report by the Investor Responsibility Research Center. Washington, DC.

Kifner, John. 1967. "Annual Stockholders' Meeting of Eastman Kodak at Flemington, NJ is the Target of Demonstrators." *New York Times* April 26: 49.

King, Brayden G. and Sarah A. Soule. 2007. "Social Movements as Extra-Institutional Entrepreneurs: The Effect of Protest on Stock Price Returns." *Administrative Science Quarterly* 52:413–442.

King, Brayden G., Keith G. Bentele and Sarah A. Soule. 2007. "Protest and Policymaking: Explaining Fluctuation in Congressional Attention to Rights Issues, 1960–1986." *Social Forces* 86:137–161.

King, Brayden G. 2008a. "A Social Movement Perspective of Stakeholder Collective Action and Influence." *Business and Society* 47(1):21–49.

2008b. "A Political Mediation Model of Corporate Response to Social Movement Activism." *Administrative Science Quarterly* 53:395–421.

Kitschelt, Herbert. 1986. "Political Opportunity Structures and Political Protest: Anti-Nuclear Movements in Four Democracies." *British Journal of Political Science* 16:57–85.

Bibliography

Klein, Naomi. 2004. "James Baker's Double Life: A Special Investigation." *The Nation* November 1 (Available at http://www.thenation.com/doc/20041101/klein, last accessed March 25, 2009).

Klein, Naomi. 1999. *No Space, No Choice, No Jobs, No Logo: Taking Aim at the Brand Bullies*. New York: Picador.

Klemesrud, Judy. 1977. "A Rally Opens Antismut Drive In Times Square." *New York Times* April 12:31.

Klotz, Audie. 1995. "Norms Reconstituting Interests: Global Racial Equality and U.S. Sanctions Against South Africa." *International Organization* 49(3):451–478.

Knight, Richard. 1990. "Sanctions, Disinvestment, and U.S. Corporations in South Africa." Pp. 67–89 in *Sanctioning Apartheid* edited by Robert E. Edgar. Trenton, NJ: Africa World Press, Inc.

Knight, Graham and Josh Greenberg. 2002. "Promotionalism and Subpolitics: Nike and Its Labor Critics." *Management Communication Quarterly* 15(4):541–570.

Koku, Paul Sergius, Aigbe Akhigbe, and Thomas M. Springer. 1997. "The Financial Impact of Boycotts and Threats of Boycotts." *Journal of Business Research* 40:15–20.

Koopmans, Ruud. 1997. "The Dynamics of Repression and Mobilization: The German Extreme Right in the 1990s." *Mobilization* 2:149–165.

Körber, Achim. 1998. "Why Everybody Loves Flipper: The Political Economy of the U.S. Dolphin-Safe Laws." *European Journal of Political Economy* 14:475–509.

Kreider, Aaron. 2005. *Sit In! A Tactical Analysis*. (Available at http://www.campusactivism.org/uploads/sit-in-tactical-analysis.pdf, last accessed March 25, 2009).

Kriesi, Hanspeter, Ruud Koopmans, Jan Willem Duyvendak, and Marco Giugni. 1995. *New Social Movements in Western Europe: A Comparative Analysis*. Minneapolis: University of Minnesota Press.

Kripalani, Manjeet. 2008. "Dow Chemical: Liable for Bhopal?" *Business Week* May 28 (Available at http://www.businessweek.com/magazine/content/08_23/b4087000856552.htm?chan=top+news_top+news+index_top+story, last accessed March 25, 2009).

Kumar, Raman, William Lamb, and Richard E. Wokutch. 2002. "The End of South African Sanctions, Institutional Ownership, and the Stock Price Performance of Boycotted Firms: Evidence on the Impact of Social/Ethical Investing." *Business and Society* 41(2):133–165.

Lagnado, Lucette. 1999. "Strained Peace: Gerber Baby Food, Grilled by Greenpeace, Plans Swift Overhaul – Gene-Modified Corn and Soy Will Go, Although Firm Feels Sure They Are Safe – Heinz Takes Action, Too." *Wall Street Journal* July 30: A1.

Lancet. 1989. "Round The World: India – Long Term Effects of MIC." Number 644. April 29: 21.

Landon, Stuart and Constance E. Smith. 1997. "The Use of Quality and Reputation Indicators by Consumers: The Case of Bordeaux Wine." *Journal of Consumer Policy* 20:289–323.

Lansing, Paul and Sarosh Kuruvilla. 1988. "Business Divestment in South Africa: In Whose Best Interest?" *Journal of Business Ethics* 7:561–574.

Larson, Jeffrey and Sarah A. Soule. 2009. "Sector Level Dynamics and Collective Action in the United States, 1965–1975." *Mobilization* September.

Ledbetter, Les. 1979. "1,000 in 'Village' Renew Protest Against Movie on Homosexuals." *New York Times* July 27:B2.

Lee, Ming-Dong Paul. 2008. "Theory of Corporate Social Responsibility: Its Evolutionary Path and the Road Ahead." *International Journal of Management Review* 10(1):53–73.

Lenox, Michael J. and Charles E. Eesley. Forthcoming. "Private Environmental Activism and the Selection and Response of Firm Targets." *Journal of Economics Management and Strategy*.

Lewis, Anthony. 1984. "Message to Pretoria." *New York Times* December 6: A31.

LiUNA. 2008. "Issue Alert: A Multi-Billion Dollar Bailout for Those at Fault: Corporate Homebuilders, the Housing Crash, and the Mortgage Crisis" (Available at http://www.liuna.org, last accessed June 12, 2008).

Lichtenstein, Grace. 1976. "Utah Group Stages Rally Against Smut." *New York Times* October 17:26.

Lipset, Seymour Martin and William Schneider. 1987. *The Confidence Gap: Business, Labor, and Government in the Public Mind*. Baltimore, MD: Johns Hopkins University Press.

Liptak, Adam. 2008. "Damages Cut Against Exxon in Valdez Case." *New York Times* June 26:A1.

Locke, Richard M., Fei Qin, and Alberto Brause. 2006. "Does Monitoring Improve Labor Standards? Lessons from Nike." MIT Sloan Research Paper No. 4612–06 (Available at SSRN: http://ssrn.com/abstract=916771, last accessed August 15, 2008).

Longman, Phillip J. 1999. "Baby Food Fight Averted." *U.S. News & World Report* 127(6):43.

Lounsbury, Michael. 2001. "Institutional Sources of Practice Variation: Staffing College and University Recycling Programs." *Administrative Science Quarterly* 46:29–56.

Love, Janice. 1988. "The Potential Impact of Economic Sanctions Against South Africa." *The Journal of Modern African Studies* 26(1):91–111.

Luders, Joseph. 2006. "The Economics of Movement Success: Business Responses to Civil Rights Mobilization." *American Journal of Sociology* 111(4):963–998.

Mackey, Alison, Tyson B. Mackey, and Jay B. Barney. 2007. "Corporation Social Responsibility and Firm Performance: Investor Preferences and Corporate Strategies." *Academy of Management Review* 32(3):817–835.

MacKinlay, Craig. A. 1997. "Event Studies in Economics and Finance." *Journal of Economic Literature* 35:13–39.

Mandle, Jay. 2000. "The Student Anti-Sweatshop Movement: Limits and Potential." *Annals of the American Academy of Political and Social Science* 570:92–103.

Manheim, Jarol B. 2001. *The Death of a Thousand Cuts: Corporate Campaigns and the Attack on the Corporation*. Mahwah, NJ: Lawrence Erlbaum Associates.

2004. *Biz-War and the Out of Power Elite: The Progressive-Left Attack on the Corporation.* Mahwah, NJ: Lawrence Erlbaum Associates.

2005. *Trends in Union Corporate Campaigns: A Briefing Book.* U.S. Chamber of Commerce.

Margolis, Joshua D. and James P. Walsh. 2001. *People and Profits? The Search for a Line Between a Company's Social and Financial Performance.* Mahwah, NJ: Lawrence Erlbaum Associates.

2003. "Misery Loves Companies: Rethinking Social Initiatives by Business." *Administrative Science Quarterly* 48:268–305.

Markides, Constantinos C. 1992. "Consequences of Corporate Restructuring: Ex Ante Evidence." *Academy of Management Journal* 35:398–412.

Marquis, Christopher. 2003. "U.S. Rules that Foreign Fleets' Use of Tuna Nets is Safe for Dolphins." *New York Times* January 1: A22.

Martin, Andrew. 2008. "The Institutional Logic of Union Organizing and the Effectiveness of Social Movement Repertoires." *American Journal of Sociology* 113:1067–1103.

Marwick, Charles. 2000. "Genetically Modified Crops Feed Ongoing Controversy." *Journal of the American Medical Association* 283(2): 188–190.

Marzullo, Sal G. 1987. "Corporations: Catalyst for Change." Pp. 371–382 in *The South African Quagmire* edited by S. Prakash Sethi. Cambridge, MA: Ballinger Publishing Company.

Massie, Robert Kinloch. 1997. *Loosing the Bonds: The United States and South Africa in the Apartheid Years.* New York: Doubleday.

McAdam, Doug. 1983. "Tactical Innovation and the Pace of Insurgency." *American Sociological Review* 48:735–754.

1989. "The Biographical Consequences of Activism." *American Sociological Review* 54:744–760.

1996. "Political Opportunities: Conceptual Origins, Current Problems, and Future Directions." Pp. 23–40 in *Comparative Perspectives on Social Movements: Political Opportunities, Mobilizing Structures, and Cultural Framings* edited by Doug McAdam, John D. McCarthy, and Mayer N. Zald. New York: Cambridge University Press.

1999. "The Biographical Impact of Social Movements." Pp. 117–146 in *How Social Movements Matter* edited by Marco Giugni, Doug McAdam, and Charles Tilly. Minneapolis: University of Minnesota Press.

McAdam, Doug, Sidney Tarrow, and Charles Tilly. 2001. *Dynamics of Contention.* New York: Cambridge University Press.

McAdam, Doug and Yang Su. 2002. "The War at Home: Antiwar Protests and Congressional Voting, 1965–1973." *American Sociological Review* 67:696–721.

McCammon, Holly J., Karen E. Campbell, Ellen M. Granberg, and Christine Mowery. 2001. "How Movements Win: Gendered Opportunity Structures and U.S. Women's Suffrage Movements, 1866–1919." *American Sociological Review* 66:49–70.

McKay, Gretchen. 2006. "Preparing Baby's First Foods Is Easy as ABC" *Pittsburgh Post-Gazette* August 17:1.

McWilliams, Abagail and Donald Siegel. 1997. "Event Studies in Management Research: Theoretical and Empirical Issues." *Academy of Management Journal* 40:626–657.

McWilliams, Abagail and Donald Siegel. 2001. "Corporate Social Responsibility: A Theory of the Firm Perspective." *Academy of Management Review* 26:117–127.

Meidinger Asset Planning Service. 1983. "District of Columbia Special Investment Study: South Africa Proposal." Harleysville, PA: Meidinger Asset Planning Service, Inc.

Meier, August and Elliott Rudwick. 1973. *CORE: A Study in the Civil Rights Movement, 1942–1968*. New York: Oxford University Press.

Meyer, David S. 2003. "Political Opportunity and Nested Institutions." *Social Movement Studies* 2(1):17–35.

1990. *A Winter of Discontent: The Nuclear Freeze and American Politics*. New York: Praeger Publishers.

2007. *The Politics of Protest*. New York: Oxford University Press.

Meyerson, Debra. 2001. *Tempered Radicals: How People Use Difference to Inspire Change at Work*. Boston: Harvard Business School Press.

Meyerson, Debra E. and Maureen A. Scully. 1995. "Tempered Radicalism and the Politics of Ambivalence and Change." *Organizational Science* 6(5): 585–600.

Meznar, Martin B., Douglas Nigh, and Chuck C.Y. Kowk. 1994. "Effect of Announcements of Withdrawal from South Africa on Stockholder Wealth." *Academy of Management Journal* 37(6):1633–1648.

Millones, Peter. 1969. "G.M. Is Picketed as Air Polluter." *New York Times* December 9:37.

Mitchell, Ronald K., Bradley R. Agle, and Donna J. Wood. 1997. "Toward a Theory of Stakeholder Identification and Salience: Defining the Principles of Who and What Really Counts." *Academy of Management Review* 22:853–886.

Mitgang, Herbert. 1978. "Authors Protest Conglomerate Deal." *New York Times* April 20: C17.

Moore, Will E. 1998. "Repression and Dissent: Substitution, Context, and Timing." *American Journal of Police Science* 42:851–873.

Morgan, Eric J. "The World is Watching: Polaroid and South Africa." *Enterprise and Society* 7(3):520–549.

Murray, Alan S. 2007. *Revolt in the Boardroom: the New Rules of Power in Corporate America*. New York: Collins.

Nace, Ted. 2003. *Gangs of America: the Rise of Corporate Power and the Disabling of Democracy*. San Francisco: Berrett-Koehler.

Nepstad, Sharon Erickson. 2008. *Religion and War Resistance in the Plowshares Movement*. New York: Cambridge University Press.

New York Times. 1962. "Psychologists Join Protest on TV Show." December 8:25.

New York Times. 1965. "Pro-Sex Group Pickets Anti-smut Drive." January 24:80.

New York Times. 1966a. "Luxury Apartment Tenants Fly Flags of Rent Protest: Laundry." October 31:30.

New York Times. 1966b. "No Heat Protest Burns Up Street." December 29: 35.

New York Times. 1966c. "Denver Housewives Boycott Markets." October 18:37.

Bibliography

New York Times. 1966d. "8 In Oregon Marching to Protest High Prices." November 6:31.

New York Times. 1967a. "Scuffle in Los Angeles." November 15:10.

New York Times. 1967b. "Dow Chief Says Protests Hurt." November 18:14.

New York Times. 1969a. "30 Protest at Sears on Welfare Credit." July 4:4.

New York Times. 1969b. "Pickets Demand PepsiCo Help Negroes." July 15:24.

New York Times. 1969c. "War Foes Adopt Business Tactic." December 28: 60.

New York Times. 1970. "Toy With Smoking Exhaust Draws Store Pickets." January 28:27.

New York Times. 1971a. "Nabisco Picketed Over Monster Toys." November 16:50.

New York Times. 1971b. "End of the Line for 'Monster' Toys." November 27:36.

New York Times. 1971c. "12 Demonstrators Seized In A&P Offices Here." February 3:41.

New York Times. 1972. "Pepsi-Cola Boycott Urged." December 10:24.

New York Times. 1975. "None Hurt as Blast In Utah Damages Kennecott Offices." September 6:15.

New York Times. 1976. "Honeywell Linked to FBI Spy Tactics." August 2: 26.

New York Times. 1977. "Humane Society Starts National Boycott of Tuna." May 13:10.

New York Times. 1978. "Protesters Greet Alumni at Princeton." February 27:NJ12.

New York Times. 1979. "GM and Ford are Sued Over Pregnancy Leaves." April 26:A18.

New York Times. 1981a. "Rights Group Will List Its Corporation Targets." August 17:B11.

New York Times. 1981b. "Feminists Protest." April 9:B5.

New York Times. 1983. "130 Arms Demonstrators Arrested in Minneapolis." April 19:A14.

New York Times. 1984a. "Settlement Ends a Suit Against Dalkon Shield." January 18:A17.

New York Times. 1984b. "Demonstration at Chemical Plant." May 6:43.

New York Times. 1985a. "Residents Criticize Carbide." August 19:A17.

New York Times. 1985b. "8 From Greenpeace Held for Plugging Waste Line." April 23:A15.

New York Times. 1986a. "Homosexuals Settle Coast Suit." December 6:56.

New York Times. 1986b. "Group Fights Forced Retirement and Other Bars to the Aged." August 17:CN2.

New York Times. 1989. "Chemical Makers Are Cleared in Lawsuit by Textile Workers." November 5:35.

New York Times. 1990. "Biochemist, 71, Fights Mandatory Retirement." October 21:45.

New York Times. 1993. "Alaska Fishermen Blockade Tankers." August 23: A8.

Niebuhr, Gustav. 1991. "Cracker Barrel Chain Angers Gay Groups With Written Policy." *Wall Street Journal* February 28:C1.

Olzak, Susan and Sarah A. Soule. 2009. Cross-Cutting Influences of Environmental Protest and Legislation." *Social Forces* September.

Orlitzky, Marc, Frank L. Schmidt, and Sara L. Rynes. 2003. "Corporate Social and Financial Performance: A Meta-Analysis." *Organization Studies* 24(3): 403–441.

O'Rourke, Dara. 2003. "Outstanding Regulation: Analyzing Nongovernmental Systems of Labor Standards and Monitoring." *The Policy Studies Journal* 31(1):1–29.

Pear, Robert. 2007. "Bush Directive Increases Sway on Regulation." *New York Times* January 30:A1.

Pedriana, Nicholas. 2006. "From Protective to Equal Treatment: Legal Framing Processes and Transformation of the Women's Movement in the 1960s." *American Journal of Sociology* 111:1718–1761.

Pescosolido, Bernice A., Elizabeth Grauerholz, and Melissa A. Milkie. 1997. "Culture and Conflict: The Portrayal of Blacks in U.S. Children's Picture Books Through the Mid- and Late-Twentieth Century." *American Sociological Review* 62:443–464.

Peterson's Guides to Four Year Colleges. 1975. Princeton, NJ: Peterson's Guides.

Peterson's Guides to Four Year Colleges. 1978. Princeton, NJ: Peterson's Guides.

Peterson's Guides to Four Year Colleges, 18th edition. 1988. Princeton, NJ: Peterson's Guides.

Peterson's Guides to Four Year Colleges, 23rd edition. 1993. Princeton, NJ: Peterson's Guides.

Pfeffer, Jeffrey and Gerald R. Salancik. 1978. *The External Control of Organizations: A Resource Dependence Perspective.* New York: Harper and Row.

Piven, Frances F. and Richard A. Cloward. 1977. *Poor People's Movements: Why They Succeed, How They Fail.* New York: Pantheon Books.

Polletta, Francesca and James M. Jasper. 2001. "Collective Identity and Social Movements." *Annual Review of Sociology* 27:283–305.

Posnikoff, Judith F. 1997. "Disinvestment From South Africa: They Did Well By Doing Good." *Contemporary Economic Policy* 15:76–86.

Pruitt, Stephen W. and Monroe Friedman. 1986. "Determining the Effectiveness of Consumer Boycotts: A Stock Price Analysis of Their Impact on Corporate Targets." *Journal of Consumer Policy* 9:375–387.

Pruitt, Stephen W., K. C. John Wei, and Richard E. White. 1988. "The Impact of Union-Sponsored Boycotts on Stock Prices of Target Firms." *The Journal of Labor Research* IX(3): 285–289.

Raeburn, Nicole C. 2004. *Changing Corporate America from the Inside Out: Lesbian and Gay Workplace Rights.* Minneapolis: University of Minnesota Press.

Rao, Hayagreeva. 2009. *Market Rebels: How Activists Make or Break Radial Innovations.* Princeton, NJ: Princeton University Press.

Richmond, Michael. 1989. "'You Guys are Way Off,' Fisherman Tells 200 Rallying to Halt Dolphin Killings." *Evening Tribune* June 13:12.

Roberts, Peter and Grahame R. Dowling. 2002. "Corporate Reputation and Sustained Superior Financial Performance." *Strategic Management Journal* 23:1077–1093.

Bibliography

Rochon, Thomas R. 1998. *Culture Moves: Ideas, Activism, and Changing Values.* Princeton, NJ: Princeton University Press.

Rock, Michael T. 2003. "Public Discloser of the Sweatshop Practices of American Multinational Garment/Shoe Makers/Retailers: Impact on their Stock Prices." *Competition and Change* 7(1):23–38.

Roe, Mark J. 2000. "Political Preconditions to Separating Ownership from Corporate Control." *Stanford Law Review* 53:539–606.

Rooney, Ben. 2008. "Foreclosures up 60% in February." CNN Money.com, March 14. (Available at http://money.cnn.com/2008/03/13/real_Estate/foreclosures_feb/?postversion=2008031410; last accessed June 12, 2008).

Rosebraugh, Craig. 2004. *Burning Rage of a Dying Planet: Speaking for the Earth Liberation Front.* New York: Lantern Books.

Ross, Philip E. 1989. "New Discrimination Charge Is Lodged Against G.M." *New York Times* February 14:D6.

Rottenberg, Simon. 1986. "The Universities and South Africa: The Campaign for Divestment." *Minerva: A Review of Science, Learning, and Policy* XXIV(2–3):223–241.

Sale, Kirkpatrick. 1973. *SDS.* New York: Vintage Books.

Schneiberg, Marc and Sarah A. Soule. 2005. "Institutionalization as a Contested, Multi-level Process: Politics, Social Movements and Rate Regulation in American Fire Insurance." Pp. 122–160 in *Social Movements and Organizations* edited by Gerald Davis, Doug McAdam, W. Richard Scott, and Mayer Zald. New York: Cambridge University Press.

Schock, Kurt. 1999. "People Power and Political Opportunities: Social Movement Mobilization and Outcomes in the Philippines and Burma." *Social Problems* 46(3):355–375.

Schor, Elana. 2008. "U.S. Labour Union's Protest Tour Targets Homebuilding Industry." *The Guardian* May 1. (Available at http://www.guardian.co.uk/business/2008/may/01/useconomy.usa1?gusrc=rss&feed=global; last accessed May 26, 2009).

Schurman, Rachel. 2004. "Fighting 'Frankenfoods': Industry Opportunity Structures and the Efficacy of the Anti-Biotech Movement in Western Europe." *Social Problems* 51(2):243–268.

Schussman, Alan and Sarah A. Soule. 2005. "Process and Protest: Accounting for Individual Protest Participation." *Social Forces* 84(2):1083–1106.

Schwartzman, Kathleen C. and Kristie A. Taylor. 1999. "What Caused the Collapse of Apartheid?" *Journal of Political and Military Sociology* Summer 27(1):109–139.

Schwartzman, Kathleen C. 2001. "Can International Boycotts Transform Political Systems? The Cases of Cuba and South Africa." *Latin American Politics and Society* 43(2):115–146.

Scully, Maureen and Amy Segal. 2002. "Passion With an Umbrella: Grassroots Activists in the Workplace." *Research in the Sociology of Organizations: Social Structure and Organizations Revisited* 19:125–168.

Scully, Maureen and W. E. Douglas Creed. 1998. "Switchpersons on the Tracks of History: Situated Agency and Contested Legitimacy in the Diffusion of

Domestic Partner Benefits." Paper presented at the annual meeting of the Academy of Management, San Diego, CA.

Seidman, Gay W. 2003. "Monitoring Multinationals: Lessons from the Anti-Apartheid Era." *Politics and Society* 31(3):381–406.

Seidman, Gay W. 2007. *Beyond the Boycott: Labor Rights, Human Rights, and Transnational Activism.* New York: Russell Sage Foundation.

Sengupta, Somini. 2008. "Decades Later, Toxic Sludge Torments Bhopal." *New York Times* July 7:A1.

Sethi, S. Prakash. 1987. "South Africa Beyond Apartheid: Reformation of Institutions and Instruments of Change." Pp. 1–37 in *The South African Quagmire* edited by S. Prakash Sethi. Cambridge, MA: Ballinger Publishing Company.

Shaw, Randy. 1999. *Reclaiming America: Nike, Clean Air, and the New National Activism.* Berkeley: University of California Press.

Shenon, Philip. 1983. "Conference Seeks Ways to Protect Animal Rights." *New York Times* August 8:B2.

Sherkat, Darren E. and Jean Blocker. 1997. "Explaining the Political and Personal Consequences of Protest." *Social Forces* 75:1049–1070.

Simon, John G., Charles W. Powers, and Jon P. Gunnemann. 1972. *The Ethical Investor: Universities and Corporate Responsibility.* New Haven, CT: Yale University Press.

Sine, Wesley D. and Brandon Lee. 2009. "Tilting at Windmills? The Environmental Movement and the Emergence of the U.S. Wind Energy Sector." *Administrative Science Quarterly* 54: 123–155.

Snow, David A. 2004. "Social Movements as Challenges to Authority: Resistance to an Emerging Conceptual Hegemony." *Research in Social Movements, Conflicts, and Change* 25:3–25.

Snow, David A., Sarah A. Soule, and Hanspeter Kriesi. 2004. *The Blackwell Companion to Social Movements.* Malden, MA: Blackwell Publishing.

Snow, David A. and Sarah A. Soule. 2009. *A Primer on Social Movements.* New York, NY: W. W. Norton.

Solomon, R. C. 1993. *Ethics and Excellence: Cooperation and Integrity in Business.* New York: Oxford University Press.

Soule, Edward. 2003. "Corporate Strategy, Government Regulatory Policy, and NGO Activism: The Case of Genetically Modified Crops." Pp. 129–156 in *Globalization and NGOs: Transforming Business, Government, and Society,* edited by Jonathan P. Doh and Hildy Teegan. Westport, CT: Praeger.

Soule, Sarah A. 1997. "The Student Divestment Movement in the United States and Tactical Diffusion: The Shantytown Protest." *Social Forces* 75:855–883.

1999. "The Diffusion of an Unsuccessful Innovation." *The Annals of the American Academy of Political and Social Sciences* 566:120–131.

2001. "Situational Effects on Political Altruism: The Student Divestment Movement in the United States." Pp. 161–176 in *Political Altruism? Solidarity Movements in International Perspective* edited by Marco Giugni and Florence Passy. Lanham, MD: Rowman and Littlefield Publishers, Inc.

2004. "Diffusion Processes within and across Social Movements." Pp. 294–310 in *The Blackwell Companion to Social Movements* edited by David A. Snow, Sarah Soule, and Hanspeter Kriesi. Malden, MA: Blackwell Publishing.

Soule, Sarah A. and Brayden G. King. 2006. "The Stages of the Policy Process and the Equal Rights Amendment, 1972–1982." *American Journal of Sociology* 111(6):1871–1909.

Soule, Sarah A. and Susan Olzak. 2004. "When Do Movements Matter? The Politics of Contingency and the Equal Rights Amendment." *American Sociological Review* 69:473–497.

Soule, Sarah A., Doug McAdam, John McCarthy, and Yang Su. 1999. "Protest Events: Cause or Consequence of State Action? The U.S. Women's Movement and Federal Congressional Activities, 1956–1979." *Mobilization* 4(2):223–238.

Soule, Sarah A. and Jennifer Earl. 2005. "A Movement Society Evaluated: Collective Protest in the United States, 1960–1986." *Mobilization* 10(3):345–364.

Soule, Sarah A. and Brayden G. King. 2008. "Competition and Resource Partitioning in Three Social Movement Industries." *American Journal of Sociology* 113(6):1568–1610.

Soule, Sarah A. and Christian Davenport. 2009. "Velvet Glove, Iron Fist or Even Hand? Protest Policing in the United States, 1960–1990." *Mobilization* 14(1):1–22.

Social Investment Forum. 2006. *2005 Report on Socially Responsible Investing Trends in the United States, 10-Year Review.* Washington, DC: Social Investment Forum.

Spar, Debora L. and Lane T. La Mure. 2003. "The Power of Activism: Assessing the Impact of NGOs on Global Business." *California Management Review* 45(3):78–101.

Stengren, Bernard. 1964. "Picketing Greets Auto Show Here." *New York Times* April 5:48.

Stillerman, Joel. 2003. "Transnational Activist Networks and the Emergence of Labor Internationalism in the NAFTA Countries." *Social Science History* 27(4):577–601.

Story, Louise. 2008. "Home Equity Frenzy Was a Bank Ad Come True." *New York Times* August 14:A1.

Strang, David and Sarah A. Soule. 1998. "Diffusion in Organizations and Social Movements: From Hybrid Corn to Poison Pills." *Annual Review of Sociology* 24:265–290.

Strange, Susan. 1996. *The Retreat of the State.* New York: Cambridge University Press.

Streitfeld, David. 2008. "In the Central Valley, the Ruins of the Housing Bust." *New York Times* August 23:B1.

Stuart, Reginald. 1977. "G.M. Plans to Raise Its Output of Fuel-Efficient Compacts." *New York Times* May 21:32.

Sussman, Barry. 1985. "Apartheid Protests Supported by Most Who Know of Them." *Washington Post* January 27:A23.

Swan, Wallace K. 1997. "The Workplace Movement." Pp. 25–33 in *Gay/Lesbian/ Bisexual/Transgender Public Policy Issues: A Citizen's and Administrator's Guide to the New Cultural Struggle* edited by Wallace K. Swan. Kirkwood, NY: Harrington Park Press.

Sylwester, Eva. 2005. "Students Protest Exxon." *Oregon Daily Emerald* November 15:1.

Tarrow, Sidney. 2005. *The New Transnational Activism.* New York: Cambridge University Press.

Tarrow, Sidney and Doug McAdam. 2005. "Scale Shift in Transnational Contention." Pp. 121–147 in *Transnational Protest and Global Activism* edited by Donatella della Porta and Sidney Tarrow. Lanham, MD: Rowman & Littlefield Publishers, Inc.

Taylor, Verta. 1996. *Rock-a-By-Baby: Feminism, Self-Help and Postpartum Depression.* New York, NY: Routledge Press.

Taylor, Verta and Nancy E. Whittier. 1992. "Collective Identity in Social Movement Communities: Lesbian Feminist Mobilization." Pp. 104–29 in *Frontiers of Social Movement Theory* edited by Aldon D. Morris and Carol McClurg Mueller. New Haven, CT: Yale University Press.

Tiesl, Mario F., Brian Roe, and Robert L. Hicks. 2002. "Can Eco-Labels Tune a Market? Evidence from Dolphin-Safe Labeling." *Journal of Environmental Economics and Management* 43:339–359.

Tilly, Charles. 1978. *From Mobilization to Revolution.* Reading, MA: Addison-Wesley.

———. 2001. "Mechanisms in Political Processes." *Annual Review of Political Science* 4:21–41.

Toftoy, Ryan P. 1998. "Now Playing: Corporate Codes of Conduct in the Global Theater. Is Nike Just Doing it?" *Journal of International and Comparative Law* 15:905.

Travlos, Nikolaos G. 1987. "Corporate Takeover Bids, Methods of Payment, and Bidding Firms' Stock Returns." *Journal of Finance* 42:943–963.

Van der Heijden, Hein-Anton. 2006. "Globalization, Environmental Movements, and the International Political Opportunity Structure." *Organization and Environment* 19(1):28–45.

Van Dyke, Nella, Sarah A. Soule, and Verta Taylor. 2004. "The Targets of Social Movements: Beyond a Focus on the State." *Authority in Contention, Research in Social Movements, Conflicts, and Change* 25: 27–51.

Van Tuijl, Peter. 1999. "NGOs and Human Rights: Sources of Justice and Democracy." *Journal of International Affairs* 52(2):493–512.

Vellela, Tony. 1988. *New Voices: Student Activism in the '80s and '90s.* Boston: South End Press.

Vienna, David. 1970. "GE Offices Here Vandalized." *Washington Post* February 9:A2.

Vietnam Labor Watch. 1997. *Nike Labor Practices in Vietnam: An Open Letter to Concerned Americans, Nike Shareholders and Consumers.* (Available at http://www.saigon.com/~nike/reports/report1.html; last accessed May 15, 2008).

Bibliography

Vogel, David. 1978. *Lobbying the Corporation: Citizen Challenges to Business Authority.* New York: Basic Books, Inc.

———. 1996. *Kindred Strangers.* Princeton, NJ: Princeton University Press.

———. 2005. *The Market for Virtue.* Washington, DC: Brookings Institution Press.

Waddock, Sandra A. and Samuel B. Graves. 1997. "The Corporate Social Performance-Financial Performance Link." *Strategic Management Journal* 18:303–319.

Waddington, David and Mike King. 2007. "The Impact of the Local: Police Public-Order Strategies During the G8 Justice and Home Affairs Ministerial Meetings." *Mobilization* 12(4):417–430.

Waddington, Peter A. 1994. *Liberty and Order: Public Order Policing in a Capital City.* London: University College London Press.

Wagner, Wayne, Allen Emkin, and Richard Dixon. 1984. "South African Divestiture: The Investment Issues." *Financial Analysts Journal* November/December: 334–336.

Waldron, Martin. 1972. "Company Will Continue to Develop Weapons, Chairman Says." *New York Times* April 27:59.

Wallich, Henry C. and John J. McGowan. 1970. "Stockholder Interest and the Corporation's Role in Social Policy." Pp. 39–59 in *A New Rationale for Corporate Social Policy* edited by William J. Baumol. New York: Committee for Economic Development.

Wallstrom, Peter and Cathy R. Wessells. 1994. "Analysis of Consumer Demand for Canned Tuna: Impact of Dolphin-Safe Controversy." Unpublished paper presented at the Conference of the International Institute of Fisheries Economics and Trade, July 12–14.

Walsh, Edward J. 1986. "The Role of Target Vulnerabilities in High-Technology Protest Movements: The Nuclear Establishment of Three Mile Island." *Sociological Forum* 1:199–218.

Washington Post. 1985. "The South African Sanctions." June 5:A22

Weber, Klaus, Hayagreeva Rao, and L. G. Thomas. 2009. "From Streets to Suites: How the Anti-Biotech Movement Affected German Pharmaceutical Firms." *American Sociological Review* 74: 106–127.

Weir, David. 1987. *The Bhopal Syndrome: Pesticides, Environment, and Health.* San Francisco: Sierra Club Books.

Welsh, Heidi J. 1988. "Shareholder Activism." *Multinational Monitor* 9(12). (Available at http://www.multinationalmonitor.org/hyper/issues/1988/12/mm1288_06.html; last accessed April 2, 2008).

Whysall, Paul. 2000. "Retailing and the Internet: A Review of Ethical Issues." *International Journal of Retail and Distribution Management* 28(11):481–489.

Widener, Patricia. 2007. "Benefits and Burdens of Transnational Campaigns: A Comparison of Four Oil Struggles in Ecuador." *Mobilization* 12(1):21–36.

Wilhelm, Brenda 1998. "Changes in Cohabitation across Cohorts: The Influence of Political Activism." *Social Forces* 77:289–310.

Wilkens, John. 1989. "Nationwide Tuna Boycott Urged to Protest Dolphin Killings." *San Diego Union* June 14:1.

Wilking, Lou H. 1987. "Should U.S. Corporations Abandon South Africa?" Pp. 383–392 in *The South African Quagmire* edited by S. Prakash Sethi. Cambridge, MA: Ballinger Publishing Company.

Williams, Dennis, George Raine, Susan Katz, Elisa Williams, and Susan Hutchinson. 1985. "A New Breed of Activism." *Newsweek* May 13: 61–62.

Williams-Slope, Mark. 1971. "A Letter to the Workers of America." United Nations Unit on Apartheid. Department of Political and Security Council Affairs. Notes and Documents. 21/71(May):445.

Wolfson, Mark. 2001. *The Fight Against Big Tobacco: The Movement, the State, and the Public's Health.* New York: Aldine de Gruyter.

Wright, Peter and Stephen P. Ferris. 1997. "Agency Conflict and Corporate Strategy: The Effect of Divestment on Corporate Value." *Strategic Management Journal* 18:77–83.

Wurf, Nick. 1986. "No Reason Not to Divest Now." *Harvard Crimson* August 8:3.

Yaziji, Michael and Jonathan Doh. 2009. *NGOs and Corporations: Conflict and Collaboration.* New York: Cambridge University Press.

Zajac, Edward J. and James D. Westphal. 2004. "The Social Construction of Value: Institutionalization and Learning Perspectives on Stock Market Reactions." *American Sociological Review* 69:433–457.

Zald, Mayer N. and Michael A. Berger. 1978. "Social Movements in Organizations: Coup d'etat, Bureaucratic Insurgency, and Mass Movement." *American Journal of Sociology* 83:823–861.

Zimmerman, Ekkart. 1980. "Macro-Comparative Research on Political Protest." Pp. 167–237 in *Handbook of Political Conflict* edited by Ted R. Gurr. New York: Free Press.

Zinn, Howard. 1997. *The Zinn Reader.* New York: Seven Stories Press.

Index

Index